"The fashion industry is the quintessential example of an industry whose marketing has profoundly shaped and manipulated consumer tastes and, indeed, society. In an update and revision of her important book on marketing in the fashion industry, Olga Mitterfellner, a London-based fashion professional and teacher, reviews marketing and communication strategies and methods used in fashion in a refreshing and interesting way."

Geoffrey T. Fong, *OC, PhD, FRSC, FCAHS, University Professor of Psychology, University of Waterloo, Waterloo, Ontario, Canada*

"This book shows that to be a fashion lover and maintain an activist's heart are not mutually exclusive. The globally minded concept speaks to an all-too-rare approach to fashion education for the student or professional. It has become commonplace to relate social responsibility to sustainability in the supply chain, but ethics plays a crucial role throughout the entire fashion industry. Olga's chapters blend history and modern practices in marketing to create a better understanding and support progressive change."

Monika Sklar, *Associate Professor and Director/Curator of the Historic Clothing and Textiles Collection, UGA, USA*

"This impressive book has a refreshing look at the fundamentals of theory and practice coupled with the past and present developments of Fashion Marketing. Students and practitioners will learn, explore, and re-evaluate the industry as Olga Mitterfellner has expertly added a much-needed dialog on ethics in marketing, prompting us to think and work responsibly."

Ilan Alon (Professor), *Dean of the School of Economics, The College of Management Academic Studies, Rishon LeZion, Israel*

Fashion Marketing and Communications

Fashion Marketing and Communications draws together interdisciplinary approaches from marketing, branding, promotion and critical media studies to provide a comprehensive and honest understanding of the commercial and ethical functions marketing plays in the fashion industry.

Offering a combination of theory and practice, the book covers subjects including historical advertising and public relations, modern consumerism, contemporary marketing techniques, international markets, and sustainable and inclusive marketing, outlining the opportunities and challenges facing the future of fashion marketers. This second edition has been fully revised to incorporate new chapters on sustainability marketing, digital marketing and future-facing trends. Interviews with practitioners have been refreshed and broadened to include a diverse range of perspectives from around the world. New case studies showcase real-life examples from Abercrombie & Fitch, Freitag, LOEWE and SOLIT Japan. This book champions new actionable theory frameworks with embedded activity sheets that invite the reader to apply the frameworks in an educational or professional context.

Examining the last 100 years of fashion marketing and communications and current theory and practice, this broad-ranging text is perfect for advanced undergraduate and postgraduate students of fashion marketing, brand management and communications as well as practitioners. PowerPoint slides and exercise questions are available to support the book.

Olga Mitterfellner, SFHEA, is Senior Lecturer in Fashion Business Management at the University of Westminster, UK.

Mastering Fashion Management

The fashion industry is dynamic, constantly evolving and worth billions worldwide: it's no wonder that Fashion Business Management has come to occupy a central position within the Business School globally. This series meets the need for rigorous yet practical and accessible textbooks that cover the full spectrum of the fashion industry and its management.

Collectively, *Mastering Fashion Management* is a valuable resource for advanced undergraduate and postgraduate students of Fashion Management, helping them gain an in-depth understanding of contemporary concepts and the realities of practice across the entire fashion chain – from design development and product sourcing, to buying and merchandising, sustainability, and sales and marketing. Individually, each text provides essential reading for a core topic. A range of consistent pedagogical features are used throughout the texts, including international case studies, highlighting the practical importance of theoretical concepts.

Postgraduate students studying for a Master's in Fashion Management in particular will find each text invaluable reading, providing the knowledge and tools to approach a future career in fashion with confidence.

Celebrity Fashion Marketing
Developing a Human Fashion Brand
Fykaa Caan and Angela Lee

Luxury Fashion Brand Management
Unifying Fashion With Sustainability
Olga Mitterfellner

Fashion Business and Digital Transformation
Technology and Innovation across the Fashion Industry
Charlene Gallery and Jo Conlon

Customer Experience in Fashion Retailing
Merging Theory and Practice
Edited by Bethan Alexander

Luxury Fashion Marketing and Branding
A Strategic Approach
Alice Dallabona

Creativity and Innovation in the Fashion Business
Contemporary Issues in Fashion Design and Product Development
Helen Goworek and Fiona Bailey

Fashion Marketing and Communications (2nd edition)
Theory and Practice Across the Fashion Industry
Olga Mitterfellner

For more information about the series, please visit https://www.routledge.com/Mastering-Fashion-Management/book-series/FM

Fashion Marketing and Communications

Theory and Practice Across the Fashion Industry

Second Edition

OLGA MITTERFELLNER

Routledge
Taylor & Francis Group

LONDON AND NEW YORK

Designed cover image: smartboy10 / Getty Images

Second edition published 2025
by Routledge
4 Park Square, Milton Park, Abingdon, Oxon, OX14 4RN

and by Routledge
605 Third Avenue, New York, NY 10158

Routledge is an imprint of the Taylor & Francis Group, an informa business

© 2025 Olga Mitterfellner

First edition published by Routledge 2020

British Library Cataloguing-in-Publication Data
A catalogue record for this book is available from the British Library

Library of Congress Cataloging-in-Publication Data
Names: Mitterfellner, Olga, 1978- author.
Title: Fashion marketing and communications: theory and practice across the fashion industry / Olga Mitterfellner.
Description: Second edition. | Abingdon, Oxon; New York, NY: Routledge, 2025. | Series: Mastering fashion management | Includes bibliographical references and index.
Identifiers: LCCN 2024025921 | ISBN 9781032582344 (hardback) | ISBN 9781032582320 (paperback) | ISBN 9781003449157 (ebook)
Subjects: LCSH: Fashion merchandising. | Advertising--Fashion. | Clothing trade. | Communication in marketing. | Branding (Marketing)
Classification: LCC HF6161.C44 M59 2025 | DDC 746.9/20688--dc23/eng/20240819
LC record available at https://lccn.loc.gov/2024025921

ISBN: 978-1-032-58234-4 (hbk)
ISBN: 978-1-032-58232-0 (pbk)
ISBN: 978-1-003-44915-7 (ebk)

DOI: 10.4324/9781003449157

Typeset in Dante and Avenir
by Deanta Global Publishing Services, Chennai, India

Access the Support Material: www.routledge.com/9781032582320

This book is dedicated to all my past, present and future students who inspire me every day. If not for their curiosity, intelligence, encouragement and motivation I wouldn't have found the patience to write so many pages, and now a second edition of this book.

Education can lift someone above and beyond their limits and I hope that the contents will do just that: elevate each reader both intellectually and personally.

Furthermore, I dedicate this book to all those (humans and animals) who have been wronged by the fashion industry and its unethical practices. We cannot fully feel your pain, but we can try and improve the past and change the future.

My gratitude also extends to my family, mentors, friends and colleagues for cheering me on in all my endeavours.

Lastly, I would like to dedicate this book to the memory of several wonderful people: my late step-father Georgi Nikolaevich Vladimov, who, as a world-famous author, would be proud of my humble literary attempts. And then, my beloved friend Mai Goya Nguyen. We met when we were so young and happy, working at the production office at Hackett London. Mai's beautiful soul left this world too soon.

Contents

About this new edition

This second edition builds on the previous first edition and considers important changes that have taken place between 2019 and 2024.

All the chapters have been extensively revised to update facts, figures and content. There are dozens of new titles that have been added to the recommended reading at the end of each chapter. Case studies have been revised with several new ones added, including an extensive one on Abercrombie & Fitch in Chapter 3. The experts interviewed in the first edition were invited to revise their contributions and check for updates.

To make studying with this book and applying it to real life most convenient, it contains many new graphics of frameworks and nine corresponding worksheets that can be used by the reader to perform analyses.

Two completely new and very relevant chapters have been written for this new edition to cover digital marketing and sustainability marketing. The new Chapter 6 covers the history and development of the internet, including Baudrillard and simulacres. It explores the evolution of e-commerce with a focus on fashion. Digital marketing and the PEO (paid, earned, owned) models are explained with a new graphic and worksheet for analysis. Furthermore, the customer journey is explained with two graphics and two worksheets. The chapter presents a fascinating case study on livestreaming and livestream commerce in China and closes with ethical considerations.

The new Chapter 11 explores the definitions of sustainability, sustainability marketing and green marketing. It covers frameworks such as the People-Planet-Profit framework of the Bruntland Report, the TBL (triple bottom line) by John Elkington, the Conceptual Framework for Sustainability by Rotimi et al. (2021), and the 3As of ethical activism with a focus on the problems of the fashion industry – both in luxury and fast fashion. A short case study on the sustainable luxury brand LOEWE is included in this chapter as well as a long case study on the Swiss brand Freitag, which has achieved circularity and sustainability.

Furthermore, four types of sustainability marketing are analyzed in depth: greenwashing, auxiliary sustainability marketing, reformative sustainability marketing and transformative sustainability marketing. Chapter 11 looks deeply at the United Nations' Sustainable Development Goals (SDGs), highlighting their strengths and problems in terms of neo-colonialism, globalization and pollution.

There is also an expert interview with Misaki Tanaka, the founder of an inclusive and sustainable brand from Japan called SOLIT.

Chapter 12 (formerly Chapter 10 in the first edition of the book) has been extensively expanded to incorporate updated trends that emerged during and post-pandemic and the developments of AI. It contains a new section on the diffusion of innovation, which connects to the economic wave theory. It covers the Consumer Trend Canvas that aids in deriving innovations from trend forecasting and offers a template for personal use.

The chapter furthermore reflects on the long-standing history of trend forecasting and features two interviews, one of which is with a Zeitgeist researcher from Germany.

As with the first edition, this updated version invites anyone interested in both fashion marketing and communications to explore the 12 chapters and find a comprehensive introduction to relevant fields of interest and understand how brands use marketing and communication strategies in the industry. Whether a practitioner or a student, you can find fresh, different ideas and sometimes a radical and unusual perspective on the subject matter.

However, this is not just a standard book but also an invitation to build your own expert opinion by exploring the past, questioning the present and contemplating the future of the industry.

This book takes a unique angle on fashion marketing, in contrast to many books which are focused on current practices and trends – surely important – because only very few take the reader back to its origins. These origins are of significance because they are the foundation of modern marketing, and only by understanding these origins and evolvement can a person evaluate modern practices and make an informed ethical judgement. By exploring these historical elements, one can become a cultured person – first and foremost – and then a professional marketer, capable of conducting an educated discourse on a variety of topics. The theory is coupled with short case examples from around the world, contextualizing some unusual approaches in practice.

Furthermore, each chapter is specifically designed to explore content independently from allowing readers to pick and choose areas of interest without having to power through it from beginning to end.

Through interviews, the book connects the reader to global professional specialists and industry experts from the UK, Germany, the USA, Japan, South Korea and Russia, offering their unique insights and a more global outlook on various topics.

Most importantly, each chapter invites the reader to reflect on ethical considerations. This is because every aspiring marketing professional and current marketer needs to be aware of the complex ethical implications of the profession. Many products and services that are marketed, and in fashion specifically, can have unethical traits and even cause harm. Sometimes the negative effects are not immediately evident in daily professional life. With this book, you can consider the pros and cons and form your own opinion of marketing practices. You can alter your course, change behaviour and implement a best-practice approach in your career. Hopefully, this book will encourage each reader to be the most ethically responsible marketer and make a difference in the world.

Fashion marketing from a historical perspective
Early days of advertising and consumerism

1

Chapter topics

How to define fashion marketing?

Marketing, and specifically fashion marketing, is part of a large industry – the fashion system – and it has a long-standing history dating back hundreds of years as well as more modern practices which are just a few decades old. Arguably, the fashion system is cyclical in its nature and is ever-changing while it recycles ideas from the past. It consists of elements such as textiles, design, production, retail, marketing, media, culture and history, but also trends and future forecasts. Hence, this book proposes a "Fashion Carousel" that summarizes this very cyclical system and is revisited in the last chapter of the book to demonstrate the necessity of ethical considerations to improve its many culprits.

Fashion marketing can take many forms and many expressions, so in order to understand the place where marketing sits within the fashion system, it is necessary to look at a few definitions that try to accurately describe it.

DOI: 10.4324/9781003449157-1

One such definition states:

> The fashion system offers a "structure, organisation and processes employed to conceive, create, produce, distribute, communicate, retail and consume fashion. [It] embodies the full supply chain of fashion and includes not only the individual components, (what the action is) but also the methods adopted to enable and realise each activity (how it is being done)".
>
> (Vecchi and Buckley, 2016)

This is a modern definition which describes the design and production of fashion, sourcing of materials, distribution and retailing (both offline and online), and consumption of fashion with all its methodologies, such as marketing, advertising and public relations (PR). The marketing of fashion specifically takes care of taking the product and getting it to the consumers, at the right price, in the right place and by successfully promoting it. These consumers – existing and potential ones – are essentially "the market".

It ties in with the "Marketing Mix", which is explored in Chapter 3 in more detail. Originally, it was McCarthy who separated Marketing Mix activities into four broad categories or elements, which he called the 4Ps of marketing: product, price, place and promotion. Later, the four Marketing Mix elements were expanded to 7Ps to include process, physical evidence and people (Kotler et al., 2009, p. 17).

An alternative definition adds a cultural and sociological aspect to the fashion system:

> The fashion industry forms part of a larger social and cultural phenomenon known as the 'fashion system,' a concept that embraces not only the business of fashion but also the art and craft of fashion, and not only production but also consumption.
>
> (Encyclopedia Britannica, 2018)

The rather complex sociological aspects of fashion theory have been written about by respected historical authors such as Roland Barthes, Bourdieu, Lipovetsky, Simmel, Veblen and Baudrillard, just to name a few. A perhaps more contemporary author for fashion students is Yuniya Kawamura, who wrote about the phenomenon of "Fashion-ology" in a modern context. Fashion-ology, according to Kawamura, is a study of fashion, but it does not focus on the apparel or process as such. Her intent is also the sociological investigation of fashion (Kawamura, 2005).

In order to understand the historical setting that brought us fashion marketing and the corresponding communication practices, in this book, we look at marketing as it initially emerged, moving on to modern practice. There is a focus on the way marketing is used to communicate with and exert influence on consumers, and an appraisal of the successful as well as dubious methods which have unethical implications.

The history of advertising, particularly in the nineteenth and twentieth centuries

The marketing methods used to reach a consumer, such as the promotion of products through advertising and public relations, can be traced back many centuries, if not millennia, into human history.

Ever since people went to market, they engaged in marketing their goods and communicating with potential and actual consumers.

About 2000–1000 BC, written advertising was recorded in places such as ancient Rome and Greece on clay boards or on artefacts. In many cultures around the world, there was a primal form of advertising (especially where literacy was absent) and this might have meant shouting loudly in the market to get shoppers' attention for one's produce. This would, of course, only reach people in the immediate vicinity of the market and was far from the global marketing we know today with large billboards, branded goods, jingles and digital channels.

Europe's cultural and economic development, particularly that of Western Europe, was hindered by the Dark Ages (lasting approximately from 500 CE to 1500 CE), during which the majority of the population, for the duration of nearly 1000 years, all but the clergy and aristocracy, had no access to literacy and culture which they had once acquired from ancient Greece and Rome. Any significant development pertaining to marketing was practically frozen during this millennium due to an overall reduction in the economy.

Then came the re-birth of Europe: the Renaissance. Early modern Europe began with the invention of the printing press by Gutenberg in the fifteenth century and gave way to mass-printed text which could be circulated to a broader audience. There is some evidence of so-called flyposting in Europe in the fifteenth century, which is somewhat similar to posters or billboards with text on them. However, in Europe, the people who could actually read were still very scarce, and so only in the nineteenth century was literacy integrated into the educational system and spread widely enough for most people to be able to read printed text and the subsequent ads (Kloss, 2012). This means that

Table 1.1 History of advertising

Medium	Dating back to	Still in use today?
Magazines (print)	18th century	Yes
Newspapers (print)	18th century	Yes
Billboards and posters	From 1850s (flyposting from 15th century in Europe)	Yes
Silent film (cinema)	End of 19th century	No
Sound film (cinema)	From 1920s	Yes
Illuminated advertising (later neon signs)	End of 19th century	Yes
Radio	From 1920s	Yes
Television	From 1920s	Yes
Internet and digital	From 1990s onwards	Yes

despite the mechanical invention of creating print, advertising in written form could only begin much later as the communicator of the message and recipient first had to be on a similar level of literacy.)

Up to the nineteenth century, however, advertising was not a necessity because the consumption of goods was restricted to the essentials, which means that the majority of people bought just what they needed and only in small quantities. In this respect, local and limited-scope advertising sufficed because consumers were personally acquainted with the butcher, the baker, the grocer and the hat maker, and chose their place of purchase based on what was available in proximity, how good the product was, and how much they liked and trusted the producer of the goods.

As for fashion, people either made garments themselves if they knew how to weave or knit, or they purchased expensive cloth from someone who did and then made a garment which would potentially last them for most of their lives so that they could pass it on to the next person. The sartorial consumption was, of course, different for the aristocracy and upper-class citizens, who had more choices and larger quantities of garments than most other citizens.

How the industrial revolution led to present marketing practices

Then, at the end of the eighteenth century until the middle of the nineteenth century, the industrial revolution happened: When the UK and US started to make great inventions, such as the steam engine or textile weaving machines, and found the right type of fuel to power the machines (steam, coal, electricity, etc.), the production of many goods became mechanized.

Replacing human labour with machines meant that the output could be increased tremendously. Thus, factories emerged, putting children, women and men into the workplace.

It must be remembered that the working conditions were poor and dangerous, the hours were long, and there were no unions to look after the workers' rights. It was normal to work for 14 hours on six days a week, no matter if you were a minor or an adult, using dangerous machines and chemicals which harmed the factory workers, the environment and close inhabitants. In fact, this might sound familiar to you if you have been following the labour conditions of modern fashion production facilities in developing countries. What we perceive as an atrocity today is an invention from around 200 years ago, tried and tested by the first industrialists and part of an era known as early democratic capitalism. The appalling working conditions of the industrial revolution went on for over a century and sometimes longer, before people were able to force the proprietors to make their workplace safer and conditions humane by joining unions, walking out to demonstrate or going on strike.

Figure 1.1 A British textile mill. Image source: Pixabay by Sue 330.

Henry Ford was one of the first industrialists to have introduced an early equivalent of today's conveyor belt with his assembly lines at Ford Motor Company's Highland Park, Michigan, factory in 1908 (Lemelson–MIT, n.d.). His economic achievement and social contribution to an American way of life is also known as "Fordism" and describes the production methods of commodities as well as the capitalist and consumerist way of life. He is credited with shifting consumerism from the few to the masses during the twentieth century (Smart, 2010).

With the subsequent use of the conveyor belt in many factories, the coordinated and fast output of goods increased dramatically. The masses of consumer goods were then transported to a multitude of stores, often far away, so that the producer and consumer no longer knew each other and products were being sold to an "unknown" customer (Zeit Online, 1955).

The huge output beyond basic needs meant that there was an imbalance in supply and demand.

Ideally, the supply of manufactured goods and the demand for goods should be in balance (Figure 1.2). In some cases, supply was scarce, so that people had to queue for basic goods such as food, which often happened during times of economic hardship and war.

In the case of the industrial revolution, suddenly more goods were being rapidly produced whilst people had no real need to increase consumption. Supply and demand fell out of balance (the imbalance is shown in Figure 1.3). Now there was no harmony between seller and buyer; no buyers had to queue for goods. On the contrary, the manufacturers had to make an effort to gain the customers' attention and secure a sale.

Thus, manufacturers of goods had two new tasks: One was to encourage people to become consumers of more goods than they actually needed by increasing demand. The other was to distinguish their product from that of their competitors and ensure preference over others.

Supply and demand in harmony

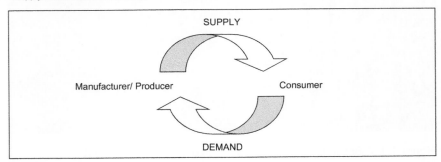

Figure 1.2 The balance of supply and demand pre-industrial revolution.

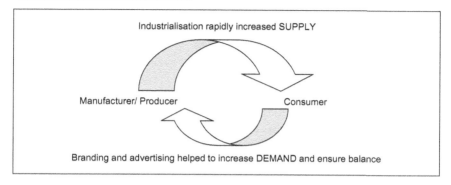

Figure 1 3 The balance of supply and demand post-industrial revolution.

The origin of modern-day consumerism and brands

As a result of industrialization, from the middle of the nineteenth century onwards, and in particular in the years around the turn of the twentieth century, the strategic professions of branding and advertising began to emerge as two instruments that would enable consumerism. In fact, advertising was thriving, and between 1867 and 1890, it grew tenfold in the USA, while similar growth was happening in industrially advanced countries such as the UK (Kloss, 2012, p. 35). In order to distinguish themselves from competitors, manufacturers began to brand their goods. According to the American Marketing Association (2024), "A brand is a name, term, design, symbol, or any other feature that identifies one seller's good or service as distinct from those of other sellers".

Since brands became increasingly competitive amongst each other, they soon began employing specialists who would design the best possible strategies in order to outwit the competitors and engage the consumer. In this context, the USA had a huge pioneering role in advertising and branding, which is why many textbooks on marketing will have a US bias. In fact, marketing professor and author of many marketing textbooks, Philip Kotler (2012), finds the roots of marketing to be quite an American commodity.

But how exactly could advertising get the brand's message through to its existing and potential customers? Which channels could a brand use if it was no longer based in its local shop or at a market stall, shouting out loudly? Here, another vital necessity for modern-day advertising came into play: mass media. Newspapers and railroads for distributing newspapers created the necessary infrastructure for modern mass communication in the twentieth century.

The development of different media channels for advertising began with print media such as posters, billboards, newspapers and magazines. *Vogue* magazine was a newspaper at first when it appeared in 1892; the *Ladies' Home Journal* was founded in 1883 (Breward, 1994).

However, in France and England, fashion magazines had been around since the turn of the eighteenth century, such as the French journal *Le journal des dames et des modes*.

Advertising for products in the first mail-order catalogues emerged around the same time, such as the Sears catalogue.

The industrial revolution equally influenced infrastructure and transportation, which means that there were suddenly new effective methods to spread printed media very quickly and widely across entire countries, including large territories such as the USA. The construction of railroads was a facilitator for advertising to really take off and grow. Steam heat and electric lights started to replace stoves, as well as oil and gas lamps, in the 1880s, whilst just ten years later electric locomotives appeared.

The *Historical Guide to North American Railroads* (Drury, 1985) describes this sudden industrial advancement of transport and infrastructure that took place roughly at the end of the nineteenth century.

Fascinatingly, before the turn of the nineteenth century, American cities and railroads used a large number of different time zones based on local solar time. Each train station thus set its own clock, making it difficult to coordinate train schedules, and once travel was accelerated from an entire day's travel to a few hours, passengers would be easily confused about the time zones.

> A few minutes difference in time between neighbouring cities made little difference when the cities were a day's travel apart. Railroads reduced the time between cities to hours, and the telegraph that accompanied them provided instant communication. To eliminate the confusion [...] in 1883 the railroads divided the U.S. into four zones with uniform times an hour apart. Gradually others adopted the standard time of the railroads.
>
> (Drury, 1985, p. 8)

The reduced time of transportation did not only influence travel but also the speed of media distribution to readers, making communication more rapid. Lane notes that in the USA, by the 1880s, over 11,000 different newspapers were available, and by 1900 a well-read newspaper such as the *Chicago Tribune* could reach about 50,000 readers. All newspapers contained plenty of advertising, of course (Lane et al., 2008).

Radio advertising began to emerge from the early 1920s onwards, and with radios being bought by many households, they could be used to reach the masses from the pin-point of a single radio station. Radios were also effective in targeting specific customer groups by means of special-interest radio stations. In fact, in the 1930s and 1940s, a majority of American radio programmes were under the control of advertising agencies who put together shows by writing the content and booking effective radio presenters from the entertainment industry (Britannica, 2017).

Case example: Yiddish radio advertising

An interesting example of targeted fashion advertising on North American radio is the case of Yiddish radio:

> In the beginning of the twentieth century, Jewish immigrants came to America from Eastern Europe in numbers of more than two million people. As the *Yiddish Radio Project* recalls, Yiddish was the language which connected those immigrants. "The recent Jewish immigrants embraced the medium, and by the early 1930s, Yiddish radio flourished nationwide. In New York alone, 23 stations broadcast dramas, variety programs, man-on-the street interviews, music, commercials, even editorials in rhyme".
>
> (Yiddish Radio Project, 2002)

The radio programmes were not only filled with music and entertainment but, of course, advertising. Radio time was sold to agencies and companies that wanted airtime.

This radio advertising included early forms of fashion advertising – for shops and products all located in the US capital of fashion, New York, and in the immediate neighbourhood of the audience. Listening to the recordings of those commercials now, you are able to feel the scope of fashion and its significance in the retail landscape of 1930s New York. From shoes to clothing stores, to famous personalities singing the skits such as celebrated cantor Moishe Oisher, who sang the theme song of the Stanton Street Clothier (Yiddish Radio Project, 2002). Male and female shoppers were both addressed.

There was a melodic jingle about Old Man Adler's elevator shoes on the Jewish Radio Hour, which catered to the short man. Elevator shoes can "elevate" the wearer by a few centimetres as they have insoles that are thickened and form a wedge (known as shoe lifts) under the heels. These shoes also promised discreetness to short men who, unlike women, could not simply elevate their height by openly wearing high heels.

In 1947, *Life Magazine* published a story on the Adler elevator shoes radio commercial and the man who was famous for delivering them: Henry Morgan. Morgan's skits were funny and even silly, which made Mr Adler initially quite sceptical about the ads. However, soon after the radio ads began, people flocked to his shop, stating that Morgan had sent them and was asking for Old Man Adler. Subsequently, Adler's profits increased (*Life Magazine*, 14 April 1947, p. 60).

Decades later, radio advertising remains a highly successful medium with an estimated 92% of US radio listeners staying tuned during commercial breaks today. (Moriarty, 2019)

From the turn of the twentieth century, poster, print and radio advertising were joined by moving pictures in silent films and later by the "talking pictures" in the 1920s.

In 1895, the Lumière Cinématographe (Camera) was shown to la Société d'encouragement pour l'industrie nationale, rue de Rennes, in Paris, together with the first silent film: *La Sortie des usines Lumière* (The exit of the Lumiére factory) by the Lumiere brothers (Lewino and Dos Santos, 2015). In the same year they publicly showed films, charging a fee from the viewers – the idea of the cinema was born. Feature films followed about 10 years later with the introduction of cinema ads in the 1920s.

Radio and cinema advertising were predominant for several consecutive decades, rather than TV. Although televisions were already available from

Table 1.2 American thinkers and pioneers of modern marketing

Name	Lifespan	Contribution to modern marketing
Ivy Lee	1877–1934	First PR activities in the USA
Edward Bernays	1891–1995	Principles of psychology used for PR
Walter Dill Scott	1869–1955	Principles of psychology used for advertising
Ernest Dichter	1907–1991	Principles of psychology used for marketing
Elias St. Elmo Lewis	1872–1948	Inventor of the AIDA model
Neil Borden	1895–1980	Inventor of the Marketing Mix
E. Jerome McCarthy	1928–2015	Inventor of the 4Ps
Abraham Maslow	1908–1970	Founder of humanistic psychology and Maslow's hierarchy of needs

Figure 1.4 A Diamond is Forever, 1955. Ad created by N.W. Ayer for De Beers. Image kindly provided by De Beers; photography by Irving Penn.

the 1920s, they only became a household staple from the 1950s onwards in countries such as the USA, offering TV advertisements directly in the home. Compared to all other media channels, once accessible by the masses, this one grew the fastest and attracted high spending by advertisers (Kloss, 2012; Lane, 2010).

And until the 1990s, when the internet was introduced as a new techno-logical platform for advertising, these original advertising media channels remained virtually unchanged, still being widely used to this day.

Case example: De Beers

"A diamond is forever", said a famous advertising agency to America in the 1940s. And everybody believed it without ever asking why.

The phrase caused social change in romantic behaviours: Women suddenly expected diamond jewellery as an engagement present. Men felt that this was the only way they could propose to their loved ones. All of the sudden, Hollywood stars began to wear diamonds, and entire movie scripts were built around the precious stone, which would be featured on red carpets and which we regularly see at events even today. All thanks to the New York-based ad agency N.W. Ayer and its client De Beers, whose profits rose to $2.1 billion by 1979 thanks to one exceptional advertising and marketing campaign that was launched in the 1940s with this phrase (*The Atlantic*, 2015).

The image shown in Figure 1.4 is one of many beautiful photographs shot by the now-deceased and famed fashion photographer Irving Penn as a series of ads for De Beers. In this image, we are peeking in from behind a palm tree plant, on an intimate moment in the relationship between a woman and a man in a glamorous public place, which is, incidentally, reinforced through a diamond gift. The copy text reads: "When love is new, and lovers share their dreams of life to be, each moment brims with happiness. It's a time that they'll recall, always, in the joyous flames of her engagement diamond". Below four sizes of sparkling diamonds the man can choose from, it boldly states: A DIAMOND IS FOREVER.

You might possibly call this an early *integrated marketing* campaign because it not only featured classic advertising and copy text, but also used celebrity endorsements by stars, product placement in the cinema and brand ambassadors such as first ladies and the late Queen Elizabeth. Whichever store you chose to buy your diamond jewellery from, the stones were by De Beers (Epstein, 1982). This helped to catapult a glitzy gemstone to stardom and make it synonymous with love, engagement, marriage and the eternal word "forever".

Yet still, hardly anyone asked why one should keep diamonds forever. Critics such as Edward Jay Epstein have said that the true reason was not a celebration of eternal love but a marketing ploy:

At the end of the 19th Century there was an ample supply of diamonds in the world and the price for the stone had been raised artificially, which would tumble immediately if everyone tried to resell their diamonds. Furthermore, De Beers controlled the supply and demand of a monopoly. "De Beers had to endow these stones with a sentiment that would inhibit the public from ever reselling them. The illusion had to be created that diamonds were forever – "forever" in the sense that they should never be resold".

(Epstein, 1982)

The USA was one of the pioneers when it came to post-industrial advertising, and many ideas, practices and case studies – which are still applicable to this day – stem from there. The first advertising agencies emerged in the latter half of the nineteenth century, such as J. Walter Thompson (founded in 1864 and still active today) and N.W. Ayer & Sons.

At the end of the nineteenth century and in the first decades of the twentieth century, when there was already an industry with many advertising and marketing professionals in the USA, professionals teamed up and founded numerous associations as well as something we'd now call "think tanks". Remarkably, most of them still exist today and have grown considerably, attracting more industry members in equal proportion to the immense growth that the advertising industry experienced in the twentieth century. The members come from all areas and industries, including the fashion industry.

• The Advertising Club of New York, founded in 1915

  In 1896, a small number of advertising men in New York City began meeting on a regular basis to share ideas on their advertising practices. In 1906, the growing group incorporated as the Advertising Men's League, ultimately becoming The Advertising Club of New York in 1915, thus celebrating 120 years of existence in 2016. Since the 1960s, the club has been giving out the ANDY award "to recognize the collaboration of creatives and marketers alike who raise the standards of craftsmanship in the industry (Advertising Club, 2024).

  The corporate members in 2016 include most of the large advertising agencies of the world such as BBDO, DDD Worldwide, J. Walter Thompson, McCann, Ogilvy & Mather, Publicis, TBWA and Young & Rubicam. TBWA for example, creates advertising for clients such as Adidas and Apple, and J. Walter Thompson – one of the oldest and largest ad agencies in the world – created a docu-fiction for the famous Italian fashion school Istituto Marangoni and featured Italian *Vogue* editor Franca Sozzani.

- The American Advertising Federation (AAF), founded in 1905

  This organization is based in Washington, DC, and claims today that it is "the unifying voice for advertising", because it provides opportunities for professionals from across the vast scope of the profession to build supportive relationships with others in the advertising industry. To accomplish its mission, it engages in grassroots activities to promote and protect its advertising activities at all levels of government. It counted around 40,000 members in 2016 (AAF, "Who we are", 2016).

  Its corporate members include publishers Condé Nast, owner of the fashion magazines *GQ, Self, Teen Vogue, Vanity Fair, Vogue, W* and *Wired;* and Hearst Magazines, owner of the fashion magazines *Marie Claire, Elle, Cosmopolitan, Esquire, Seventeen* and *Harper's Bazaar.*

- The Association of National Advertisers (ANA), founded in 1910

  It is one of the US advertising industry's oldest trade associations. Today, the ANA's membership includes nearly 1,000 companies with 15,000 brands that collectively spend or support more than $300 billion in marketing and advertising annually.

  Some of the current members are fashion and beauty companies, including Crocs, Fashion Institute of Technology (F&S), JCPenney, L'Oréal USA, Nike, Mary Kay Inc., Victoria's Secret and Walmart (ANA, 2024).

- The American Association of Advertising Agencies (AAAA, 4A's), founded in 1917

  It was founded in New York as a national trade association to represent US advertising agencies and claims on its website that today "4A's members are responsible for about 80 percent of the total advertising placed by agencies nationwide" (4A's, 2016).

  Some of AAAA's clients closely work with fashion brands: Luxe Collective Group, a media agency, has done work for Hermes, Karl by Karl Lagerfeld and John Hardy, as well as luxury watchmakers such as Blancpain and Breguet. Branding experts Select World have a project portfolio that includes luxury fashion brands Balenciaga, Roberto Cavalli, Marni, Ermenegildo Zegna and Joop!

- The Advertising Research Foundation (ARF), founded in 1936

  Founded in 1936 by the Association of National Advertisers and the American Association of Advertising Agencies, this is a non-profit industry association for sharing knowledge in the fields of advertising and media. Its stated mission is the active development of "leading and bleeding-edge solutions" and to "evangelize the leaders that lead them into action". The

ARF wants to "challenge conventions and discover new insights that benefit our member network". Its membership today consists of over 400 advertisers, advertising agencies, research firms, media companies, educational institutions and international organizations, and there are a few fashion brands amongst those: Levi Strauss & Co., Nike and retailer Walmart.

It also publishes the academic *Journal of Advertising Research* and has renowned academic members such as Stanford University, New York University and New York Institute of Technology, as well as the Wharton School (The ARF, 2016).

Equally, similar associations were formed in Europe, such as the Advertising Association in the UK, which was founded in 1924, and the Reichsverband der Anzeigenvertreter e.V., founded in the 1920s in Germany. In France, L'Autorité de Régulation Professionnelle de la Publicité (ARPP) was founded in 1935. However, it was in the USA that the advertising industry was thriving exceptionally well in this particular time period. It also benefitted from early studies in psychology and disciples of Sigmund Freud (who either had studied directly with him or learned his theories) arriving in America and applying psychology to consumer behaviour. Famous thinkers who were mostly active from the turn of the twentieth century onwards were Walter Dill Scott, Edward Bernays, Ernest Dichter, Neil Borden and E. Jerome McCarthy, Ivy Lee, Elmo Lewis, and Abraham Maslow.

Their contributions to modern marketing practices were highly progressive and significant, as most of their theories are used to this day and, in the case of the AIDA model, have been used for more than 110 years. Of course, their ideas have undergone modification and further development, but just like the theories of Sigmund Freud, as a foundation, they are still relevant.

Despite the benefits that their work provided for marketing as a new discipline, there are also many reasons why these marketing men were highly criticized. Their practices were often unethical and harmful to the masses, as they were based on manipulation, propaganda and disrespect for individual's physical and psychological health, which is in stark contrast to the original ideas of Freud. The influences and consequences of some of these practices are discussed in the next chapters.

Ethical considerations

Prior to the onset of the industrial revolution, production and consumption were in harmony. However, the rate of fashion production (and production of many other goods) has been steadily increasing since the dawn of the industrial revolution. It has increased to a point where we now have "fast fashion" and "throwaway fashion", and fashion styles quickly become obsolete. Coupled with the evolution of modern marketing practices, people have been trained to consume more than they need, regardless of the consequences. In most developed countries, we are now used to fashion consumption as a learned behaviour, difficult if not impossible to unlearn. This can be traced back to the invention of mass media instruments such as newspapers (and transportation for their distribution), cinema, TV and radio, without which advertising would not have such power and influence over masses of people simultaneously.

As illustrated through the example of the "Diamonds are forever" campaign, it becomes evident that advertising can change society and manipulate our behaviour, even influencing the romantic traditions of people. This is just the tip of the iceberg that was created in our consumer society by highly unethical and manipulative tactics, deliberately engineered in a way so that we are not aware of how much influence this has on our behaviour. The following chapters will reveal more of what lies beneath.

Progressively, many activists inside and outside the fashion industry have expressed criticism and believe that the true problems of today's fashion industry lie in our long-standing habit of consuming, causing global problems such as production controversies, human rights issues, and pollution on land and in oceans. (These issues relating to sustainability are discussed in depth in Chapter 11.)

It is therefore the purpose of this book to encourage the reader to actively understand, critique and change the system that has been established and apply their personal understanding of ethics in marketing and brand communication – both during studies and at work.

Further reading

ANA (2024) Member Companies. The Association of National Advertisers (online). Available at: https://www.ana.net/members/list

Bernays, E. and Miller, M. C. (2004) *Propaganda*. New York: Ig Publishing.

Diamond, J. (2015) *Retail Advertising and Promotion*. New York: Fairchild.

Dichter, E. (1971) *Motivating Human Behavior*. New York: McGraw-Hill.

Epstein, E. J. (1982) Have you ever tried to sell a diamond? The Atlantic (online). Available at: https://www.theatlantic.com/magazine/archive/1982/02/have-you-ever-tried-to-sell-a-diamond/304575/

Heimann, J. and Nieder, A. A. (2016) *20th-Century Fashion: 100 Years of Apparel Ads*. Cologne, Germany: Taschen.

History of Advertising Trust (Learning Resources) www.hatads.org.uk

Lane, W. R., Whitehill Kink, K. and Russel, T. J. (2008) *Kleppner's Advertising Procedure*. 17th edn. New Jersey: Pearson Prentice Hall.

Lane, R. et Al. (2010) Kleppner's Advertising Procedure 17th Ed. Prentice Hall: Saddle River

Laird, P. (2001) *Advertising Progress*. Baltimore: Johns Hopkins University Press.

Smart, B. (2010) *Consumer Society: Critical Issues and Environmental Consequences*. Sage: London.

The Atlantic (2015) How an Ad Campaign Invented the Diamond Engagement Ring. www.theatlantic.com/international/archive/2015/02/how-an-ad-campaign-invented-the-diamond-engagement-ring/385376

Tungate, M. (2007) *Adland: A Global History of Advertising*. London: Kogan Page.

Tye, L. (2002) *The Father of Spin: Edward L. Bernays and the Birth of Public Relations*. New York: Henry Holt.

Veblen, T. (2005) *Conspicuous Consumption*. London: Penguin.

Yiddish Radio Project (2002) Sound Portraits Productions. www.yiddishradioproject.org

Fashion promotion and public relations

2

Chapter topics

The early days of public relations

Public relations, a most effective marketing tool, has been present in our history for several centuries and in the early days it was called propaganda – a term that was changed in the 1940s to public relations (or PR). This is because of the original Latin definition of propaganda or propagare, which translates to "propagate" in English. What exactly does it mean to propagate? According to the *Macmillan Dictionary* (2019) it means "to spread ideas, beliefs etc to a lot of people".

Propaganda:

Macmillian (2019) gives the modern definition of *propaganda* as "information, especially false information, that a government or organization spreads in order to influence people's opinions and beliefs".

DOI: 10.4324/9781003449157-2

Public relations:

> However, the modern definition of *public relations* is "communication with various internal and external publics to create an image for a product or corporation" (Lane, 2008).

In both the original form of propaganda and in modern public relations there is an organization of political or commercial interest which wants to spread information in order to shape the opinion of the public. Tracing the use of propaganda back a few centuries, Cull, Culbert and Welsh (2003) found evidence from the 1500s in their attempt to create a "Historical Encyclopedia" of such events. One example from those early days is Queen Elizabeth I, who employed propagandists and cleverly shaped her relationship with the general public. This is particularly interesting because her "PR strategy" had a strong emphasis on fashion and thus connects the past to the present.

Case example: Queen Elizabeth I

So how exactly did propaganda and PR work in the sixteenth century when Queen Elizabeth I reigned?

There was great pressure on Queen Elizabeth to marry as the political stability of the country and international relations depended on it. However, in the middle of the sixteenth century, it became evident that she was not going to marry and remain a single woman and ruler, which caused much mistrust and discontent.

She is said to have used clever rhetoric (which you could also call propaganda) to persuade parliament to respect her decision. But that was not enough because she had to make her choice viable to her people. She decided to live out her choice of being the "Virgin Queen" who is married to her country and make it publicly visible through the means of fashion.

It was now up to her and her close assistants to develop a specific wardrobe, which would signal her chaste lifestyle to the people she ruled. During the era, there was an implicit language of colours, accessories and fabrics, which were read like words. For example, white represented virginity and an embroidered crescent moon meant chastity (Howley, 2009).

From 1566 onwards, the queen's sartorial choices were political ones. Even her portraits were constructed with great calculation to make sure that no physical flaws were ever revealed whilst paying great attention to the symbolic power of her dress. If her subordinates and her people were

Figure 2.1 "The Ditchley portrait". A painting of Queen Elizabeth I by Marcus Gheeraerts the Younger, ca. 1592, oil on canvas. The queen's symbolic sartorial choice represented her virginity. © National Portrait Gallery, London.

to accept that she was married to her country, they literally had to see it to believe it. Any doubts about her political power, ability as a ruler and choice to remain single had to be eliminated. Nevertheless, it remains a mystery until this day whether she really was chaste or had some "bedfellows", as Dr Anna Whitelock (2013) called them.

It is comparable to today's sartorial choices of women in power such as the wardrobes of Jackie Kennedy, Michelle Obama or Carla Bruni, who, although not monarchs or single rulers, did have to use their clothing in order to establish and maintain a political and social stance. Jackie Kennedy, for example, employed Oleg Cassini, a Russian aristocrat who had fled from the Russian Revolution to the USA. The husband of Hollywood beauty Gene Tierney, Cassini created Dior-like tailored costumes for Kennedy and made her look feminine, effortlessly chic and beautiful as America's first lady. She had to be perfectly dressed for her role and Cassini was highly experienced in exactly that: He had already dressed many Hollywood leading ladies as a film studio costumier.

Across the Channel and nearly two centuries after Elizabeth I, in France, during the French Revolution, which lasted from 1789 to 1799, pamphlets, music, plays, art and festivals were used to spread revolutionary thoughts and convince the masses to join in. Then, once Napoleon took control over the country, he too used similar propaganda material to secure his role as the emperor by adding new national holidays (such as his birthday) and organizing fireworks, parades and public balls. He too, had portraits painted of the image he wanted to instil: a military leader, the emperor (Cull et al., 2003).

In fact, you could easily call these political figures "opinion leaders" – a term which we know in the context of popular culture today and which is discussed in Chapter 5.

When did propaganda get its new name of "public relations"?

To answer this question, one has to look at Edward Bernays, an important shaper of modern-day PR and advertising. He is often called the father of PR or "spin" or the inventor of PR and other times credited as the father of advertising.

In fact, it can be said that he used both communication instruments. Bernays, who was Sigmund Freud's nephew, closely worked with his uncle's theories on psychology. However, his goal was not to help unlock the inner self of the people but instead by knowing human psychology he wanted to influence and

Figure 2.2 Model with cigarette holder. Fuselage Fashion Couture show in London 2002 presenting a collection inspired by the fashion of the 1920s to 1940s and the aesthetic of women smoking at that time. Author's own design, photography and styling.

unleash secret desires to manipulate them. He created full campaigns to sell cigarettes to women, bacon to the USA, war to countries and much more as he was hired by banks, corporations and governments. Without his ingenious advertising and PR inventions, such as the testimonial, there would not be the type of advertising we know today. He called his activities "propaganda" but changed it to "public relations" once the former term had been hijacked and gravely misused by the Nazis of WWII.

Case example: Torches of Freedom

Edward Bernays also worked with fashion, as early as in the 1920s. One of his significant media stunts was the "Torches of Freedom" campaign. Among his clients, which included companies, corporations, politicians and the US government, was the tobacco producer Great American Tobacco of Lucky Strike cigarettes. The brief was to raise the female consumers' cigarette consumption. But in the early twentieth century, smoking was considered unthinkable for women, especially in public. Bernays contrived a publicity stunt: He summoned famous and well-regarded women to march down central New York during the 1929 Easter Sunday parade with a lit cigarette in hand. He also summoned journalists to the site so that they could report on the event. No one knew that the parade was not initiated by women who were demonstrating for freedom but by a tobacco company (Amosa and Haglund, 2002).

A lot of money had been spent to advertise the 1920s green package of Lucky Strikes and Bernays's goal was to make this colour fashionable, too. Turning to fashion, Bernays organized the "Green Ball" at the Waldorf-Astoria which was attended by leading debutantes of New York. The colour green would be the ball's motif and everyone attending would be required to wear the colour from head to toe: green ball gowns, green shoes, green gloves, green handkerchiefs, green jewellery (Tye, 2002, p. 39).

To ensure the effective spreading of the message, fashion editors were invited to a Green Fashions Fall Luncheon to dine on green menus. Consequently, and as planned, after the ball, magazines such as *Vogue* praised both the colour green and the event itself.

This green fashion craze initiated by Bernays for Lucky Strikes made other tobacco brands uncomfortable, so much so that even the rival tobacco company Camel produced an advertisement depicting a girl wearing a green dress.

A large amount of press coverage was generated by the "Torches of Freedom" campaign and the season's most popular colour, yet the public did not question any of it or consider that the news was artificially staged. The authors of *Propaganda and Mass Persuasion* insist that even today, "propagandists will continue to invent stories about adversaries, falsify statistics, and 'create' news. From the propagandist's point of view, lies must only be told about unverifiable facts" (Cull et al., 2003).

Bernays had more involvement with the fashion industry, which fascinated him. He found fashion PR to be extremely powerful and exemplary in what propaganda can do, such as make women change their hairstyles or opt for a completely different look. According to Véronique Pouillard

(2013), Bernays wrote about his fascination with fashion in 1928 in his book *Propaganda* and did not make a distinction between using the words "PR" or "propaganda" as this was interchangeable at that time.

Bernays worked with fashion on numerous occasions, including in the 1920s when he was hired by French couturier Charles Frederick Worth to help combat the downturn of French fashion at that time and promote it in America (Pouillard, 2013).

Brand communication

Since the advent of PR during the early twentieth century, PR has been the tool which fashion brands use to communicate with a wide audience of their stakeholders. In Figure 2.3, you can see the two-way communication between a fashion brand and the public. The public can be divided into three groups of people:

- The media people, including fashion journalists and editors, bloggers, and celebrities, who can often be opinion leaders (or influencers) and shape the public's attitudes.

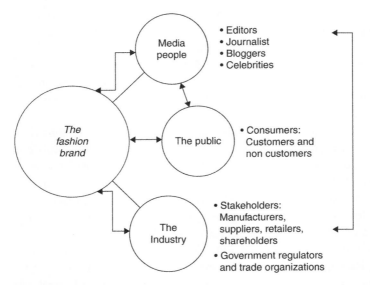

Figure 2.3 Connections between the fashion brand and the public. Author's original illustration.

- The public, including all people who might be reached by the brand's communication activities, be it existing customers, potential customers or those who will not buy the brand but might talk about it.
- The industry, which, simply put, is everyone behind the scenes of a brand. Those people will be stakeholders with an interest or investment in the brand such as suppliers and manufacturers, retailers and shareholders. Governments of countries where clothing is produced or sold will have a relationship with the brand, starting from the taxes that need to be paid or production standards that are set in place for the workers. Trade organizations form an important part of a fashion brand's business practices.

There is a direct connection among these three main groups, which the fashion brand interacts with, and the interaction goes both ways. Media people will react to news from the brand and so will the public. The public will hear about a brand's development from different sources, including the media. As an example, when Tom Ford decided to replace his catwalk show with a fashion film in 2015, consumers found out about this from the brand as well as from publications that wrote about it. The consumers can have a positive or negative attitude towards the brand and media communication which feeds right back to both. However, the general public rarely has any communication with the professional industry.

Understanding the core differences between advertising and PR

The Public Relations Society of America defines public relations as "a strategic communication process that builds mutually beneficial relationships between organizations and their publics" (PRSA, 2016).

In contrast, here is the definition of advertising by marketing-guru Philp Kotler (Kotler et al., 2009): "Advertising is any paid form of non-personal presentation & promotion of ideas, goods, or services by an identified sponsor". In simple words, "advertising is a means of informing and communicating essential information".

Yet again Kleppner's Advertising Procedure states: "Advertising consists of paid notices from identified sponsors normally offered through communication media" (Lane et al., 2008).

Both have similarities and both are designed to work together, supporting all communication efforts of the brand, and usually a brand will try to coordinate advertising and public relations activities within its communications strategy and, of course, the entire Marketing Mix.

Table 2.1 The main differences between advertising and PR

	Advertising	Public relations
Frequency of single campaign	Repeated as often as necessary	Works only once
Cost intensity	Very cost-intensive	Variable from low to high cost intensity
Control over final outcome	Complete control	Little control if working with journalist
Goal of campaign	Increase sales and revenue	Improve reputation, awareness
Reaction of consumers	Mistrust ads	Trust PR
Marketing goal	Influence opinions and reactions	Influence opinions and reactions

Even though advertising and PR work best in combination and sometimes share a campaign, there may be some basic differences in terms of frequency, cost, control and the reaction of the consumers.

The marketing goals of a promotion are to increase sales and revenue, adjust the image, or increase awareness and public acceptance, and are usually shared between PR and advertising.

Table 2.1 shows the main differences between advertising and PR.

In terms of the frequency of a campaign, the clear difference is that in advertising, an ad campaign can be shown as often as necessary through the various media channels. However, with PR activities, a journalist might write a single feature in a magazine for the current issue and the same article will not reappear again. The same goes for an event such as a product launch or a fashion show which is only staged once and reported on around the time of it taking place.

The cost intensity is still very high for advertising with one page of a four-colour ad in *Vogue* costing around $200,000. However, in public relations, it is possible to use low-cost measures such as digital press releases or invite the press to the premises of the PR company and its showrooms. Of course, events and especially fashion weeks can raise this cost, giving PR a wider range in terms of cost intensity than advertising.

In advertising, there is a lot of control over the final outcome of a campaign. From the idea and the design of an ad, for example, to the decision of where it will be shown and for how long – all this is determined by a brand. But with public relations, a large part of work for the PR professional means liaising with journalists, bloggers and opinion leaders from the industry with the hope that they will feature the brand in an editorial piece or on their media channel. It is usually impossible to completely control the outcome.

Normally, the goal of the advertising campaign is primarily to increase sales and revenue. Public relations is more concerned with raising awareness of the existence of a brand or product, improving its reputation and acceptance. Ultimately, this is meant to help the brand grow in the marketplace and, of course, achieve more sales.

Because the customer is aware that with advertising the brand is directly talking to him and trying to sell him something, he is likely to ignore or even mistrust the brand. When PR is used and an industry expert talks about the brand, customers show much more trust. The downside is that in an ad campaign the brand has complete control over the message that it is sending to the target customer, but it has very little control over, say, a journalist who is writing about the brand. Overall, advertising can be very costly because any traditional media such as magazines, TV or cinema charges high prices. Public relations can be expensive if it includes an event or show, but usually the expenditure is much lower as no direct media space is purchased.

There is one thing that both advertising and public relations have in common when they promote a brand or product: they want to influence the consumer's opinions and reactions. With both promotional tools, the goal is a positive attitude of the consumer towards the brand, the desire to buy it and brand loyalty, which help the overall marketing strategy for the growth, resilience and success of the brand.

Today's fashion brands tend to use both communication tools in their marketing strategy, with a mixture of PR and advertising initiatives such as the use of ads in magazines and simultaneous events which journalists could report on.

But of course, there are also exceptions: Zara is a brand that up to now has hardly ever invested in classic advertising. You will not see any Zara billboards, TV commercials or magazine spreads. For a brand which is known for copying catwalk looks at the speed of light, there is perhaps no need to advertise because this is already done by the high-fashion brands.

A competitor from the same fast-fashion segment that does rely on advertising heavily is H&M. Its campaigns are often seen in the city landscape and can feature celebrities.

The role of PR and how it complements advertising

For fashion brands, public relations might work closely with fashion magazines on behalf of a fashion brand.

The PR agency might be a separate department within the fashion brand's headquarters. But this in-house agency will work with smaller local agencies which are knowledgeable about the local market.

Independent PR agencies will take on a number of clients, be their sole PR agent or, as in the earlier example, be an additional PR agent and form a network and cluster of agencies that their client – the fashion brand – works with.

One might wonder if it is not sufficient for a brand to simply purchase advertising space in glossy fashion magazines and guarantee sales. However, just as advertising plays a huge role in the Marketing Mix of a brand, it is equally important for brands (some might argue that it is imperative) to be mentioned by an editor of the same fashion magazine in an editorial piece. This is the equivalent of "free advertising" as it is generally much cheaper than if the same page size had been purchased for an ad. For example, one full-colour page of advertising in American *Vogue* costs over $200,000, but if the editor writes an article the size of the same page, the only cost that the brand has to pay is to the PR agency. The price for the PR work comes at a fraction of the cost of a print ad.

Furthermore, because readers tend to trust PR more than open advertisements, this can be very important for shaping a positive relationship with a brand's audience. This makes the job of public relations professionals quite challenging because liaising with fashion magazines or opinion leaders such as bloggers does not necessarily guarantee a story.

However, there is an unspoken rule that most magazines do give some "editorial" love to clients who have purchased several pages of advertising. If you look through a *Vogue*, *Elle*, *Cosmo* or *Harper's Bazaar* and see which fashion brands are featured on the back cover, first pages and fold-outs, you will most likely find their products mentioned in an editorial within the same magazine. In this case, if the PR agency is working for a brand which also purchases advertising, they will have a much easier job of securing press coverage in the issue.

The power of the press is quite substantial: A brand might invest a lot of money in advertising, but when Anna Wintour, Suzy Menkes, Hillary Alexander or Emmanuelle Alt mention a fashion label, it can catapult it into stardom. For the PR professional, it is thus highly important to know the editors and journalists of each publication that they would like to work with and approach them accordingly. They also have to genuinely understand the brand which they are working for and find suitable media.

In addition to that, today's influencers (or opinion leaders), such as bloggers and stylists, are just as important as the classic journalists, even though there are many discussions on whether opinion leaders can be considered journalists in a classic sense of the word. This is because journalism is supposed to report independently and not be biased by any brand affiliations. However, it is well known that influencers such as bloggers will report on products which they were gifted or paid for, so much so that blogging has developed into a new profession and pays a decent wage.

Press pack and press release

When a PR company is looking to get a brand into glossy fashion magazines, to get journalists talking or the media reporting – both print and digital – it will prepare and send out press kits, a physical or digital compilation of the most important information on the fashion brand, including the latest press releases, photographs of the collection (called look books) and information on the season's inspiration. A press kit might also contain background information on the brand, market data, videos or links to downloadable material and, of course, small gifts and trinkets.

An important element of the press kit is the press release. A press release is usually a short written text which states the most important information about an event or newsworthy story but is written in an inspiring way which captures the reader's attention. Sometimes the press release is called a press statement, media release or news release. It can be of any length ranging from just 300 words to 1,000. The press release can be part of the press kit or it can be sent on its own if it is noteworthy.

The information contained in the press release should be built like a pyramid with the most important and short sentences at the top, descending to more text throughout the body of the entire press release and allowing for larger sections of text farther down the page (see Figure 2.4).

1. The very first paragraph must provide answers to the five W questions:
    Who? Who are the key players – your company, anyone else involved with the product? Who does your news affect/who does it benefit?
    What? What is the news?
    Why? Why is this happening and why should the reader care?
    Where? Where did this happen or will happen?
    When? Is there a precise timing or time frame?
    The 5Ws might be accompanied by the "H" for how. How did this come about?
2. The second section gives more details on the elements mentioned in the first paragraph. It still has to be concise and to the point.
3. Further down, the next section can give details on the brand, its background or history, statistics and an interesting story that supports the main message of the release.
4. Any other details, information or text can be written here but should not contain vital facts of high importance as they might get omitted by the reader. The most important information goes to the top of the pyramid.

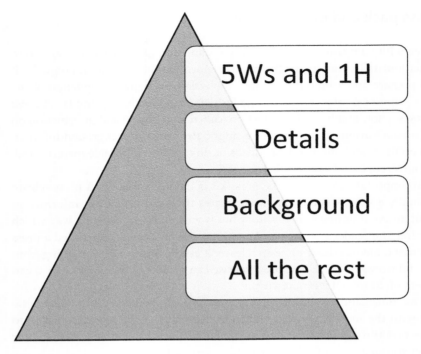

Figure 2.4 The press release pyramid. Author's original illustration.

Finally, the press release should state the media contacts with instructions on how to contact the PR agent or PR department of the fashion brand for further information. If the press release is not part of a press kit, then it is good to indicate that further media and look books can be obtained in physical or digital format upon request or through a link.

In Figure 2.5, you can see examples of two physical look books by Hugo Boss: one for the Boss Men's Collection of Fall/Winter 2016 and the other for Boss Women's Collection Fall/Winter 2016. The spiral-bound booklets show images taken directly from the catwalk show for the women's collection and photo stills for the menswear collection. Both booklets include stills of accessories and feature the name and product number of each item. These are handy for journalists when they want to request more information on the item but are also designed for buyers who need the product code for orders.

The booklets offer an internet link to the Hugo Boss press service portal where a trend report and all of the look book pictures can be downloaded for further use.

Good PR must not only know which journalist might be interested in writing about which product, they must also know the profiles of the

Figure 2.5 Hugo Boss look books: Fall/Winter 2016 with menswear accessories on the left and a runway shot of womenswear on the right. Image kindly provided by Hugo Boss.

readership. This is another area where both advertising and PR use the same information.

A professional who is constantly working with the same media will know these things by heart, but in case the information is not at hand, it can easily be looked up.

Every publication usually offers something called "media data" on its website. More than the content of the magazine, this is the information which is vital for advertising and PR alike. The media data will contain rate cards, or the prices for buying advertising space in the magazine. In the case of *Vogue*, one full-colour page costs around $200,000 in the USA. There will also be data on the cost of digital advertising space.

Furthermore, there is data on the readership with a look at the lifestyle (or demographics). This usually includes the average age or age span of the readers, whether they are male or female, if they are educated, how much they earn and what their lifestyle is generally like.

Both advertising and PR must understand what audience they want to communicate with when they launch a campaign. Is their target reader (and thus target customer) an affluent, urban female in her 30s with a high interest in designer brands? Or is the reader a teenager who still lives at home and can only buy cheaper products with their pocket money? Perhaps the target customer is a man who likes to do sports and nature, and who needs durable and eco-friendly clothing.

Case example: The Lawn Tennis Association – a social purpose for a niche audience

The successful PR agency in London called Exposure PR has worked for established and well-known clients such as Levi's, Jaeger, Barbour and Uniqlo and was responsible for successfully reviving Doc Martens with its fresh campaigns.

The agency worked for large brands with broad target audiences as well as localized and small brands, and in this case, it was a world-famous organization based in London, looking to work on a small local scale and with a social purpose.

In 2004, the Lawn Tennis Association (LTA), the national governing body for tennis throughout the UK which also organizes the world-renowned Wimbledon tennis championships, approached Exposure to help it spread the word about playing tennis to young people in the vicinity of London. The LTA had only managed to train one tennis star on home turf and wanted to get more young people to take up tennis but had difficulties encouraging Londoners to do so. Furthermore, tennis is a sport that was normally connected to the upper-middle and upper classes and perhaps off-putting for youths outside of this demographic.

So how could the PR agency reach the target market of its client? Exposure decided to target the hip and style-conscious youths of Greater London through the medium of fashion. Exposure PR recruited a graduate from the famed Central Saint Martins University to design an innovative and unusual capsule collection of tennis clothes. The mini collection featured hand-made adjustable textiles made from a combination of different types of mesh fabrics and featured three outfits that were adjustable, interchangeable, could be worn inside-out and be suitable for actively playing the sport (see Figure 2.6). This was relatively groundbreaking at the time because no tennis brand had delved away from functional athletic wear to fashion and there were no tennis brand collaborations with tennis stars that are common today.

After the collection was produced, a professional photo shoot was organized with a model at a local tennis court in London's Hackney – an area which is gentrified and very popular now but was considered rather deprived in the early 2000s. The images were published not in high-fashion glossy magazines but in daily and local papers which would be read by a wide demographic and spoken about. No advertising was used along with the PR campaign, illustrating that local campaigns and word-of-mouth might be more effective in reaching the target group than pure advertising.

Tennis Collection for Lawn Tennis Association

Olga Mitterfellner Designs

Figure 2.6 Original drawings, textile designs and the finished hand-made garments on a model showing an innovative tennis collection for the Lawn Tennis Association. Author's original designs, styling and photographs.

Other activities that PR companies do can include the organization of fashion shows, product launches or shop launches, securing celebrity endorsements, blogger relations and social media projects.

PR can also be quite serious: Strategic and financially focused PR companies might be in charge of dealing with all the publicity for the financial activities of a company. It is not only large corporations that offer an IPO (initial public offering) and join the stock market, but also fashion companies which are active on the stock exchange such as LVMH, Richemont or Farfetch. PR can help them here as they are obliged to report their financial results and activities at specified intervals. The same can be observed when there are takeovers of businesses or new owners, such as, in 2013, the takeover of Valentino by the financial vehicle Mayhoola, owned by the second wife of the former Emir of Qatar, Her Highness Sheikha Mozah bint Nasser Al Missned; and the takeover of Balmain in 2016.

Strategic public relations can also deal with crises or when a company is involved in a scandal. A good example is when, in 2014, the German clothing brand Tom Tailor was accused of using cat fur for the bobbles of its winter knitted hats, even though the company had a no-fur policy.

In such cases, advertising would not be of much use to shape the public's opinion and PR is the best method to proceed.

Interview with Teresa Havvas on Lipcote

Teresa Havvas is a creative communications expert and educator, co-founder of The Advisory & and head of brand for Lipcote & Co. (Lipcote [iconic lipstick topcoat] and Browcote [brow gel] are award-winning products.)

Q: Please tell me about yourself.

TH: Mentoring self-belief as part of a mission to safeguard creativity, I live by a 'for us, for others' philosophy, where the act of creative communication is to blend and collaborate the principles of branding, marketing, PR and advertising in service of great storytelling strategies and value innovation.

I have been in the industry for over 15 years, launching and championing independent and on-the-rise designers, hair and beauty salons, accessory labels, a style magazine, as well as in-house with a global lifestyle brand.

I graduated from LCF [London College of Fashion], class of 2000, in what was then one of the few holistic, BA Fashion Promotion

Figure 2.7 Teresa Havvas. Image by photographer Julia Sterre Schmitz.

degrees; a course that was innovated by industry's best teaching from the world of PR, marketing, journalism, culture and broadcasting. This is what provided me with the ultimate platform from which to launch my career as a PR consultant. Stories that connect audiences to brands in an authentic, engaging way is what drives me.

Q: What inspires you?

TH: Connection; the art of collaborative intelligence where we respect and decode mind patterns by way of revealing true possibilities ... I am inspired by industry friends who consciously go against the grain in pursuit of something better, cultivating messages that mean something, with positive social impact for people and planet. I am ever in awe of the new creatives I teach/mentor; a mutual alliance where my expertise and their fresh skill set collide to ignite ideas with intention. I'm inspired when my energy for a project ignites a person's inner confidence to be bold.

I welcome all opportunities to partner with those open to push parameters so we can free a new perspective and stories that make you feel something.

I surround myself with a lot of multi-disciplinary, image makers and visual storytellers, who come from all walks and backgrounds, so that I am constantly learning, challenging and being challenged. I am inspired by process and specifically *play* through honest yet facilitated ways of communication that can truly enable all to bring their unique selves to the conversation. It is our uniqueness that will define a new position from which to promote with purpose and cause.

Q: Tell me about the frameworks you apply to bring campaigns to life?

TH: "Social for social" is one approach developed for Lipcote & Co. to celebrate the launch of a new look and sister product to the brand. Dedicated to true followers, this *social* event, captured and produced in real time, organically generated on-site digital content assets used to tell stories post event and co-authored with those who have a genuine relationship with Lipcote & Co.

We wanted to push the traditional launch party format with an experience that captured community, conversation, self-expression and above all fun – key pillars to the brand.

All elements: from a specially selected beauty-inspired co-working venue, personalised catering and floristry; to independent embroidery body positivity workshops and mini spa retreat, were aligned to express and ignite conversations about lipstick. With Lipcote being the original lipstick sealer, each touchpoint resonated beyond the functional attributes to how it makes wearers *feel* when applying it to keep colour in place (see Figure 2.8). From this emotional perspective, Lipcote is also a tool for *sealing* self-confidence.

Friends and family of the brand also had an opportunity to meet those behind the brand face to face and learn more about our partnering charity – Get Lippy by Eve Appeal. A self-contained studio to capture photos of participating guests from press, bloggers, industry and internal team would become the makings of our campaign.

We broke tradition with a one-day event, held on a Sunday, and it was a full house filled with an invite-only crowd we knew would care and resonate.

We explored and embraced what it is to be social in all aspects and took time to acknowledge and celebrate brand-to-people relationships, to be remembered for the right reasons. With the landscape operating at such a fast pace, sometimes the bravest thing to do is to what I like to call "presentproof" … to pause, audit, and reaffirm intention so that we can *futureproof* customer journeys and experiences that connect in a more human way. Social for social is to frame events as experiences that facilitate making connections on and offline and in honour of a social cause that brings people together.

Figure 2.8 Lipcote lipstick sealer. With kind permission from Teresa Havvas and Lipcote.

Q: How do you understand the audience?

TH: Research and development are vital; hands-on and approached strategically. I spend time auditing and explore angles and avenues to establish how best to reach out and connect. It's a behind-the-scenes process that takes commitment, creative thinking, emotional and collaborative intelligence to ensure the correct to brand relationships are being made.

It is a grass roots, effective approach, and a long-term process, which you need to keep working on and we look at all media channels to listen and learn.

I put myself out there to meet as many people as possible, to discover as much as possible about them from a mind set and ethnographic point of view, so that understanding can inspire new ways to reach them with messages that are relevant.

This could involve enrolling insights and forecasting professionals, select creative and media teams as well as buyers to validate and challenge thinking.

My teaching also enables me to focus group new ideas and set live project briefs, so that young creatives and illustrators have an opportunity to work with us on projects.

Q: How do you go about setting your goals and achieving them?

TH: Goals are often set as series of mini – short- to mid-term – strategies that we roll out throughout the year, aligned to key retail partnerships and collaborators.

While reactive, I also forward plan as much as possible. From a commercial perspective, it's important to focus on a balance of trade and consumer-integrated strategies within reasonable set budgets.

We achieve by doing and learning from what worked/did not work to consistently get better.

Q: How do you deal with limitations?

TH: Creativity is of course limitless! That leaves the age-old budget constraints, which, while challenging, do encourage focus to best strategise. A modest budget for example means that we need to allow for a longer time frame to reach our potential and the time to negotiate the partnerships, so that they are mutually beneficial.

A larger pot of investment means that the process can be accelerated with opportunity to broaden the scope, the team and awareness.

Q: Do you see a link of PR and advertising working together?

TH: Yes, I think that it's circular, one feeds the other. It all radiates out from Creative Communication. I believe that the best PRs think like advertisers and that the best in advertising thinks as a PR. It's all about connection and it takes a holistic approach with above and below the line blending to form a cohesive interface that channels the message for an experience. I have learnt that without an experience being felt, there is no story to tell.

Q: How do you see ethics and social responsibility when working in PR? And what about beauty standards?

TH: It's fundamental that practitioners also give time to educate and create platforms that seek out talent to nurture and guide future communicators. I feel that all campaigns should consider positive social

Figure 2.9 Lipcote packaging. With kind permission from Teresa Havvas and Lipcote.

impact – a cause to pioneer so that the power goes further with intention, integrity and above all transparency. PR when delivered well can drive change and inspire visionary thinking.

Beauty standards is an illusion. What's important is to educate and inspire through promotional campaigns that are carefully curated. I'm fascinated with the term 'Edutainment' to cleverly produce both informative and captivating content that helps people make better choices.

I'm of the thinking that follower numbers do not act as a barometer for status. I would like to see the term 'beauty standards' dissolved because the industry recognises difference and diversity as standard. I'm a philosopher at heart and Beauty for me is Truth.

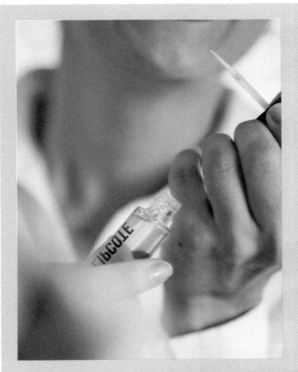

Figure 2.10 Lipcote product close-up. With kind permission from Teresa Havvas and Lipcote.

Q: What are your recommendations for current and future PR professionals?

TH: To honour your creative spirit. Research and explore, be curious and challenge; respectfully disrupt and build campaigns with heart. Remember the R in PR is Relationships; connect and communicate responsibly.

Ethical considerations

Public relations is an evolvement of propaganda and is nearly identical in its content. The only difference is the official name. Whatever term you use to describe it, it has the power and the goal to actively manipulate the minds of masses of people to the advantage of a particular brand, person or organization. The relationship between the two is one-sided by default and only benefits one party. We are now at an age where PR has evolved so much that there are trusted practices of the profession and measurable outcomes, making it a lucrative instrument for any fashion brand. The art of PR includes understanding the psychology of individuals and the masses and using the most suitable mass media instruments to influence if not control society.

PR stunts are often disguised as a real social occurrence, taking inspiration from the success of the "Torches of Freedom" by Bernays in the 1920s. By means of deception, consumers are fooled and cannot make an informed decision about a particular product or brand.

When working in PR or with a PR team, it is imperative to consider the ethical implications of any such action, especially when negative, unhealthy or unfair things are falsely portrayed as something positive (such as portraying cigarettes as healthy and highly fashionable).

Further reading

Bernays, E. and Miller M. C. (2004) *Propaganda*. New York: Ig Publishing.

Chomsky, N. (1995) *Manufacturing Consent: The Political Economy of the Mass Media*. London: Vintage.

Cope, J. and Maloney, D. (2016) *Fashion Promotion in Practice*. London: Bloomsbury.

Diamond, J. (2015) *Retail Advertising and Promotion*. New York: Fairchild.

Dowson, R. and Bassett, D. (2018) *Event Planning and Management: A Practical Handbook for PR and Events Professionals*. London: Kogan Page.

Graham, B. and Anouti, C. (2018) *Promoting Fashion*. London: Laurence King.

Moore, G. (2012) *Basics Fashion Management: Fashion Promotion 02: Fashion Promotion: Building a Brand through Marketing and Communication*. Lausanne, Switzerland: Bloomsbury Publishing PLC; Imprint: AVA Publishing SA.

Perlman, S. and Sherman, G. J. (2012) *Fashion Public Relations*. New York: Fairchild.

Reic, I. (2017) *Events Marketing Management: A Consumer Perspective*. Abingdon: Routledge.

Smith, P. R. and Zook, Z. (2016) *Marketing Communications: Offline and Online Integration, Engagement and Analytics*. 6th edn. London: Kogan Page.

Tye, L. (2002) *The Father of Spin: Edward L. Bernays and the Birth of Public Relations*. New York: Henry Holt (Owl Books).

Wilcox, D. L. et al. (2015) *Public Relations: Strategies and Tactics*. 11th edn. Harlow: Pearson.

The Marketing Mix and communications tools

3

Chapter topics

The original Marketing Mix

As demonstrated in the first two chapters, some of the important people who developed the foundation of modern-day marketing by developing advertising and public relations were Edward Bernays, Ernest Dichter, Ivy Lee, Elmo Lewis, Walter Dill Scott, Abraham Maslow, and the inventors of the "Marketing Mix": Neil H. Borden and E. Jerome McCarthy.

Prior to that, although marketing activities were carried out, there was no specific term or theoretical framework to conceptualize them. The Marketing Mix was invented by one of the many famous thinkers of the twentieth century, Neil Borden, who contrived it in 1940, and it went on to become a significant foundation of former and current marketing theories as well as a widespread framework used in higher education for marketing.

DOI: 10.4324/9781003449157-3

Traditional Marketing Mix

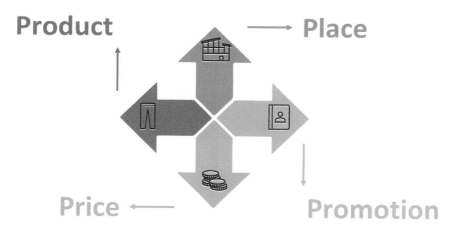

Figure 3.1 The Marketing Mix. Author's original illustration based on the original Marketing Mix.

The mix includes all the important basic elements that need to be in place and in harmony in order to make a brand successful as well as profitable (see Figure 3.1). In 1960, E. Jerome McCarthy took the theory a step further and segmented those elements into separate groups, called the 4Ps:

Product
Price
Place
Promotion

The four basic Ps determine the product which needs to be produced and distributed, the place where it is on offer, its price and its promotion through communication strategies. Thus, the concept of advertising and public relations is grouped into one of the four Ps (promotion). According to the theory, the Ps can be controlled and used to ensure that the business is profitable. It is also taught to students first as a holistic concept, looking at promotion later on. However, historically and chronologically, the promotional tools were the first and arguably the most significant marketing concepts that were developed by the Western capitalist world and implemented successfully, so this book looks at these theories according to their developmental chronology.

The 4Ps in detail plus 3Ps: process, physical evidence, people

In the 1980s, the four Marketing Mix Ps (Product Price, Place, Promotion) were expanded further to 7Ps, and had more of a focus on services: process (service process), physical evidence and people (participants) (Kotler et al., 2009, p. 17).

Much literature and consequent discussions refer to the 4, 7, 8 or more Ps with various adaptations and expansions. This chapter looks at the classical four Ps in depth and examines the additional three which Booms and Bitner proposed in 1981.

Product

The product is arguably a key component of the Marketing Mix and is most important to any fashion business which sells tangible and physical products, such as clothing, shoes, accessories, etc. This might also include perfume, cosmetics, jewellery and watches. Some fashion brands consciously opt for a so-called brand-extension or brand-stretch into other segments, meaning that they might also offer travel experiences such as hotels, restaurants, food, homeware, flowers and others.

A prime example is Armani, which offers several fashion brands (i.e. Giorgio Armani, Emporio Armani, Armani Exchange) and all the items listed above (i.e. restaurants, hotels, flowers, beauty), at various price points from true luxury to affordable luxury and premium prices.

Zara is another brand whose focus is on the clothing segment in the fast-fashion price range but also has Zara Home stores, separate from their fashion stores, offering homeware and lifestyle products.

An important part of making a fashion product desirable for consumers is branding.

A brand, according to Kotler, is "a name, term, sign, symbol, design or a combination of these, that identifies the maker or seller of the product or service" (Kotler et al., 2009, p. 511).

As mentioned in Chapter 1, brands became prevalent with the onset of the industrial revolution to better distinguish products from various manufacturers, and branding has grown into an art and profession of its own over the last centuries. The brand name, logo and features are an integral part of it – they make up a fashion brand's reputation regarding quality and performance. The packaging of a brand might also add to the way consumers perceive and enjoy it.

Table 3.1 The 7 Ps

Product/service	Price	Promotion	Place	Physical evidence	Process	People
Product or service	Regular price	Advertising	Global channels	Tangible service environment and evidence	Service design	Staff
Design features	Discount price	Public relations	Assortments		Self-service technologies	Customers
Brand name	Payment conditions	Sales promotion	Locations	Sound		
Packaging	Pricing strategies	Direct marketing	Inventory	Sight		
Services		Online and offline	Transport	Smell		
				Taste		
				Touch		
				Packaging		

Source: Based on Kotler et al. (2009).

For fashion consumers, the brand's image can sometimes overshadow the product itself and give way to accepting hefty prices. Brands like Supreme have been changing the way luxury fashion is perceived and purchased in recent years, since the streetwear brand teamed up with luxury fashion including Louis Vuitton, Burberry, Tiffany and Co., The North Face and others. The association with Supreme led to customers anticipating a "product drop" weeks in advance, later queuing up at the stores and hoping to get a product before it is "sold out". The quality of the product was hardly at the forefront of customers' minds as they did not get to test and inspect it prior to purchasing. The affiliation of the brands was enough to cause hype.

The fashion product can also be complemented by a service or experience, such as a beauty treatment, an app or an event, but is ultimately tied to the fashion brand and the core product that it is known for. For businesses that have a focus on service, the supplemental 3Ps (as described later in this chapter) are an essential element of their Marketing Mix.

Price

The pricing strategy of a fashion business determines how much customers have to pay in order to receive the goods or services. Most of the time, the price is directly connected to the market level, the quality and possibly the reputation, with haute couture being highly expensive and fast fashion (or throwaway fashion) being most affordable.

The various price levels of a fashion product can be categorized within a hierarchy of price and quality in the pyramid shown in Figure 3.2.

Figure 3.2 Hierarchy of price and quality pyramid. Author's original illustration.

The price is determined by the production and distribution costs, as well as the mark-up that the brand can achieve. A mass-produced item might have a low mark-up, but the business remains profitable due to the sheer volume of items sold. A hand-crafted luxury piece such as a watch might be of limited production numbers and would need a high mark-up and price to justify the reduced quantity made, as well as the time, effort and materials that are used in its manufacture.

A brand also has to monitor competitors' pricing carefully, understand what the customer is prepared to pay and whether he or she will return for repeat purchases.

In terms of product promotion, pricing can be used through discounts, deals (i.e. buy one get one 50% off) or vouchers in order to entice the customer to make a purchase.

Place

This "P" is predominantly involved in the transport, logistics and distribution of fashion through various sales channels. Enough merchandise must be produced or sourced so it can be offered at the "place", which can be online, offline, through mail-order catalogues or even directly from the manufacturer. The brand must ensure the correct assortment and carefully monitor its inventory. Furthermore, in a very globalized business, the place is no longer necessarily fixed to one place of origin and local distribution. Luxury fashion brands might still produce their products in one atelier, the place where the brand originated many decades ago, but their consumers will expect to purchase the products in a myriad of global locations. The mid-market and fast-fashion brands often produce in several countries and in quantities which need a high level of management. Time management also plays a role, as the product must reach the place or be available through any sales channel in the correct quantities.

Furthermore, consumers now want the physical and digital place of purchase to be highly engaging, entertaining and experiential. Chapter 9 takes a closer look at how this can be achieved through sensory branding and digital integration.

Promotion

This "P" is the main focus of this book, and it stands for effective communication with the target customer and prospective customer with the goal of increasing awareness, profit or both. Promotion includes advertising and public relations, sales promotion and direct marketing, and can be conducted online, offline and in person, through visual merchandising, celebrity endorsement, sponsorship and guerrilla marketing.

As mentioned in Chapter 1, the USA was one of the pioneers when it came to post-industrial advertising, and the first advertising agencies emerged there in the latter half of the nineteenth century, such as J. Walter Thompson (founded in 1864 and still active today) and N.W. Ayer & Sons.

Promotion is also highly reliant on the mass media landscape such as newspapers, cinema, TV, radio and, of course, digital media. The choice of promotional channels is part of the communications strategy planning that a business has to establish. This involves setting goals, budgets and measurable key performance indicators (KPIs) to monitor the outcome of the communications endeavours.

Promotion is also a question of cost because campaigns and appropriate channels can be very expensive. Equally, a well-planned and executed promotional activity by a brand can have a high return on investment. Most brands cannot exist without promotional activities.

Marketing communications tools

The business strategy of any company will likely include overall objectives, and the marketing department will make an appropriate marketing plan. This is then transferred onto an operational plan, which describes how marketing communications should be executed, as part of the marketing communications plan.

The marketing communications plan will establish a time frame in which the most appropriate tools will be implemented and how. (In terms of the Marketing Mix, it is the "P" for promotion.)Nowadays, the most effective communications plan should use a braod selection of available tools and strive for Integrated Marketing Communication.

Figure 3.3 shows an approach to the Integrated Marketing Communications plan and the various tools available. Depending on the business needs, this can be reduced, expanded or changed to best fit the strategic and marketing goals and usually a combination of on-line and off-line measures is used, which can be classified into Above-the-Line and Below-the-Line activities. These are explained in more detail in Chapter 4 and generally consist of:

- Public relations
- Advertising
- Social media activities (across various platforms and in collaboration with social media personalities)

Figure 3.3 Integrated marketing communications. Author's original illustration.

- Trade shows, conferences, presentations and events
- Sales promotions (direct mail, in store or online)

In order to choose the appropriate tools, it is important to understand whether the fashion brand wants to use mass communication (mass marketing) or very targeted communication (target marketing).

Mass marketing

Mass marketing is intended to appeal to all, with no specific target market in mind. This can work especially well with staple products such as basic socks, basic underwear and cotton T-shirts because – one might argue – everyone will need these items in their lives, no matter who they are. In this case, to boost a bland staple product, differentiate the brand from its competitors and reach a mass market, collaborations between brands can be very useful, as was done in the case of H&M that collaborated with David Beckham for its underwear.

NB: Above-the-line communication is most suitable for mass marketing.

Target marketing

With target marketing, you spend time (and money) researching your customer. The advantage here is that from then on your marketing efforts are streamlined and efficient – you can reach the people who will actually spend money on your brand. The brand communications plan will be tailored to address these specific customers. Chapters 7 and 8 are dedicated to understanding target marketing in great detail, for both national and international consumers.

NB: Below-the-line communication is most suitable for target marketing.

The supplemental 3Ps

People

People are those who are directly and indirectly connected to the consumer and play a role in the product or service that is offered. These people might be involved in the design, production, and distribution or delivery of the product. They might be sales assistants or customer service employees online and offline.

In terms of customer service, this is a pivotal contact point, and businesses must take this very seriously to achieve a positive and lasting relationship with the consumer as well as repeat sales. A prime example comes from the aviation industry, where airlines compete for passengers. No matter what the booking process and pre-flight experience were, the ultimate test is the flight itself. The cabin crew and flight crew represent everything the airline stands for, in a confined space, within a limited amount of time and with a predetermined selection of service items for the passenger. Their service, appearance and competence often determine whether a passenger will choose the same airline for their next flight.

It is the same for fashion brands, where the sales assistants only have a limited amount of time to really impress the customer and make him or her return next time. In addition, contrary to aviation, the product might not have been purchased yet, and it is up to the staff to entice the consumer to buy.

Furthermore, there are the management and marketing personnel within the business who play a significant role behind the scenes of a brand but with a powerful effect on consumers. As the case example at the end of this chapter shows, unethical or unwise behaviour can actively disappoint customers and cause a brand to decline.

Process

The word "process" can be substituted with the word "system". This is the system any and every business needs to have in order to thrive because it is responsible for delivering a service to the customer. It might be the technological processes, which would include the process of manufacturing goods and adapting them for the needs of clients, as well as supply chain management (SCM) (digitalerra, 2016), the electronic process or a transaction process (payment systems), aftersales process, and all elements of the customer journey which is the end-to-end customer experience and explained in more detail in Chapter 6.

A prime example of "process" in place is the subscription business trend in fashion and especially in beauty and cosmetics. Birchbox is one company that offers a seamless customer journey from signing up online for the beauty products to receiving regular product deliveries and customizing the subscription. The brand can only do well if its process is completely thought through and offers customers a satisfactory end-to-end experience.

Physical evidence

These are tangible elements of the brand where the customer experiences the service or receives evidence of the brand's ethos. For example, the tangible elements within the service environment might be the building or store; the sound, sight, smell, taste and touch within those premises; as well as any material cues. Brochures, flyers, business cards or a website could be considered as part of the service environment and its evidence. Physical evidence is therefore connected to the "P" for place, and elements of this have been extracted and separated as "physical evidence".

Further elements of this evidence can be packaging, such as the shopping bags, wrapping paper, and tags and labels on the garments. If one buys a luxury item, careful packaging in quality material is expected, whereas a fast-fashion store might ask the customer to pay extra for a plastic bag.

The brochure by a watchmaker or jewellery brand might be printed on glossy, good-quality paper, and this again will signal the brand's positioning, identity and market level to the consumer.

Overall, the physical evidence has to show consistency not only with one retail place but across all stores and even online.

According to the Oxford College of Marketing (2013), the staff have to look smart and tidy, be dressed appropriately, and might benefit from wearing uniforms or adhering to a dress policy that leads to a consistent image for existing and potential customers. Chapter 8 looks at the point-of-sale in more detail.

The New Marketing Mix: 4Ds replace the 4Ps

The twenty-first century calls for a New Marketing Mix, and due to global changes, it is questionable whether the old Marketing Mix would still be relevant to all types of fashion businesses.

Arguably, a New Marketing Mix would be useful where the 4Ps are replaced by 4Ds.
What are those 4Ds?

Diversity replacing place: This "D" has two elements: local diversity and global diversity that replace a traditional look at a particular marketplace. Companies need to think globally because they are trading in diverse regions and cultures. China and India are set to supersede the American market in the near future, so all companies should consider how they could sell to new markets and hire knowledgeable staff. The marketplace is now virtually everywhere and anywhere, very diverse and international.

Even in the home country, increasingly, fashion consumers want to see their own diversity respected and reflected in the way brands communicate with them. The UK's *Vogue* magazine has, for example, changed its editorial team to include a broader spectrum of races and ethnicities on its staff, which is a step that was much celebrated within the fashion industry. The UK is a highly diverse country, London in particular, so it is no longer possible to ignore this fact at a fashion publication.

Digitalization replacing promotion: Reliance on the old types of promotion does not suffice to ensure success for brands today, and a digital strategy is crucial. Fashion brands have to engage with consumers through different devices and platforms, specifically tailored to the preferred communication channels of the age group and geographical location. A brand can do well with digital promotion only, ignoring traditional communication channels altogether, and this is especially true for pure play online retailers that do not have physical stores.

On the other hand, when you add digital technology in a brick-and-mortar store, you can use it to promote your product at the POS and connect it to your digital offering, creating a 360° experience.

Design replacing product: Trends in fashion and lifestyle are changing rapidly, with very few brands still adhering to a few collections per year, as was the norm only a few decades ago. As brands drop or release collections frequently, consumers pay more attention to the design and style of the product.

It has to be trendy and interesting for a brand to make a sale, and design is the key to this. There are also new technologies revolutionizing the way products are designed, embedding functionality or smart properties that play a role when consumers make a choice. This can include nanotechnology, smart textiles, and 3D or 4D printing. Therefore, in fashion, the overall design is the key to any successful product.

Desire replacing price: With neuroscience revealing the mysteries of the consumer's brain, science and marketing realize what makes people tick. Although a suitable pricing policy is still important, it is more important to create desire within the consumer's mind. This can be achieved if a brand has a great story, promotes itself through the right channels and creates products and a brand identity that are unique. Consequently, the consumer will long for this brand and agree to the price, rather than the other way around where the price dictates the decision to purchase. This is particularly true for all the young generations: The great consumer group called Millennials is more concerned with a brand's image and sustainable approach rather than the price or even the quality. Generation Z lives online and has to be persuaded by brands on social media and through purpose and social causes such as inclusivity and diversity. The youngest consumer group, Gen Alpha, needs personalized content and role models who endorse their products. It is imperative for fashion brands to understand how to tap into the emotion of desire with all young generations while not alienating the older ones.

NEW Marketing Mix with 4 Ds

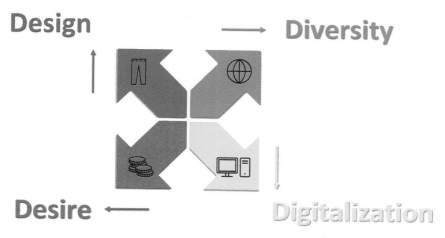

Figure 3.4 The New Marketing Mix: 4Ds. Author's original illustration.

Interview with Sharon Hughes and case example on Donna Sharp

Figure 3.5 Sharon Hughes.

With a dynamic presence in the global educational landscape, Sharon N Hughes is not only a seasoned educator but also a strategic leader known for challenging conventions and transforming innovative ideas into impactful realities. Her dedication to fashion studies, coupled with a commitment to equality and inclusive cultural expressions, has positioned her as a thought leader in the realms of arts, technology and business. She is skilled in digital strategy, integrated marketing communications, events coordination, creative management, consumer behaviour and project management. Boasting over a decade of teaching experience, Sharon's extensive academic contributions extend globally, from the UK to Asia, the US to the UAE, as well as consulting in Africa and Portugal. She has delivered lectures and convened symposiums on diverse topics, such as the evolving landscape of African fashion, social media marketing and digital trends in the fashion industry. Her academic and journalistic contributions extend to publications in journals, conference papers and articles exploring themes such as Black beauty, fashion ethics and museum exhibition reviews on Black British fashion. Her teaching and research interests reflect her passion for inclusivity and cultural diversity in the arts. Her focus spans a wide array of topics, including Black women's identities through digital lenses, decolonization in the arts, historical and contemporary expressions of Black and Brown identities in fashion, and STEAM initiatives for marginalized youth in art and design.

With over 20 years of industry experience in marketing management with lifestyle brands such as Macy's and Instyle UK, and creative arts education firms, Sharon began her career in fashion retail management in the US before transitioning to the corporate world of marketing by way of event planning, advertising and creative management with creative firms and non-profits globally. Her expertise in navigating the dynamic landscape of digital marketing in the fashion industry is commendable. Notably, her consulting engagement with brands like Chanel underscores her ability to drive brand developmental marketing strategies.

Q: What does marketing mean to you?

SH: Marketing means to me presenting the right product, at the right price, to the right target audience, and in the right place. It is about establishing relationships with consumers by appealing to their lifestyle and maintaining those relationships by understanding their needs and wants as they progress through life.

Figure 3.6 New brand imagery for the Donna Sharp brand. With kind permission from Sharon Hughes.

Q: Please tell me about the project you did for the Donna Sharp brand. How did you use the principles of marketing for it?

SH: As Director of Marketing for American Heritage Textiles (a bedding brand), I've been charged with rebranding a new company with an old but well-established '90s brand, Donna Sharp. Changing the mindsets of people who are very loyal to a former company is very challenging. I would say the most challenging element of my role.

But as the new owner took over Donna Sharp [the company], it was set to change as Donna Sharp, the brand. With the establishment of a new mission and brand values, I took the Head of Departments, our CEO and owner through strategic branding seminars in which I used the 4Ps to discuss our new plans. From redefining our product (who is the Donna Sharp brand, what do we stand for, who do we create products for – our customers), our pricing strategy was reestablished for there wasn't one prior to my entry. Therefore, as you can see from the chart, products will be launched within four pricing and positioning ranges, as well as priced and launched accordingly throughout the seasons. Our collections (via e-commerce) will be launched sporadically throughout the year' this will keep our e-commerce as fresh as possible. This feeds the current drive of online shoppers, for studies show consumers shop more often and have a desire for new arrivals and sales as they enter e-commerce sites.

As a manufacturer and retailer, we had to establish our place in the market, for not only do we sell on our own website, but we sell on partner websites such as Wayfair, along with wholesale clients such as boutique shops and catalogue sites.

Regarding promotions, previously, Donna Sharp's promotional material had been quite bland, uninviting and confusing. The campaigns prior to my arrival featured models aged in their 20s when Donna Sharp's youngest consumer is in their 50s. Therefore, the face of the brand was not representative of the shareholders of the brand. Therefore, for our spring campaigns, we launched an integrated strategy utilizing print and digital mediums, website, PPC [pay-per-click] and social media. We chose models that were aged appropriately to our existing and aspirational customers and was much more diverse. With $1.2 trillion in spending power, African-American consumers are an important population for smart brands that want to grow market share and brand preference. Therefore, you can see the results of this campaign attached. Our marketing materials and promotions are looking cleaner, sharper and more approachable. Most importantly, they are up-to-date, current and diverse. [Sharon modelled herself in the campaign to represent diversity.]

Q: Do you think that you used all seven Ps and if so, how did you use them?

SH: Eventually, yes. People, process and physical evidence have fallen in line with how we position our parent company to our existing customers as they age; maintain relationships they set for their children (Gen X); and establish products, and diverse promotions that will attract new customers (older Millennials).

Q: Did you use any marketing and branding communications tools?

SH: Yes.

Q: What was the outcome of the project?

SH: Still ongoing. However, our sales have increased by 21 per cent. Website traffic has increased by 53 per cent. Our social media engagement has increased. Our review average is 4.7 out of 5.0, and we have launched a modern brand called Your Lifestyles to service the new customer we wish to attract. Therefore, I would say we are moving in the right direction.

Figure 3.7 New brand imagery for Donna Sharp. With kind permission from Sharon Hughes.

Our product and pricing strategy

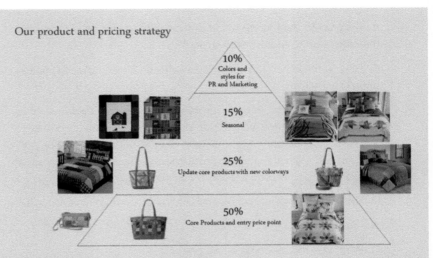

Figure 3.8 New product and pricing strategy for Donna Sharp. With kind permission from Sharon Hughes.

Q: Did anything surprise you?

SH: Yes, how challenging it is to train internal teams to new brand standards and how loyal customers over 55 really are.

Retail should be adapted to fit product develop

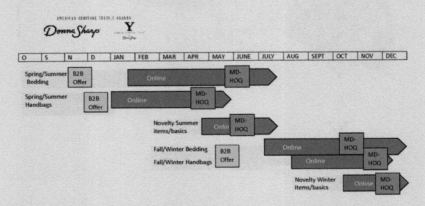

Figure 3.9 Planning of product launch for Donna Sharp. With kind permission from Sharon Hughes.

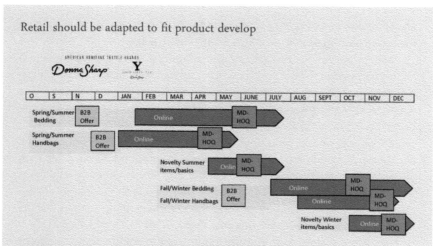

Retail should be adapted to fit product develop

Figure 3.10 New brand imagery for Donna Sharp featuring diversity. With kind permission from Sharon Hughes.

Case example: Abercrombie & Fitch – a brand built on the absence of ethics

Abercrombie & Fitch (also known as A&F) is an example of historically unethical brand leadership that was consciously embedded into its marketing and communication tactics, ultimately driving the brand into decline. A&F has learned from these past mistakes and, under the management of a new CEO, has applied new marketing tactics that attempt to repair the past issues and steer it in a more ethical and inclusive direction.

Mike Jeffries, the CEO

The American fashion brand Abercrombie & Fitch started out as a hunting company in the early 1900s and consequently went through several phases of acquisitions and rebranding. In its famous incarnation as a casual-wear fashion brand from the early 1990s, it was led by controversial CEO Michael Jeffries for a total of 22 years. Jeffries is said to have run the brand very much like a toxic cult (Armitage, 2014).

For example, the highly secretive headquarters and training facilities of A&F were purposely built in 2002 in the middle of nowhere in New Albany, Ohio, isolating staff from the outside world while insulating them with constant music playing. It was also known as "the campus" and was designed by Anderson Architects, which created open-plan interiors with worktables and sheds, as well as space for the brand's own advertising posters, making the space highly immersive (Office Snapshots, 2024).

Reportedly, Jeffries brought store managers around a campfire where he then revealed the latest sales numbers and achievements in a very informal setting. According to Denizet-Lewis (2006), everyone at the site was young, and wore torn jeans by the brand and flip-flops. The mode of transportation in the camp was foot-powered scooters.

Jeffries was said to have been obsessed with youthful and good looks and underwent numerous plastic surgeries attempting to save his own appearance from natural ageing. According to Robin Lewis, a retail consultant, the CEO aligned his soul and entire persona to the image of A&F through the surgeries and by wearing the brand's clothing such as T-shirts and ripped jeans (Bloomberg Businessweek, 2015).

This personal style gave a strong identity to the brand and its strategies as well as policies. For instance, Jeffries's recruitment policies were controversial: Only good-looking people were allowed to apply as "models" – a term used in lieu of the usual term "sales assistant". For those models, A&F provided handbooks which dictated appearance such as clothing, hair and even nail varnish colour. Controversially, only good-looking, white, young and slim people were Jeffries's preferred staff and customers, and the brand was built to exclude those who did not fit this stereotype.

To Jeffries, sexual attraction was vital in what he saw as the "emotional experience" he created for the customers, as the CEO revealed in his infamous interview with *Salon* magazine: "It's almost everything. That's why we hire good-looking people in our stores. Because good-looking people attract other good-looking people, and we want to market to cool, good-looking people. We don't market to anyone other than that" (Denizet-Lewis, 2016).

How was this marketing vision embedded into the Marketing Mix?

Product

The products included t-shirts, casual tops and bottoms, knitwear, jeans, and personal care products and were priced higher than competitors, putting the brand in the premium segment.

The brand refused to serve diverse customers by deliberately limiting the clothing sizes. The colour black was banned from the collections, the logos were ever-present and a big part of the necessary brand recognition and identity.

It was an all-American style that was created from Jeffries's vision with denim, polos, T-shirts and smart-casual khakis, all embellished with large and recognizable logos.

Figure 3.11 Billboard advertising of Abercrombie & Fitch depicting a topless model during the leadership of CEOJeffries.

Brand communication and promotion

Abercrombie & Fitch was perhaps most famous for the advertising and promotional material which drew much interest but also caused plenty of controversy. It predominantly had the visual language of inappropriate adult material; it was deemed racy, sexualizing teens and showing them scantily clothed or nude – much to the dismay of the teen customers' parents. Until approximately 2004 and the outcome of a lawsuit, most teenagers featured in the ads were predominantly white. Many of the campaigns were shot by famous fashion photographer Bruce Weber (*The Guardian*, 2012).

A&F did not just create oversized billboards in busy urban areas, but to reach absolutely anyone anywhere in the US, the brand produced a magazine called *A&F Quarterly*, which was accused of promoting "alcohol and group sex" to teenagers (*The New Yorker*, 2013). The magazine was discontinued in 2003.

According to Denizet-Lewis (2016), the magazine "boasted articles about the history of orgies and pictures of chiselled, mostly white, all-American boys and girls (but mostly boys) cavorting naked on horses, beaches, pianos, surfboards, statues and phallically suggestive tree trunks". The American Decency Association was so outraged that it called for a boycott and started selling anti-Abercrombie T-shirts: 'Ditch Fitch: Abercrombie Peddles Porn and Exploits Children.' Meanwhile, gay men across America were eagerly collecting the magazines, lured by photographer Bruce Weber's taste for beautiful, masculine boys playfully pulling off each other's boxers.

(Denizet-Lewis, 2006)

As much as this brand communication approach was clearly unethical, it worked perfectly well for A&F creating toxic role models for gullible teenagers who embraced the idea. The young male customers were emulating the male models, and girls customers were enthusiastically wishing to have those boys (Chen, 2021).

Place: in-store promotion and visual merchandising

One of the main attractions of physical A&F stores were young, buff and good-looking topless men standing outside, luring in customers who first lined up to have their photos taken. Once inside, there were more large images of half-naked models covering the walls; the lights were dimmed to create a dark and club-like atmosphere. There was loud music, and the signature scent "Fierce" was sprayed throughout the stores. This scent was described by A&F as "lifestyle ... packed with confidence and a bold, masculine attitude" (Shopify, 2016). In fact, these ideas were guidelines that came directly from CEO Jeffries. According to Chen (2021), Jeffries dictated to the stores to play the music loudly, diffuse the scent, ensure dark lighting and for staff never to wear dark colours and black.

A&F ethical faux pas and lawsuits

The first racial discrimination lawsuits emerged as early as 1999, when it became evident that A&F hardly hired ethnic minorities or women, and if it did, those individuals would be made invisible to customers by working in the back offices or cleaning the premises. In 2004, A&F was penalized with a payment of $40 million to all the plaintiffs and made small efforts to improve its diversity (Beachler, 2014). Furthermore, A&F had to change its strategy for recruiting staff, which was done by actively "targeting particular predominately white fraternities or sororities" (LDF, 2006).

Product scandals

In 2002, A&F produced T-shirts which made fun of Asians. For example, one shirt featured a print of comic-style Asians (reminiscent of discriminatory drawings of the early twentieth century) with the caption "Wong

Brothers Laundry Service: Two Wongs can make it White". This was not just a play on words but also a strong discriminatory message. The laundry service was a direct attack on laundry services run by Asian Americans.

Another shirt in the series featured a printed Buddha and the words: "Abercrombie and Fitch Buddha Bash – Get Your Buddha on the Floor", with Buddha being used as a substitute for the word "booty". When Asian Americans felt stereotyped and discriminated against, a PR spokesperson from Abercrombie & Fitch showed no remorse and argued that the brand thought Asians would love the shirt (Strasburg, 2002). Even though the T-shirts were eventually pulled from the stores, it left a bitter taste with consumers and the media alike, prompting many to go out on the street to protest against the discrimination.

All this did not transpire to the A&F staff. In 2006, A&F was preparing to launch stores in the UK and held a recruitment event in London for store managers. The recruitment process included events in London bars where two American A&F recruiters made jokes about the T-shirts, finding them very entertaining.

Just a year prior to that, in 2005, A&F launched a line of T-shirts that featured slogans which offended many girls and women. The copy included "Who Needs a Brain When You Have These?" and "Gentlemen Prefer Tig Ol' Bitties" and "Do I Make You Look Fat?" (Danowitz et al., 2012). The T-shirts were later discontinued.

Exclusion, not inclusion

In 2006, Jeffries was interviewed by Benoit Denizet-Lewis of *Salon* magazine – an infamous interview which had a big impact on the brand – where Jeffries unapologetically stated that his brand is intended only for cool kids, definitely excluding others. His words became synonymous with the brand's image. The reporter called Jeffries "The Willie Wonka of the fashion industry" thereafter (Armitage, 2014).

Denizet-Lewis (2006) observed that for the CEO, America's overweight, unattractive and undesirable teens should shop elsewhere, quoting Jeffries's following words:

> In every school there are the cool and popular kids, and then there are the not-so-cool kids. Candidly, we go after the cool kids. We go after the attractive all-American kid with a great attitude and a lot of friends. A lot of people don't belong [in our clothes], and they can't belong. Are we exclusionary? Absolutely. Those companies that are in trouble are trying to target everybody: young, old, fat, skinny. But

then you become totally vanilla. You don't alienate anybody, but you don't excite anybody, either.

The alienation was also targeting employees, discriminating on the grounds of physical disabilities, religion, ethnicity and much more.

In 2007, a girl had applied for a job at the retail store and wore a hijab during the interview process. She did not get the job, and it was later revealed that this was because she wore the religious head covering. A lawsuit lasting an astounding eight years followed the incident, and ultimately the plaintiff won – in 2015. This was picked up by the media and caused much scandalous press, such as Aljazeera (2015), which critically reported that Elauf was denied the job by A&F "on the grounds that wearing the scarf violated its 'look policy' for members of the sales staff, a policy intended to promote the brand's East Coast collegiate image".

In 2009, a former employee in the UK took Abercrombie & Fitch to an employment tribunal. The plaintiff was born with a deformity of her arm (with a lower part missing) and allegedly had to work in the stockroom of the London store in the UK. This was due to her not fitting the company's strict "look policy" for shop floor staff. Although she received £8,000 for unlawful harassment, it was ruled that she did not suffer disability discrimination (Saner, 2012)

In 2011, Abercrombie & Fitch implemented a brand strategy to deter an unintentional brand ambassador from the Italian-American community. The brand tried to pay off reality TV show star Mike Sorrentino, also known as "The Situation", to stop wearing A&F shirts on *Jersey Shore* because it supposedly brought a negative image to the "aspirational nature" of the A&F brand. The Italian-American cast was famous for being "loud, foul-mouthed, hyper-groomed, spray-tanned, sex-obsessed" and might be alienating faithful A&F fans (Sweney, 2011). A spokesperson from A&F stated:

> We are deeply concerned that Mr. Sorrentino's association with our brand could cause significant damage to our image. We have therefore offered a substantial payment to Michael 'The Situation' Sorrentino and the producers of MTV's Jersey Shore to have the character wear an alternate brand. We have also extended this offer to other members of the cast and are urgently awaiting a response.

Controversially, at the same time, A&F began marketing shirts with the printed words "The Fitchuation", which were profiting from the television

A&F Marketing under Mike Jeffries

Toxic, unethical and discriminatory policies were embedded in the Marketing Mix

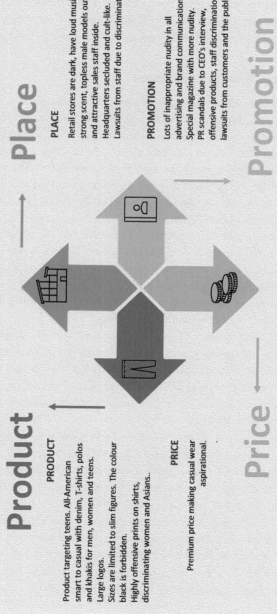

Product

PRODUCT

Product targeting teens. All-American smart to casual with denim, T-shirts, polos and khakis for men, women and teens. Large logos.
Sizes are limited to slim figures. The colour black is forbidden.
Highly offensive prints on shirts, discriminating women and Asians..

PRICE

Premium price making casual wear aspirational.

Place

PLACE

Retail stores are dark, have loud music, strong scent, topless male models outside and attractive sales staff inside.
Headquarters secluded and cult-like.
Lawsuits from staff due to discrimination.

PROMOTION

Lots of inappropriate nudity in all advertising and brand communication.
Special magazine with more nudity.
PR scandals due to CEO's interview, offensive products, staff discrimination lawsuits from customers and the public.

Promotion

Price

Figure 3.12 The Abercrombie & Fitch Marketing Mix during the times of CEO Jeffries.

star's popularity and association with the brand (Shontell, 2011) The confrontation turned into a lawsuit with Sorrentino filing against Abercrombie & Fitch, claiming the company abused his name, image and trademark when asking him publicly not to wear the brand's clothes on the show and then making T-shirts like "The Fitchuation". Unfortunately, Sorrentino lost as he had not secured trademark rights to the words used by A&F (Gardner, 2013).

Financial growth and decline

From the 1990s onwards, A&F saw continuous growth, and in 1996 the brand went public with a listing on the stock exchange. In 2006, the company was valued at $5 billion and had a profit of nearly $1 billion a year. In 2007, the net income was a staggering $475 million. According to Statista, A&F continued to open flagship stores and owned 363 stores worldwide. At its peak, the growing revenue was being brought in from more than 800 points-of-sale as well as several successful subsidiary brands, such as Hollister (Denizet-Lewis, 2016).

This is particularly interesting, considering how successful A&F was despite the extremely unethical recruitment and employment policies, the exclusionary sizing, the sleazy advertising and lawsuits. Still, the brand went from financial strength to strength.

However, a turning point began around 2007 when sales began to fall, and with it, the brand went into decline.

A&F tried to save its reputation in 2012 when it launched a dedicated website on diversity and inclusion, listing statistics of racial diversity amongst employees. It also held a Diversity Week twice a year and brought to life the Abercrombie & Fitch Diversity Scholarship Program together with the National Society of High School Scholars to award leaders on these issues (Danowitz, 2012).

Despite these efforts, the downward spiral was unstoppable. In 2013, the scandalous interview with CEO Jeffries resurfaced in the press and outraged many people once more, triggering body-positivity activism. Plus-size blogger The Militant Baker spoofed A&F ads with the slogan "Attractive & Fat" where she was emulating the A&F visual identity. An American man named Karber created a video on YouTube suggesting viewers take their old Abercrombie clothes and donate them to homeless people. The video went viral with the hashtag "Fitch the Homeless", featuring the words: "Together, we can make Abercrombie & Fitch the world's No. 1 brand of homeless apparel" (*The New Yorker*, 2013).

In the same year, the brand's stores had declined by nearly 100 to only 275 stores (Statista, 2016). Furthermore, in 2014, expected profits were estimated at $106 million, which would have been less than half of A&F's profits in 2012.

The decline was very clear and had a ripple effect on CEO Jeffries, who not only saw a reduction in his pay by about 70 per cent but was also no longer the chairman of the board, with his employment contract due to expire in early 2015 (Bloomberg Businessweek, 2015). But he found an ingenious way out of this conundrum: In 2014, shortly before the expiration of his contract, Jeffries simply did not turn up to work – without any prior warning – never to be heard from again.

Two years after his departure, in 2016, a statement issued by the company confirmed a decline in profit by 81 per cent (Safdar, 2016).

A&F rebranding strategies

With the sudden disappearance of CEO Michael Jeffries in 2014, A&F was left without a leader and saddled with a tainted reputation. Sales were steadily decreasing because the original core customers had grown up over the decades and were not buying from the teenage brand any longer.

A&F had to reinvent and rebrand itself in order to survive but was struggling to find a new, strong identity that would be effective and ethical.

The first step was to appoint new and diversified management, which in 2014 consisted of not one but four leaders: Fran Horowitz, Christos Angelides, Jonathan Ramsden and Arthur Martinez, who were already senior members of the company.

Some short time later, Fran Horowitz became the single CEO of Abercrombie & Fitch, whilst sub-brands Hollister and Gilly Hicks were given their own new CEOs to ensure that each brand would find its own identity. It was Horowitz who proclaimed that she no longer wanted guys without shirts or the sexualized marketing, and she very much meant what she said (Chen, 2021). Her changes to the Abercrombie & Fitch brand were implemented across the entire Marketing Mix.

Place: in-store promotion and visual merchandising

Some of the changes Abercrombie & Fitch applied in its stores presented a significant change in brand identity.

As Horowitz promised, there were no more topless male models outside the stores (or inside), and the music volume was decreased inside the stores. The in-store perfume was reduced by 25%, while 60 stores had to close in 2017 (Colon, 2017).

Then, in the same year, a new store concept was introduced which saw interiors using natural materials such as cork and wood, moving away from the feeling of a nightclub by including lighter colours and brighter lighting in general (Anyanwu and Muller, 2017). Furthermore, a move to online retail proved to be very successful in securing around 30 per cent of sales revenue (TextilWirtschaft, 2018).

In 2022, A&F had 233 stores worldwide, with the Abercrombie & Fitch Group generating US$3.69 billion globally (this includes sub-brands such as Hollister) (Smith, 2023).

Product

Horowitz implemented something very new at A&F: customer-centric research. This was completely omitted by Jeffries but was highly important if the brand was to rebuild itself out of a reputational and financial slump.

The research helped to target a new and young consumer, who was no longer a teenager but rather a young adult, in their mid-20s (so a Millennial) looking forward to an extended weekend (96 hours) and needed the outfits to fit the leisurely occasions.

Logically, the product was adapted to suit the new consumers' needs, who might do anything during this long weekend from partying to socializing to attending gatherings. The range now includes the staples of leisurewear, smart shirts, trousers, denim, activewear and smart-casual "office approved" combinations, as the Millennial is likely to have a job. There is also a collection for weddings, catering to both brides and their guests.

Jeffries loved logos on the brand's clothing to build the brand identity, but at this point, customers did not want to be associated with the brand and show off the logo. Thus, in 2015, A&F completely removed the logo from the collection (Spiegel, 2014). After that, the logo was redesigned and used sparingly, in a smaller size to attract less attention.

The collections also included the colour black for the first time, since Jeffries did not allow it.

Production and stocks of clothes in larger sizes were another significant change to make the brand inclusive of larger body types at last. By 2020, A&F was connecting the product to body-positivity campaigns.

Price

There have been few changes in the pricing of A&F apparel, which remains at a premium price level. Some cheaper items such as baseball caps retail at £22, men's jeans cost £65 on average, a women's dress is around £100 and a women's wool-blend coat costs £175. Of course, you can still purchase the signature perfume "Fierce" for £58, and this is one of the few items that features a nude male torso on the bottle (Abercrombie & Fitch, 2024).

Brand communication and promotion after rebranding

Along with the cancellation of nude males and all-American white models in and outside of the stores, the marketing communication campaigns were also adjusted to become less explicit and provocative, with the website redesigned to reflect an all-inclusive approach. As Econsultancy reported on the brand's new online communication: "Using words like 'evolving', 'reinventing' and 'welcoming' – the brand is reassuring both old and new consumers that change is a positive thing" (Gilliland, 2016).

In 2018, A&F appointed Carey Collins Krug as a marketing manager. She further developed the brand online, where it was likely to be seen by its target audience. She reiterated the focus on the long weekend, which was established through customer-centric research. In a recent interview with the *Wall Street Journal*, Collins Krug described the lifestyle of the target customer in detail: They are at work, finish a Zoom call, then dash to the gym for a workout, order a drink during happy hour, or jump on a flight to attend a bridal shower, bachelorette party or a wedding (Deighton, 2024). Thus, for these latter needs, A&F introduced a bridal shop online with outfits for all occasions.

Collins Krug's strategy has been gaining momentum across several social media platforms. On Instagram, the brand had 5 million followers in 2024 and shows diverse customer types. There are influencers of various ethnicities and body sizes filming A&F hauls on social media and cooperating with the brand on TikTok, YouTube and Instagram, which now boasts an "army of brand advocates" (Deighton, 2024).

In 2024, the website proclaims its new and clear vision: "This is Abercrombie Today. Today—and every day—we're leading with purpose, championing inclusivity and creating a sense of belonging".

This is apparently not just good copy, but also one important change that A&F implemented since the arrival of Fran Horowitz. A&F engages in philanthropy and corporate social responsibility activities. The company supports several global initiatives, such as GLSEN, which helps to ensure a safe school environment for LGBTQ+ students where they are not confronted with bullying or harassment. For the well-being and mental health of students of colour, A&F cooperates with The Steve Fund. In the long list of A&F partnerships there are also efforts in sustainability, such as the Blue Jeans Go Green project, which works on collecting and recycling denim (Abercrombie & Fitch, 2024).

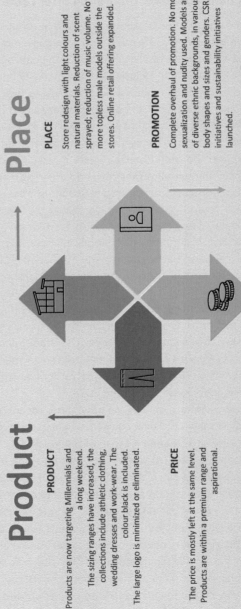

A&F Marketing under Fran Horowitz

Inclusive, diverse and ethical policies were embedded in the revised Marketing Mix

Product

PRODUCT

Products are now targeting Millennials and a long weekend.
The sizing ranges have increased, the collections include athletic clothing, wedding dresses and work-wear. The colour black is included.
The large logo is minimized or eliminated.

PRICE

The price is mostly left at the same level.
Products are within a premium range and aspirational.

Place

PLACE

Store redesign with light colours and natural materials. Reduction of scent sprayed; reduction of music volume. No more topless male models outside the stores. Online retail offering expanded.

PROMOTION

Complete overhaul of promotion. No more sexualization and nudity used. Models are of diverse ethnic backgrounds, in various body shapes and sizes and genders. CSR initiatives and sustainability initiatives launched.

Price

Promotion

Figure 3.13 The Abercrombie & Fitch Marketing Mix during the times of CEO Fran Horowitz.

NEW Marketing Mix Analysis for A&F

Inclusive, diverse and ethical policies were embedded in the revised Marketing Mix

Design

Products are designed with Millennials in mind and a long weekend. Designs include increased sizing ranges; the collections include athletic clothing, wedding dresses and work-wear. The colour black is included. The large logo is minimized or eliminated.

A&F wants to remain desirable and aspirational as a premium brand. Therefore, the price is mostly left at the same level. The product prices are attuned with Millennials who have an income and want to spend on their social life.

Desire

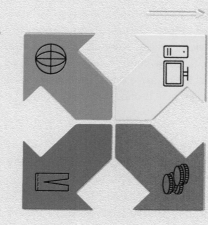

Diversity

Diverse customers are welcomed through a redesign of the store, making it inviting through with light colours and natural materials, reduction of scent sprayed; reduction of music volume and no topless models. Online retail offering expanded to reach diverse customers globally. Visuals show diverse people.

Digital channels are used to showcase a new brand identity through a complete overhaul of promotion. No more sexualization and nudity used. Models are of diverse ethnic backgrounds, in various body shapes and sizes and genders. CSR initiatives and sustainability initiatives launched.

Digitalization

Figure 3.14 The New Marketing Mix (4Ds) applied to Abercrombie & Fitch during the times of CEO Fran Horowitz and after rebranding.

Is this change enough?

This case study shows that any changes to the ethical principles of a brand must encompass the entire Marketing Mix, with the product, place and promotion taking centre stage.

But with all the new steps taken to revive the brand, the question remains whether this is enough or indeed the right kind of change to help pick up sales, gain new customers and save the brand from extinction. CEO Jeffries was a crucial element to the brand's ethos and image. Despite his controversial comments as well as his unusual leadership, one could argue that his very style was responsible for shaping the brand into a successful business that worked at a particular time for a specific consumer group. However, the terrible reputation and ethical faux pas sent the brand into a steep decline.

The new CEO, Fran Horowitz, is happy with the results that A&F has achieved since its rebranding. Customers seem to have forgiven and forgotten the previous ethical scandals and do not associate the new A&F with its old self. Sales revenues have been stabilized and there is a strong, unified vision for an inclusive brand that caters to many diverse customers from one particular age group. It remains to be seen how A&F continues to develop.

References

Abercrombie & Fitch (2020) Available at: https://www.abercrombie.com/

Abercrombie & Fitch Co. (2023) Annual Report for the Fiscal Year Ended January 28, 2023: Form 10-K 2022, page 55. Available at: https://abe rcrombieandfitchcompany.gcs-web.com/static-files/38057e1f-28b2 -4a32-84a0-17e8c4089cb4

Abercrombie and Fitch (2024). Our Partners. Available at: https://corporate .abercrombie.com/our-impact/partners/

Al Jazeera (2015). US Muslim Wins Hijab Case Against Abercrombie & Fitch. Reuters. Available at: http://www.aljazeera.com/news/2015/06/ rules-clothing-label-discrimination-case-150601141831931.html

Anyanwu, O. and Muller, M. (2017) Abercrombie mit neuem Store-Konzept. FashionNetwork. Available at: https://de.fashionnetwork.com/news/ Abercrombie-mit-neuem-store-kon-zept,790074.html

Bloomberg Businessweek, 2015. The Aging of Abercrombie & Fitch. Available at: https://www.bloomberg.com/businessweek

Button, D. (2023) Abercrombie & Fitch's Rebranding Is Paying Off. The Street. Available at: https://www.thestreet.com/retail/abercrombie-fitchs-rebranding-is-paying-off

Chen, C. (2021) Abercrombie & Fitch's Brand Reinvention. Business of Fashion. Available at: https://www.businessoffashion.com/case-studies/retail/abercrombie-fitchs-brand-reinvention-download-the-case-study/

Colon, A. (2017) Let's Pour a Mall Slushie Out for the 60 A&F Stores to Close in 2017. Refinery 29. Available at: http://www.refinery29.com/2017/03/143486/abercrombie-fitch-closing-stories-rebranding

Deighton, K. (2024) Abercrombie & Fitch Is Reaping the Rewards of Taking Adult Women Seriously. The Wall Street Journal. Available at: https://www.wsj.com/articles/abercrombie-fitch-is-reaping-the-rewards-of-taking-adult-women-seriously-d3e11dbe

Denizet-Lewis, B. (2006) The Man Behind Abercrombie & Fitch. Salon. Available at: https://www.Denizet-Lewis.com/2006/01/24/jeffries/

Denizet-Lewis, B. (2006) The Man Behind Abercrombie & Fitch. Salon. Available at: https://www.Denizet-Lewis.com/2006/01/24/jeffries/

Gardner, E. (2013) 'Jersey Shore' Star Loses 'Fitchuation' Lawsuit to Abercrombie & Fitch. The Hollywood Reporter. Available at: https://www.hollywoodreporter.com/business/business-news/jersey-shore-star-loses-fitchuation-579759/

Gilliland, N. (2016) A Closer Look at the Re-brand of Abercrombie & Fitch. Econsultancy. Available at: https://www.econsultancy.com/blog/68436-a-closer-look-at-the-re-brand-of-abercrombie-fitch

Armitage, J. (2014) Mike Jeffries: Beauty and the Beast of Abercrombie & Fitch. Independent. http://www.independent.co.uk/news/business/analysis-and-features/mike-jeffries-beauty-and-the-beast-of-abercrombie-fitch-9914131.html

LDF (2006) NAACP Legal Defense and Educational Fund, Inc. Case: Abercrombie & Fitch Employment Discrimination. Available at: http://www.naacpldf.org/case-issue/abercrombie-fitch-employment-discrimination

Office Snapshots (2024) The Abercrombie & Fitch Headquarters Campus. Available at: https://officesnapshots.com/2012/03/01/the-abercrombie-fitch-headquarters-campus/

Safdar, K. (2016) Abercrombie & Fitch profit tumbles as it rebrands. Market Watch. Available at: https://www.marketwatch.com/story/abercrombie-fitch-profit-tumbles-as-it-rebrands-2016-11-18

Saner, E. (2012) Abercrombie & Fitch: for beautiful people only. The Guardian (online). Available: https://www.theguardian.com/fashion/2012/apr/28/abercrombie-fitch-savile-row

Shontell, A. (2011) Abercrombie & Fitch Says Jersey Shore Member Is Tarnishing Its Brand, But It Sells "The Fitchuation T-Shirts. Business Insider. Available at: https://www.businessinsider.com/abercrombie-and-fitch-jersey-shore-mike-situation-fitchuation-2011-8?r=US&IR=T

Shopify (2016) How Retailers Manipulate Sight, Smell, and Sound to Trigger Purchase Behaviour in Consumers. Available at: https://www.shopify.com/retail/119926083-how-retailers-manipulate-sight-smell-and-sound-to-trigger-purchase-behavior-in-consumers

Smith, P. (2023) Number of Abercrombie & Fitch stores worldwide from 1998 to 2022. Statista. Available at: https://www-statista-com.uow.idm.oclc.org/statistics/268507/number-of-abercrombie-und-fitch-stores-worldwide/

Spiegel (2014) Abercrombie & Fitch will wieder cool werden. Available at: https://www.spiegel.de/wirtschaft/unternehmen/abercrombie-fitch-modefirma-ver-kauft-kleidung-ohne-logo-a-988812.html

Statista (2016) https://www.statista.com/statistics/268507/number-of-abercrombie-und-fitch-stores-worldwide/

Strasbourg, J. (2002) Abercrombie recalls T-shirts many found offensive. Sfgate. Available at: https://www.sfgate.com/news/article/Abercrombie-recalls-T-shirts-many-found-offensive-2849480.php

Sweney, M. (2011) Jersey Shore's The Situation offered cash not to wear Abercrombie & Fitch. The Guardian. Available at: https://www.theguardian.com/media/2011/aug/17/jersey-shore-situation-abercrombie-fitch

TextilWirtschaft (2018) Nachhaltiger Turnaround bei A&F. Available at: https://www.wiso-net.de/document/TW__20181206478568%7CTWA__20181206478568

The Guardian (2012) Abercrombie & Fitch: For Beautiful People Only. https://www.theguardian.com/fashion/2012/apr/28/abercrombie-fitch-savile-row

The New Yorker (2013) The Story Behind Fitch the Homeless. Available at: https://www.newyorker.com/culture/culture-desk/the-story-behind-fitch-the-homeless

Figure 3.15 4Ps Mkt Mix Worksheet.

Figure 3.16 4Ds Mkt Mix Worksheet.

Ethical considerations

Ethics should be considered with every "P" and every "D" of the Marketing Mix.

Product

Is it sustainable or can it be recycled? Is it safe to use for the intended target group, both in a physical and mental sense? In other industries, the impact of an unethical product can be more obvious, such as the marketing of fast food, gambling, alcohol and tobacco. When Abercrombie & Fitch launched its T-shirts with prints that were racist and insulting to Asians and Asian Americans, those individuals joined in protest. The company was unapologetic and reluctantly pulled the products from the shelves after the negative press became extensive.

Mintel published a study on ethical attitudes in the US in 2015 and found that over 60 per cent of consumers find ethical issues important, and 35 per cent of customers will stop purchasing products from brands they deem unethical. Furthermore, consumers do not feel comfortable when a brand is successful by exploiting someone (Mintel, 2015). This means that ethics are not only a personal issue for a marketing professional but also a strategic issue for a fashion company, possibly causing a decline in revenue when not addressed appropriately. In 2021, Mintel confirmed the trajectory, stating that transparency is not enough to help consumers understand the impact of a brand, the impact they make by choosing a particular brand or whether the brand is making progress on stated goals. Therefore, brands need to make "fundamental and structural changes" to meet "heightened ethical expectations from consumers in the future". (Li, 2021)

This is why it is important to ask: How is the product manufactured? Is the supply chain sustainable, and does it respect nature, humans and animals along the way? If not, can any of these points be improved?

Promotion

Promotion is a very prominent ethical concern, as detailed in the two preceding chapters, and it has evolved due to highly unethical practices. Promotion can often be manipulative, misleading and cause harm to the users. (Chapter 10 is dedicated to the harmful side effects of promotion, especially in advertising.)

Place and retail spaces are often full of deceit and manipulation. A prime example is Abercrombie & Fitch which used topless young men to lure consumers into shops. Online, consumers are often bombarded with messages, targeted advertising and aggressive newsletters designed to extort a purchase.

Furthermore, as discussed later in Chapter 9, retail buildings and shops can gentrify entire areas, driving out small and diverse businesses and changing the social and urban life of inhabitants.

Price

This leads to the question of price: What is a fair price and what is an unjustified mark-up? When something is very cheap and affordable or highly discounted, how little is the pay that factory workers receive? There are many concerns that revolve around pricing. Consumers are often persuaded to buy now and pay later, pay in instalments or run up their credit card or store card bill. Whilst paying in instalments can arguably be a great invention and help consumers buy expensive things that they normally they would not be able to afford, the pricing strategies can often leave people in serious debt.

People

Finally, people and the sales force of many fashion brands are trained and forced to behave in an unethical way. Sales staff are trained in techniques of psychological persuasion, and consumers do not tend to realize this. How often is the service provided by a sales assistant the ultimate decision factor? How often do they appear to be as nice as our best friends? Whilst great service is a benefit, a fashion company needs to have clear guidelines on an ethical code of practice where service is not the same as manipulation.

Authors such as Naomi Klein, Jean Kilbourne and Naomi Wolf, and organizations such as Adbusters have written about the problems with manipulative, globalized and unethical marketing targeting adults and children, which is discussed in depth in Chapter 10.

Some brands have taken the ethical approach very seriously and tried to implement a best practice initiative at every step of their business. Sadly, there are only a handful of such brands, but there are several positive examples in this book, like Abercrombie & Fitch after its rebranding efforts, and the brands LOEWE, Freitag and SOLIT Japan, which are featured in Chapter 11.

Further reading

Easey, M. (2009) *Fashion Marketing*. 3rd edn. Oxford: Blackwell (available as an e-book).

Hooley, N. et al. (2020) Marketing Strategy and Competitive Positioning. 7th edn. Harlow: Pearson.

Jackson, T. and Shaw, D. (2009) *Mastering Fashion Marketing*. New York: Palgrave Macmillan.

Jobber, D. (2010) *Principles and Practice of Marketing*. 6th edn. London: McGraw Hill.

Keller, K. L. and Swaminathan, V. (2020) *Strategic Brand Management: Building, Measuring, and Managing Brand Equity*. 5th global edn. Harlow: Pearson.

Kotler, P. et al. (2009) *Marketing Management*. 13th edn. Harlow: Pearson Education Ltd.

Kotler, P., Armstrong, G., Wong, V. and Saunders, J. (2012) *Principles of Marketing*. 5th European edn. Harlow: FT Prentice Hall.

Kotler, P. and Lane Keller, K. (2016) *Marketing Management*. Global Edition, 15th edn. Harlow: Pearson Education Limited.

The advertising agency **4**
Branding and marketing communications

Chapter topics

The advertising agency

Around the turn of the nineteenth century, the first advertising agencies were formed, which are quite similar to the type of agencies we know today. However, the original advertising agencies usually provided a fraction of the services that are on offer now. In the 1980s, when small agencies merged with others and became large networks, they were able to operate on a worldwide scale. This is highly relevant in today's business world, which is mostly global. With a global marketplace, agencies have also seen a transformation of the services they offer.

Today's agencies might be a "full-service agency" which not only creates classic advertising but also conducts market research, provides content for digital platforms, stages events, engages in public relations and purchases all the media where the campaign will be shown. The aim is to offer a 360° service to the client.

DOI: 10.4324/9781003449157-4

The way agencies secure work is by pitching their ideas to a prospective industry client who wishes to advertise. In this pitch, the agency presents its credentials and an initial idea of what type of advertising it could create for the client and which media channels would be best suited. If the client is happy with the presentation, a contract is signed and the real work begins.

Whether it is just the pitch or the full-on campaign that has been signed, the agency needs some important data from the client, which is usually put in a client briefing. Without this information, an advertising campaign might fail completely.

The client briefing

The client briefing is basically a set of instructions written by the client for the agency. According to Schneider and Pflaum (2000), the foundation of the briefing is the marketing strategy, which generally explains which products are offered to which target customers through which methods and in which market. The briefings are highly individual, but ideally should contain the following points:

1. Analysis of the status quo
- Information about competitors, such as their market share and products of competitors.
- Information on the market, such as market data and data collected through experience.
- Information about the product and the brand itself, including strengths and weaknesses, acceptance, origin or history;and the overall development of the marketing strategythus far
- External influences, beyond the control of the brand, such as trends, politics or society;

2. Objectives/strategy
- Size of the campaign, type of campaign, plan of action.

3. The goal
- Communication goals, such as increasing usage of the product, penetration of the message into the market, changing consumer attitude or behaviour, changing the brand image and making the brand more known or more popular.
- (Immediate goals to increase revenue and market share should not be the primary goal of an ad campaign because this is only possible through the implementation of the entire Marketing Mix.)

4. Target market
- Customer profiling (socio-demographic structure, psychological typing).
- Demographics such as age, income, education, etc. (This topic will be discussed in depth in Chapter 5.)

5. Timing
- When should this campaign be launched, and how does it fit with other marketing activities?

6. Budget
- How much is the brand ready to spend on ad creation, the media and any additional services such as PR or events?

Agency briefing

Once the agency gets the job, it will turn the client's briefing into an internal briefing that will most likely change into an "agency briefing", which is used for internal purposes and actually getting the job done. It will be broken down into tasks for the different departments and employees, including the creative team (Schneider and Pflaum, 2000). The creative department and the creative director are the ones who are responsible for inventing the concept and the campaign. The creative concept is highly important to brands today, as this can set them apart from competitors and convey a unique brand message to the consumer.

But, whilst the creative process is highly important to a successful campaign, for the client, it is rather "cheap" compared to how much it then costs to show the ad in various media channels. This is because the media channels can come with a hefty price.

A 30-second ad during the Super Bowl is world famous for costing several million dollars; *Vogue* magazine charges around $200,000 per one full-colour page! The infamous September edition, often referred to as the "September Issue", consists of over 600 ad pages on average (out of 900-plus magazine pages in total), and you can calculate just how much the magazine makes in that one month. In 2013, the fashion magazine generated a total advertising revenue of US$460 million (Statista). For fashion branding, this means that only the most successful brands can afford to advertise there, squeezing out a lot of the competition. Startups and small designers have to accept advertising in less glamorous media or use public relations to get some editorial content in top-range magazines.

In brief, brands spend billions on advertising and media globally with a forecast of ad spending and ad volume of $552 billion and combined advertising, media, and marketing spending surpassing $1 trillion in 2017 (GroupM, August 2, 2016). Today, this trajectory keeps growing and global advertising revenue is estimated to continue growing in 2024, reaching $989.8 billion and surpassing one trillion in revenue in 2025. (GroupM, 2024) Equally, the media channels and their advertising space are worth billions.

Considering the expenditure, the brand wants the ad to have the most impact, which is why it needs to be shown in the right media channels, at the right time and to the right audience.

This is where the media planning department starts working. This department, which can be part of the agency in-house or a separate business, has the task of finding and booking suitable media, using the client's budget. The goal is to reach the right audience at the right time with the right message to generate the desired response and then stay within the designated budget.

Media planners perform various calculations to determine how many individuals will be reached, how many times on average, how much this will cost when using the various media, and how much impact this will have on the target audience.

Old and new communication channels

So what are today's media platforms where one can advertise?

Generally, the advertising channels are separated into BTL and ATL, which is short for below-the-line and above-the-line media, respectively. According to the Advertising Club, these terms emerged in the 1950s and classify media into mass media and targeted media. Most of the available media channels have been in use for decades and are very effective (Manral, 2011).

ATL usually describes conventional media such as television and radio advertising, cinema advertising, print in magazines and newspapers, billboards, as well as online ads (search engine ads). This type of communication targets a wider audience, is not specific to individual consumers and has a very broad reach.

BTL advertising is more adjusted towards the individual (or smaller but specific target groups) using less conventional methods of advertising, such as sales promotions at the point-of-sale (POS), public relations, direct marketing, fairs and trade shows, sponsoring, event marketing, product placement, and most innovative communication forms such as guerilla marketing, ambient marketing, social media marketing, viral marketing and Bluetooth marketing. It can be a much cheaper, yet more effective way of reaching the consumer.

The choice of media channels will depend on several factors, such as the message the brand wants to send out, the target customer group, the budget and the overall goal. It might choose to use ATL media, BTL media, or mix and match from both.

ABOVE

Target:	Media:
Mass audience	Television advertising Radio advertising Cinema advertising Print in magazines and newspapers Billboards On-line ads (search engine ads etc.)

THE LINE

BELOW

Target:	Media:
Specific consumer group	Sales Promotions at the POS Public Relations Direct marketing Fairs and trade shows Sponsoring Event marketing Product Placement Fashion Film Innovative communication forms such as guerilla marketing, ambient marketing, social media marketing, viral marketing, Bluetooth marketing etc.

Figure 4.1 ATL (above-the-line) and BTL (below-the-line) media. Author's original illustration.

Case example: MINI

The self-proclaimed lifestyle car brand MINI (which is owned by BMW) is known to have used guerrilla marketing to promote its car, where it appeared in unusual places and in unexpected situations.

In 2009, the Amsterdam-based ad agency JWT (J. Walter Thompson Amsterdam) produced a series of giant cardboard gift boxes which were placed on the streets of Amsterdam just after Christmas, together with a heap of trash. Each box had a large diagram of the car with the words "MINI COOPER" and the logo printed across the top, a barcode and price of 99,- (currency not stated). It was made to look as if someone was gifted a Mini Cooper in this giant box for Christmas and had now discarded the box and the wrapping for municipal trash collection. Images and videos of people passing the installation went viral shortly after.

In 2010, MINI once again surprised people with an installation on the beaches of Zandvoort (a coastal town outside of Amsterdam) and in Knokke (a coastal town in Belgium, bordering the Netherlands) with a campaign featuring a giant bottle which seemingly had washed up on the shore with a life-size MINI car inside.

For this campaign, MINI teamed up with FEL, an Amsterdam-based agency specializing in brand experience. According to the agency, literally, FEL means "fierce".

> And that's exactly what we do. Create fierce communication, with ideas and concepts that stand out. Using clever creativity, we're looking for more attention for the same budget. We want to create campaigns where consumers want to be part of. So our best campaigns are the ones where there's no media budget involved, like this MINI case. For MINI we've been the BTL agency in Holland (activation, guerrilla marketing, social) for 5 years now, with occasional assignments in Belgium and for MINI international. We also work for brands like Sony, ABN, Save The Children, Neckermann and Shell.

Figure 4.2A A real MINI in a giant inflatable bottle on the beach of the Netherlands. Image kindly provided by the creative agency FEL.

Figure 4.2B Continued.

According to Jay Conrad Levinson, guerrilla marketing "works because it's simple to understand, easy to implement and outrageously inexpensive". He should know, as he was the one who invented the term back in the 1980s (Levinson, 2016).

So how expensive is "outrageously inexpensive" and what sort of costs are we comparing it to, you might wonder. Let's see which of the ATL and BTL are most expensive and which ones are cheap.

Most media will publish their advertising costs online. It can be tricky to find it via the website, but if you search for the media's name and add the words "rate card" or "media kit" (sometimes "media pack" or "media data"), you will be able to access the data.

Table 4.1 shows some examples of what advertising can cost as of 2022, from very reasonable to excruciatingly high.

Consumer trust

According to research conducted by Statista in 2021, 45 per cent of global respondents mistrusted text ads on mobile phones and 38 per cent mistrusted online banner ads (Statista, 2023a). Generally, social media has been deemed the least credible advertising medium by consumers worldwide, despite the

Table 4.1 Advertising costs as of 2022

Media type	Example of one purchased unit	Cost
TV: NBC (US)	30 seconds on NBC's *Sunday Night Football*	$828,501
TV: NBC (US)	30-second commercial during the Super Bowl	$7 million
Print magazine: *Vogue* (UK)	Monthly edition	£15,000 to £160,000
Print magazine: *Vogue* (US)	Monthly edition	$187,609 to $225,000
Billboard: London Underground (UK)	£1 week for a small business	£300
Billboard: Times Square NYC (US)	15 seconds	$40
Supplement print magazine: *Financial Times* HTSI	Worldwide edition, colour page (including cover)	£ 5,788 to £ 70,829
Social media: Instagram ad	Cost per click to destination URL	$0.50–$0.95
Social media: Weibo (China)	1,000 ad views	RMB 5
Social media: WeChat (China)	Cost per follow	RMB 80–100

rising level of use. Interestingly, the least trusted but most used channel of digital advertising has seen global spending of US$522.5 billion in 2021, with an estimated increase to US$836 billion by 2026 (Statista, 2023b).

On the contrary, the most trustworthy ad channels were brand websites and brand sponsorships (including brand-sponsored sporting events), only outranked by recommendations from friends and family, which accounted for a 90 per cent trust level (Navarro, 2023). Television has remained a popular channel for brands since its inception more than 100 years ago, with high levels of trust in many nations. In North America, TV ad spending was projected to reach nearly US$67 billion in 2022, contributing to a global TV ad revenue of US$132 billion (Majidi, 2023).

Interview with Thorsten Voigt

Thorsten Voigt has been a copywriter and creative director at Serviceplan for more than nine years and recently switched to freelancing. Serviceplan is the largest advertising agency in Germany and one of the largest advertising groups in Europe. Its headquarters is in Munich.

Figure 4.3 Thorsten Voigt.

Q: Do brands choose to work with just one agency now that advertising agencies are offering 360° service?

TV: Large, successful brands like Adidas, Nike, BMW like to choose the best possible agencies for each communication strategy. So they will take the leading agency for their print advertising, another leading agency for their PR and yet another for digital strategies. In-house, the brand usually has a vision and smart marketing plan, which ensures that all their agencies create concepts that fit their vision. However, smaller brands might choose the one-stop option and use just one agency for all of their communication needs.

Q: How do brands find their agency?

TV: Through recommendations or by directly contacting the best possible agencies, if that is what they are looking for. Serviceplan, for example, has a really good reputation in Germany and a top creative ranking.

Q: What happens then?

TV: A client will ask five or six agencies to do a pitch for him. Often-times the brands will not pay for the pitch (or may offer a small pitch fee), which might cost the agency tens of thousands of euros to prepare. This is because the agency develops the strategy, creates nearly finished layouts and mood-movies to sell the idea.

Q: When the client has chosen you over the others, what are the next steps?

TV: The consultant gets a briefing from the client and develops a strategy on how to reach the target customer. This strategy information and the goal of the campaign are passed on to the creative team, who has to develop the campaign.

Q: What does the creative team do, and who is involved in creating the campaign?

TV: For a campaign, the team consists of a senior copywriter and a senior art director. The creative director makes sure that their work is creative enough and fits the briefing and strategy. The strategy comes from the consultants who received all the relevant information from the client. Other people who might be involved are online experts if you are creating a 360° strategy, media planners and others. The creative process itself is quite tenacious because the first idea we get is usually not the best one. The first idea is the one that will come to the minds of many. We look for the one that has not been done before and is unique. Many ideas get tossed in the garbage, and you might work extra hours while brainstorming.

Q: How do you know which ideas have not been done before?

TV: In the creative department, you have to keep up to date and know what the competition is doing. In a way, everything has already been done at some point, but it's the fresh take that counts, and we try to use new impressions and new combinations to create something great.

Q: What skills do you need to work on the creative team?

TV: As an art director you need to know all the graphic programmes and understand layouts, illustrators need to be good with drawing, and a copywriter just needs to be really good with language and just know words. The trick is to make a point in as few words as possible.

Q: How about media planning?

TV: It can be an in-house department or a separate firm that the agency closely works with. The agency might recommend the media firm, but ultimately it's the client's choice which one he uses. He might just want a creative campaign.

Q: What happens if you receive a request from two competing brands, let's say Nike and Adidas, who want a campaign from your agency?

TV: Some clients will request that you do not work with a competitor; they want to be the only client of a certain segment. Others request a different creative team to work on their account if they know that you work on a close competitor. It really depends on the brands.

Q: How are fashion brands different from other clients?

TV: Fashion brands can easily do all the creative work themselves and might not need an agency for that. They know photography, model casting, fittings, etc. They might need help with the media planning.

Q: What about the classic advertising channels, the so-called ATL? Are they dying out?

TV: It's still very important. But ultimately the communication channel depends on the target customer. A young person is always in touch with their mobile device, while an older person will read a magazine or newspaper. Billboards and posters will probably remain effective for everyone because when we are out and about we look at the street ads.

Creative direction at the agency and the fashion brand

Large fashion companies, especially those in the luxury segment, usually have one famous creative director or sometimes a creative duo of directors, such as Maria Grazia Chiuri and Pierpaolo Piccioli at Valentino until 2016. There is no need to rely on an agency for the creative input because the creative director has a certain vision for the brand's advertising, photography and promotion, and oftentimes is gifted in all these areas.

Thus, the creative director might be engaged in a broad spectrum of creating the fashion imagery used to promote the brand. In the case of Karl Lagerfeld, he was – like many creative directors – a multi-talent and designed buildings, interiors, published books, engaged in photography and other very creative practices.

For the brand Chanel, he was known to cast models, take photos and even shoot advertorial movies himself. When he had a new muse, he or she would appear on the catwalk and in the promotional images, just like Claudia Schiffer,

Tilda Swinton, Cara Delevingne, Brad Kroenig, Baptiste Giabiconi and, more recently, Kendall Jenner.

In 2015, *The Observer* reported that Kendall Jenner was styled by the infamous Grace Coddington and then photographed by Karl Lagerfeld for a spread in *Vogue*'s September issue. She also got to play with Karl Lagerfeld's famous cat Choupette.

For Marc Jacobs, his muse has been Sofia Coppola, who starred in several ad campaigns for him over the span of 13 years, including for the perfumes Blush and Daisy.

If the creative director is not taking the photos him- or herself, or does not have a talented movie director to help, the fashion house will closely work with a fashion photographer to produce high-quality images and communicate the brand's vision.

Brands that have distinct creative vision and heritage thrive on a creative director. He or she has the task of delivering a unique creative vision that will influence all brand elements, from the collections to the brand communication, forming a unique brand identity. This is the USP of the fashion brand, and therefore a creative director's vision might better know what type of visual communication is suitable.

The great influence on the fashion brand has been documented in popular and somewhat voyeuristic fashion documentaries, starting with Loic Prigent in 2005, who filmed Karl Lagerfeld at Chanel. Since then, many more such documentaries have emerged, showing Yves Saint Laurent and his partner Marc Jacobs at Louis Vuitton, Raf Simons at Dior, Frida Giannini at Gucci, Valentino in his many homes and other creative directors hard at work. The documentaries show a secret world behind the closed doors of the most celebrated luxury brands and their temporary geniuses, who are leaving due to old age, being ushered out by the brand or getting poached by others. In the last few years, the luxury fashion business has evolved into the Mad Hatter's tea party where all of a sudden everyone changes places but remains at the same table. These increasingly frequent movements have been named the game of "Fashion Musical Chairs" by editors from *Vanity Fair*, *The New York Times*, *Vogue* and *Harper's Bazaar*.

When the creative director dies or departs, luxury fashion brands face the challenge and the opportunity of revitalizing the brand identity with a new creative director.

For instance, in the case of Yves Saint Laurent, the brand saw a 180° makeover when Hedi Slimane took the creative reins in 1999. He moved the headquarters of the brand from Paris to Los Angeles; changed the look from romantic and feminine to grunge and unisex; and brought in sneakers, sickeningly thin models in his much-criticized ad campaigns and a monochrome colour palette.

He is famously known for having created most of the fashion ad campaigns where he cast the models, styled them and photographed them himself.

But what made many fashion veterans scream was the change of the brand's name from Yves Saint Laurent (YSL) to Saint Laurent. There was a small revolt of printed T-shirts that read "Ain't Laurent without Yves" in a clever wordplay.

Despite all the commotion, his new vision for the brand was a commercial success and brought the ageing brand high profits within a short period of time.

In 2016, Slimane left the company, and a new creative director is in place: Anthony Vaccarello, who has to live up to the fame and success of his predecessor.

Similar influences on a brand's identity and its communication can be observed with the brands Dior, Balmain, Gucci, Lanvin, Burberry, Balenciaga, Givenchy and others.

The challenges for fashion media today

Although advertising today uses all sorts of media channels, including online advertising and social media, most fashion brands (especially in the luxury segment) still use the traditional fashion magazine as the main platform for advertising, and perhaps surprisingly it still works well for them. It is also part of a long-standing history of advertising in fashion magazines dating back to the first issues of *Harper's Bazaar* or *Vogue in the 19th century*.

As the cover and fold-out pages are highly expensive, there is often a lot of competition between luxury brands that want to secure the best possible spot. Furthermore, if brands spend a certain amount of money on advertising in the magazine, the chances are very high that the brand will also appear in a free editorial of the issue.

When you look at the rate card or media kit of a glossy magazine, there will also be prices for digital media such as tablets and smartphones, as well as demographic data on the core reader of the publication.

Digital channels are becoming increasingly important, while print notes some decline.

Business of Fashion wrote as far back as August 2016 that most editorial content is currently consumed digitally, which publishing houses not only acknowledge but also embed in their future strategy. "Indeed, Hearst, Condé Nast and Time Inc. have each announced plans to significantly boost their digital offerings [which] means trimming the budgets of their print magazines" (Hoang, 2016). However, a recent report by Statista has shown an unexpected resilience of magazines (as opposed to other print media such as newspapers):

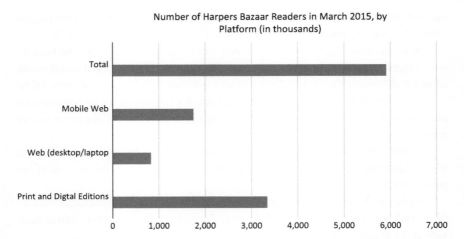

Figure 4.4 The number of *Harper's Bazaar* readers in the United States in March 2015, by platform. The magazine reached 1.74 million readers over the mobile web. Data from Statista (2015).

the total number of magazine readers in the US remained above 220 million in every year between 2016 and 2020. Furthermore, in the US, consumers continue to prefer print magazines over digital, and consequently there has been a steady increase in print consumer magazines in the United States from 2017 until 2024 (Watson, 2024).

In a snapshot of the readership platforms of *Harper's Bazaar* in March 2015, you can see that of 5,909,000 readers, 257,100 – or more than a third – are looking at digital content either on the internet or on a mobile device. In addition to the regular print, there are digital editions, and as a statistic, both are put together rather than looking at them separately.

> The fashion magazine is still a classic choice for fashion advertising despite e-commerce and m-commerce. However, as digital media becomes increasingly popular with consumers, fashion brands and fashion publications need to urgently catch up.

So what is the future for fashion print magazines? And how does this affect traditional print advertising?

Let's look at the average revenue of magazines from advertising: According to Statista, in 2013, *Vogue* US magazine made more than $US460 million in advertising revenue. During the same period, *Elle* magazine made more than $US392 (Statista, 2014).

One short-term reflex type of strategy by fashion "glossies" is to increase the price of their magazines. This is because apart from the advertising revenue, the magazines live off the circulation or the number of copies sold. However, this cannot be done blindly. The publications need to analyze the current target readers and evaluate which type of platform corresponds to which age group. Generally, Generation Z (and younger Millennials) are consuming their fashion editorials on mobile devices. This is where fashion ads should be happening. But the division by age and generation closes when it comes to luxury fashion, which was revealed in a recent study by McKinsey and Altagamma in 2015. Older luxury consumers also like to use the same digital and mobile platforms (Remy, Catena and Durand-Servoingt, 2015) so switching to advertising on digital platforms might thus be lucrative as it reaches many age groups and many potential readers at once.

Looking at platforms such as Instagram, WeChat, YouTube and other globally used apps (or own-brand apps), there is room to place editorials and advertising, which can link to an extensive version in the printed edition, thus closing the publishing and ad loop. Global digital marketing options are discussed in more detail in Chapter 6.

The interesting and challenging element is that the popularity of digital platforms fluctuates strongly and changes rapidly – something that sturdy fashion magazines have been getting used to. With digital platforms, they can go in and out of style within a few years or a few months, and their popularity can differ from country to country and from age group to age group. The new challenge for classic fashion magazines is to keep up with the changing nature of digital content and their audiences, and in order to do so, they must invest in new talent – the digital natives who grew up with those platforms. Until recently, some of the sales teams of those platforms might have been older and not digital natives themselves, so it is crucial for their success to employ young people as part of their team to teach the older generations.

If the brand does not want to employ digital natives, it can work together with a media agency that helps brands to clearly define the right channels in order to reach the target customer. This type of agency will make sure that the advertising message reaches its maximum potential. It is solely focused on getting the brand's message and content to the target audience by using the most suitable media channel. Furthermore, the agency can negotiate prices and book slots or space with the channel providers and platforms directly.

The following interview shows some insights about the work such an agency does.

Interview with a renowned media agency in Germany

Q: How large is your agency?

A: We have a very large international network of agencies, which has about 80,000 employees.

Q: How would you sum up the services that you offer to your clients?

A: We offer our clients comprehensive support in terms of all media activities. To put it short, we make sure that our clients' products (or services) and their advertising campaigns reach potential customers at the right place and at the right time. We work out the suitable target group by analyzing and defining it; we analyze and interpret the entire market and the specific competitors of our clients. We develop strategies for exactly how and where the products or services should be marketed, continuously lead the entire campaign management on behalf of our clients and optimize the return on investment and much more. We are always at the side of our clients and continuously consult them on anything and everything media.

Q: How many clients do you work with?

A: Overall, our agency deals with more than 150 different clients.

Q: Do you have clients from the fashion industry, and are there any differences when working with them?

A: Yes, we have fashion and accessories luxury brands as well as online retailers. When working with fashion clients, one has to be open to new trends and be quick to "jump on the bandwagon" when a new trend emerges in order to stay ahead in a very competitive market. Furthermore, social media is a very important topic (especially Facebook or Instagram) as it appeals to the target market and is convenient for them.

Q: Do you work with advertising agencies or directly with the marketing and communication departments of the various companies?

A: We work directly with the marketing and communications departments of companies and brands, with a constant exchange of ideas and joint planning.

As a media agency, we then take care of the realization of the media strategy and manage the campaign. Sometimes we connect with other agencies – but those are PR agencies or creative agencies. Since we are responsible for the media performance of a product, our work may cross over into PR activities and this is why we are also in constant exchange with the PR agency. The same goes for creative agencies, because we have to know the creative work in order to assess which channels might work best.

Q: Have media preferences changed over the last few years?

A: Yes, and very much so! TV is still a popular type of media, which has a high reach for commercials. However, today there is a lot of streaming mainly because people work more, are out and about and have very little time for classic TV. This means there is a strong trend in increasingly using online videos or video-on-demand because it gives more flexibility and choice as to when you want to watch your favourite show. In addition, it is more pleasant for consumers because commercials are much shorter during streaming than on classic TV.

Moreover, global digitization plays an increasingly important role. Everyone is everywhere, always online, constantly leaving data behind and simultaneously being tracked. This means that many brands and products now have to play off their precisely target-oriented and "catchy" advertising messages against each other in a highly competitive market of the digital world.

Even though there are many possibilities to place an advertising message, this has to happen in the right environment and with the right message, or else it will not motivate anyone to buy or consume but rather be perceived as "annoying" and "disruptive", and enhance a negative connotation in consumers' minds.

Considering digitalization, one should not underestimate the power of social media and its current role. This is precisely the virtual place where many consumers are at during their leisure time. And during leisure time, they are relaxed and more open to advertising messages of all kinds. This is where they can be reached extremely well with a suitable offer or even product information. Here it is easier to like a page, be redirected to another website or to interact with a product in a different way.

Especially in this regard, the so-called programmatic advertising is gaining increasing importance, where the purchase and sale of advertising space happens in real time. This offers specific possibilities of targeting (the brand buys media directly) and reaching the perfectly suitable consumer by analyzing his online surfing behaviour in advance. The consumer is in the right environment, at the right time and receives the right ad message.

Ethical considerations

What sort of ethics must an advertising agency or media agency consider?

If you look back at the history of targeted advertising and marketing (in Chapters 1 and 2), any client and any product were accepted, and the main goal was to launch a successful campaign. This was true for selling cigarettes to women (including pregnant women as demonstrated by ads of the mid-twentieth century), alcohol, unhealthy food, slimming products, overpriced fashion and cosmetics, and products that would not meet standards pertaining to social, environmental, and sometimes even legal codes of good practice. The ethical marketer must carefully examine the product and the company and decide whether it is something worth promoting, as this promotion naturally reaches hundreds, thousands or sometimes millions of people. A choice will affect the public and therefore this choice must be made responsibly.

There are several advertising agencies that have made a strong stance on their ethical practices,with the leadership of Wally Snyder who became the president of the American Advertising Federation (AAF) in 1992 and promoted the regulation of ethics in advertising.

As the director of the Institute for Advertising Ethics (IAE), the IAE aims to "inspire advertising, public relations and marketing communications professionals to practice the highest personal ethics in the creation and distribution of commercial information to consumers".

The IAE is built on eight principles and practices which convey what all forms of communication should be based on, including advertising, public relations, marketing communications, news and editorial.

The principles include truth and ethical standards in their daily work, abiding by the law, clearly marking sponsored content by bloggers or influencers (versus a blogger's own opinion), and taking special precautions when addressing vulnerable members of society such as children, among others. The eighth principle is arguably the most important one for any marketing professional: "members of the team creating ads should be given permission to express internally their ethical concerns" (Richards et Al., 2023).

Discussing ethical concerns is the first step to creating awareness within a marketing company, and the logical second step is then to integrate the best practices into the projects.

Further reading

Bartlett, D. (2013) *Fashion Media: Past and Present*. London: Bloomsbury Academic.

Diamond, J. (2015) *Retail Advertising and Promotion*. New York: Fairchild.

Fennis, B. M. and Stroebe, W. (2010) *The Psychology of Advertising*. Abingdon, UK: Psychology Press.

GroupM (2024) This Year Next Year: 2024 Global Midyear Forecast. Available at: https://www.groupm.com/2024-global-midyear-forecast/

Keaney, M. (2007) *Fashion & Advertising. (World's Top Photographers Workshops)*. Mies: RotoVision.

Kelley, L. D., Jugenheimer, D. W. and Sheehan K. (2015) *Advertising Media Planning: A Brand Management Approach*. 4th edn. New York: Routledge.

Lane, W. R., Whitehill Kink, K. and Russel, T. J. (2008) *Kleppner's Advertising Procedure*. 17th edn. New Jersey: Pearson Prentice Hall.

Lea-Greenwood, G. (2012) *Fashion Marketing Communications*. Hoboken: John Wiley & Sons.

Moore, G. (2012) *Basics Fashion Management: Fashion Promotion 02: Building a Brand Through Marketing and Communication*. London: Bloomsbury Publishing.

Matharu, S. (2011) *Advertising Fashion Brands to the UK Ethnic Market: How Ethnic Models Influence Ethnic Consumer Purchase Behaviour*. Verlag, Germany: VDM.

Moriarty, S. et al. (2019) *Advertising & IMC: Principles & Practice*. 11th edn. Harlow: Pearson.

Richards, J.I., McAlister, A.R., Susman, A., and Snyder, W. (2023). Advertising Ethics: Documenting Its History and Evolution. Advertising & Society Quarterly 24(4), https://dx.doi.org/10.1353/asr.2023.a916297

Schneider, K. and Pflaum, D. (2000) Werbung in Theorie und Praxis. 5th ed. M&S Verlag: Waiblingen.

Statista (2014) Leading magazines in the United States based on advertising revenue in 2013 (in million U.S. dollars). Available at: https://www-statista-com.uow.idm.oclc.org/statistics/202481/top-20-us-magazines-by-advertising-revenue-in-2011/

IAE (2024) Principles & Practices. The Institute for Advertising Ethics (online) Available at: https://www.iaethics.org/principles-and-practices

Springer, P. (2008) *Ads to Icons: How Advertising Succeeds in a Multimedia Age*. London: Kogan Page.

Tungate, M. (2007) *Adland: A Global History of Advertising*. London: Kogan Page.

Advertising news, sites and resources

Advertising Age. https://adage.com

Ad Asia Online. www.adasiaonline.com

Adweek. www.adweek.vom

Branding in Asia. https://brandinginasia.com

Campaign Asia. www.campaignasia.com

Campaign. www.camaignlive.co.uk
Digiday. https://digiday.com
The Drum. www.thedrum.com
The Institute for Advertising Ethics https://www.iaethics.org/
MediaPost. www.mediapost.com

Influencers, opinion leaders and KOLs

5

Who is leading your opinion?

Chapter topics

The general meaning of an opinion leader

Two-step flow of communication

The precursor to the two-step flow of communication hypothesis, which emerged in 1944, was the brainchild of Paul Lazarsfeld, Bernard Berelson and Hazel Gaudet. The purpose of the study was to examine what influenced people to vote during political campaigns. The research showed unexpected results, as the biggest influence on the people was personal and quite informal contacts rather than exposure to targeted content on the radio or in newspapers. Based on these findings, it was Katz and Lazarsfeld who developed the

DOI: 10.4324/9781003449157-5

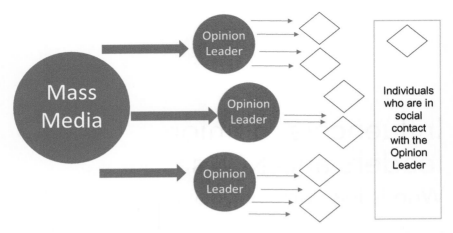

Figure 5.1 Two-step communication model. Author's interpretation of original by Lazarsfeld.

two-step flow theory of mass communication, which is still widely used today or has been amended and developed further for present times.

As the name states, the theory is based on two steps of information flow. First, information from the mass media will reach opinion leaders, who are people paying attention to and following the mass media. Then opinion leaders will interpret this information and, being quite influential, they will disseminate their interpretation to a large group of people with whom they are socially connected (University of Twente, 2017).

This model, which was first developed in the 1940s (the golden age of marketing innovation in the USA as mentioned in the previous chapters), became relevant once again in the twenty-first century when blogging emerged and with it the possibility to achieve a certain reaction from a mass of people.

Influencers essentially work the same way: There is one influencer who has followers. This influencer will receive sponsored goods and information from brands, which are then presented in a personal, authentic style on the influencer's media channel (or multiple channels and platforms). The information reaches the followers, and his or her opinion leads the opinion of a multitude of followers.

The only change today from the original framework is an evolution of cross-communication between the followers, strengthening the message which is spread, as well as a multitude of media platforms that can link to each other. However, the psychological and sociological mechanisms remain the same.

The two-step flow model by Lazarsfeld in the 1940s can still be used today to demonstrate how opinion leaders bring a message to their followers, thus spreading it to very specific groups.

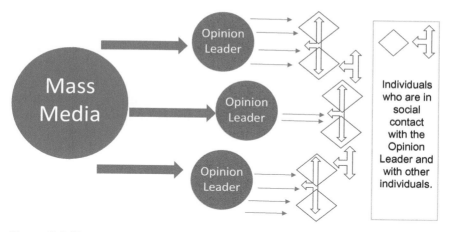

Figure 5.2 Two-step communication model applied for use today. Author's interpretation based on original by Lazarsfeld.

For a brand it can be beneficial not to broadly spread a message to everyone possible but to seek out an opinion leader who will get the message to those who are most likely to respond to it positively.

Understanding bloggers and influencers and what they can do for fashion brands

When looking at the first fashion-related influencer content in the early days of the internet, it was the bloggers who started it. It began in the early years of the twenty-first century as a sort of personal diary, a diary that was not quite yours nor that secret because its aim was for everyone to read it and comment on it. To the reader, it offered 24-hour access and was location-independent at the same time. This was a novelty at that point and was met with some resistance.

In the first years of the new millennium, people began setting up personal style blogs and showcasing fashion on them. One of the very first people to do so was the now-famous Scott Schuman with his "The Sartorialist" blog. Schuman (2005) states in his biography that he "began The Sartorialist with the idea of creating a two-way dialogue about the world of fashion and its relationship to daily life". He posted street shots of stylish people, sharing his creative life as well as his perspective on fashion with the world.

Schuman would have been considered an "industry blogger", which means that he was with a background in the industry, either fashion journalism, design, styling or similar. In this particular case, he had a degree in apparel merchandising and photography.

The other type of blogger was called the "citizen blogger". According to Gwyneth Moore (2012), this person is a "passionate consumer of fashion", sharing their lifestyle and clothing habits, style and opinions with followers, but essentially an amateur in terms of professionalism.

In 2016, about ten years after the first blogs emerged, there were already hundreds of thousands of successful and high-earning bloggers, and it had become a staple of the growing digital landscape which was developing simultaneously, offering new apps, platforms and user-friendly interfaces.

Mark Briggs writes that bloggers, unlike journalists, have the privilege of far more freedom in what they write, who they talk to and what other people they link their posts to. They might start out small, but as more people read their blog, they will reach a tipping point after which the audience takes over. This is a benchmark that indicates when a blog has become really successful and profitable (Briggs, 2016).

However, the quality of their posts needs to be considered in order to achieve the best result. Thus, in 2016, about 18 per cent of private bloggers turned to the help of professional editors before posting, and around 50 per cent asked someone to look over the post before making it live (Crestodina, 2018).

The power of blogs became so pertinentt that even the classic printed media resorted to launching their own blogs on their websites, like *Vogue* magazine, which poached Suzy Menkes away from a career at *The International Herald Tribune* (spanning 25 years) to become the editor of *Vogue*'s in-house blog in 2014.

The term "blogger" morphed into "influencer" and increasingly opened up to other people of influence and new content formats. Influencers and content creators now include self-made influencers (the former citizen blogger), film and television personalities, celebrities, athletes and vloggers, becoming a new profession and a new lucrative business sector. (It is rare that one witnesses the emergence of a completely new profession within their lifetime, particularly within the fashion industry, which makes this quite remarkable.) What has also changed is that now influencers are paid by brands, endorse products or services, and receive large payments for their work.

If a brand and an influencer are the right fit, the amount they earn can be substantial. As early as 2011, Schuman stated in a controversial interview with The Talks that American Apparel bought advertising space on his The Sartorialist site for one year and Net-a-Porter for the rest of 2010.

> So those two ads alone are a good fraction of a million dollars: more than a quarter million and less than a half a million. [...] My audience is so much larger than everybody else's that advertisers, well at least American Apparel told me that I am not in their internet budget. My order is so big and they have to pay so much that I am actually in their magazine budget. That comes from having a good size audience.

Interestingly, this statement caused quite a stir in the fashion world, being quoted numerous times on other blogs and websites. However, the original publisher of the interview no longer has it on its website (Oyster, 2011).

So how exactly is an influencer and content creator the right fit for a fashion brand?

Here is a list of potential characteristics and business options a fashion brand might be looking for when it wants to do business with an influencer:

- The fashion influencer (FI) is in tune with the current trends, and their posts are highly relevant to his or her audience.
- FI comes across as authentic and is considered an authority in fashion.
- The content of the posts is highly visual (photo/video); it is engaging because it is original and creative.
- The content is informative so that the brand's message can be transferred. FI has a good writing style and is an excellent communicator (including grammar and spelling) when it comes to storytelling, should the written contribution be required.
- FI is happy to report directly on location about fashion events, sometimes live.
- The blog posts by FI can be timed with other important marketing activities of the brand, such as store openings, shows and product launches.
- FI has several thousand or hundreds of thousands of followers, and they are a perfect fit for the brand.
- The followers are the correct target group for the fashion brand in terms of age, gender, income, fashion preference, shopping habits, etc.
- The followers react to the influencer's content, so a high rate of engagement can be expected.
- FI does not promote competing brands, or FI does promote competing brands, but there is minimal risk of losing customers this way.
- FI has a presence on different platforms, such as a blog, YouTube, Instagram, Twitter, etc. The brand can choose to do a campaign either on several platforms or just the strongest one.

What brands get in return for working with a blogger/ influencer:

- Engagement.
- Reach.
- Targeting the existing and new consumers who are likely to respond positively to the message.
- Potential increase in product or service purchases.
- Fast access to data on consumer behaviour.

Research is still emerging on how social media works or why indeed it does. But some say that searching, finding, liking, sharing, commenting and the self-presentation on social media are deeply embedded in our primal instincts and connect to feelings of reward.

> Dopamine is stimulated by unpredictability, by small bits of information, and by reward cues—pretty much the exact conditions of social media. The pull of dopamine is so strong that studies have shown tweeting is harder for people to resist than cigarettes and alcohol.
>
> (Seiter, 2016)

Perhaps it is the dopamine that has helped the industry grow exponentially. In 2016, the influencer marketing market size worldwide was worth US$1.7 billion, but in 2024, it was worth US$24 billion, with Instagram and YouTube being the most popular social media platforms to date (Dencheva, 2023). That is, however, only true for the global West, because Asia has its own set of platforms, with China boasting Little Red Book (Xiaohongshu), Weibo, WeChat, Douyin, Tencent QQ, Baidu Tieba, Tencent Video, Zhihu and Bilibili.

Interview with blogger Navaz Batliwalla aka Disneyrollergirl

Figure 5.3 Navaz Batliwalla aka Disneyrollergirl. With kind permission of Navaz Batliwalla and Emma Miranda Moore.

Navaz Batliwalla is a London-based fashion editor, brand consultant and founder of the culture of fashion blog Disneyrollergirl.net. She has also published two books: *The New Garconne: How to be a Modern Gentlewoman*, and *Face Values: The New Beauty Rituals and Skincare Secrets* (Laurence King Publishing).

Q: I believe that you have had professional training and a fashion industry background. Could you please tell me a bit more about that?

NB: My background isn't design but fashion media. I have worked in print and digital publishing for over 20 years, including working as the fashion director of *CosmoGIRL!* and the launch fashion editor of *Grazia India*. In 1999, while I was a freelance stylist, I was approached to contribute a fashion advice column and articles to a women's online publication (called Handbag.com which was owned by Telegraph Media and later Hearst). I also contributed to their discussion forums, which I enjoyed very much as I felt this gave me great insight into the consumer. For me, the forums were almost a precursor to social media.

Q: Do you think it is essential to have this background to be a successful fashion influencer, or would you say that those with no formal training do it just as well?

NB: No, it's not anymore because brands just want access to people who are interested in fashion and have a big audience. It used to be that luxury brands preferred to stick to what they know, i.e. print, journalists or those who have proven credentials.

For me, having those established relationships meant I already had "access" and a level of trust.

On the other hand, if you're someone posting outfit pictures on Instagram in which the subject is you rather than brands, then it's not necessary to have a fashion industry background. That said, any experience in business is a benefit, and the fashion industry has many unspoken codes. Now it is more important that you have an audience and proven engagement that doesn't necessitate an industry background. That being said, more recently, we are seeing a return to experts (which can be designers or journalists) who have proven expertise that consumers can trust.

Q: How many years have you been a fashion influencer, and is this your full-time job and career now?

NB: I have been blogging at Disneyrollergirl.net for seventeen years. I combine it with freelance writing and consulting, which means that although the blogging generates income, I'm not beholden to it and don't need to monetize every single opportunity. Being more choosy increases my credibility and value.

Q: How much time do you need to spend weekly to tend to your social media activities?

NB: Sadly, I'm a one-man band, so for me social media is 24/7. However, as a fashion writer, it is also my news source.

Q: Do you use a tool or platform to manage all your social media accounts?

NB: No, I do everything manually.

Q: How important is it to be based in a large fashion capital, like London?

NB: For the work I do it's essential. It gives me creative stimulation and also allows me to create visually interesting content. Networking and maintaining relationships with publicists is an important part of what I do and that has to be done in London.

Q: What is your USP, or how are you unique and different from other bloggers?

NB: I am an established "fashion insider" and have been working in the industry for a long time. I write from an informed journalistic perspective, so the blog is not about me but my observations on fashion, the industry, retail and anything in those spheres that's emerging. So I covered subjects such as the emerging markets, gender-neutral fashion, social media, content and commerce, and omnichannel retail early on. Once they start to infiltrate the mainstream, I move on to explore other emerging areas.

Q: Do you ever turn off your phone, computer, ignore all messages and go out for a walk?

NB: Of course.

Q: How did fashion brands start approaching you back in the day?

NB: For the first three years I didn't have an email address for my blog. Eventually I decided to get one so I didn't miss out on commercial opportunities. I was anonymous at the time but decided to "go public". Brands would email me and invite me to press days, fashion shows or coffee meetings to understand how I work. But I also knew many brands already so they felt safe with me as a blogger.

Q: If possible, please name some brands you have worked for.

NB: Chloe, Dior, Levi's, Chanel, Smythson, Jigsaw, Harrods.

Q: What would you say brands are looking for in a blogger/influencer with whom they'd like to work? And what do you, as an influencer, expect from them?

NB: The best and most clued-up brands expect a genuine interest in their brand/sector/product and a real point of view. The not-so-good brands expect lots of clicks and sales and do not always have realistic expectations (i.e. they don't research the blog to check if it's a good fit). I have high expectations and prefer to work with brands on projects over a long period of time rather than one-off campaigns. That way I invest time to understand the brand and create lasting content that works for both of us. I have to consider all of my channels including social media and Pinterest to make sure the content has the best reach. Often the brand only cares about your unique users, which is short-sighted.

Q: Is it usually the marketing team or the PR team or the advertising team that works with you?

NB: They usually go via an influencer agency in the first instance.

Q: Do the brands have a clear vision of what they want to communicate and how you can do that?

NB: Increasingly yes.

Q: How much freedom do brands grant you, also in terms of creativity and the channels you use?

NB: It varies. The most high-end brands give me the most freedom; they take time to nurture a lasting relationship and make sure the brand and product are a good fit. Quite often I will go to them with an idea. The more mainstream brands tend to be box tickers. "We need this many eyeballs, we have this much budget, let's get ten bloggers to do the same campaign, here's the hashtag". It's a blanket approach and not very interesting. It's easier for them to manage this way than managing ten very different individual campaigns, even if a tailored approach would probably be more engaging to each person's audience.

Q: Blogging (influencer work) has turned into a whole new profession, and some of the successful bloggers need to employ entire teams, including photographers, digital artists, etc. Do you employ any "helpers" or can you do it all by yourself?

NB: It's not sustainable or scalable to do it yourself if it's a full-time job. If I'm doing a collaboration, I need to work with photographers and models. I have a tech person to help with the back end from time to time, but in an ideal world I would have the means to pay for ongoing tech services. Obviously I want to be informed but keeping up with developments in web design, social media, affiliates and so on is too much for one person after a certain point. I do have an agent to help with negotiations and some production work, but they don't always have the manpower to go out looking for new clients. So I have to do a certain amount of personal brand building and relationship building myself, which is time-consuming. In fact, self-marketing is increasingly important in the age of fast, bite-sized content. People want to know who's talking to them.

Q: There is a stereotypical idea of what a blogger's life is like, based on the imagery that they communicate: Sleeping in and waking up in 5-star hotels, eating fancy food, being chauffeured around to fashion events and clinking glasses with all the "it" people. All this while wearing designer clothes and getting lots of dosh for it. Please give us a wake-up call and insight into the reality!

NB: The reality is of course nothing like this. People need to understand that, like all creative industries, the above scenario may be the reality for the 0.01 per cent, but as with other fashion jobs, we all collude in portraying an illusion. Why? Because the illusion and fantasy of fashion is what pays our bills. The reality is more like spending around four hours on each blog post (researching, writing, editing, coding, taking/editing/resizing/tagging images), promoting with social media, engaging with followers/commenters, answering up to 250 emails a day, managing PR's expectations on whether you can attend an event/meeting or write about an unsolicited product you've been sent, attending press days, shop openings, etc. to "support the brand", keeping up with every new platform that comes along, making sure your outfit is on brand every time you go to an event, in case you are photographed or filmed. Quite often I work until late at night as I am more productive when there are no emails coming in. Yet I'm still expected to attend breakfast meetings at 9 am. A lot of it is just like any other desk job. But of course we don't talk about that! Creating outfit posts or editorial shoots really does take some considerable pre-production, post-production and endless social media promotion. There's a lot of donkey work connected to it.

Q: Would you say that blogging or being a social media influencer is more advertising or is it public relations? Perhaps it is journalism based on advertorials?

NB: At the level where it's being monetized it's a combination of all four. It should be a balance, and I think when the advertising and commercial aspects overshadow everything else, then you have a problem. The readers get bored and your content has no substance.

Q: Are there any bloggers who inspired you when you were starting out, and who do you look up to now?

NB: Most of the bloggers I looked up to in the early days aren't around anymore. I don't know if I looked up to them as much as admiring their writing and tone of voice.

Q: What comes when all the blogging has been done? There are bloggers turning into designers, others (like you!) publish serious books. Blogs based on personal youth and beauty can't be eternal. What do you see in this profession for the next 10 to 20 years?

NB: No one said blogging was or should be about personal youth and beauty, although commercially it feels like it has become that. For a while it became saturated with the new wave who came along because they wanted the fame and ego-stroking rather than because they had something to say. That cohort moved onto social media and we're now seeing blogging and thoughtful writing return in the form of Substack newsletters. It's a recognition of the intimacy you build with your reader as a regular blog writer.

Q: What inspires you to keep going? What do you envision for your influencer future?

NB: I don't envision my influencer future as such. My goal is to maintain a living as a freelance fashion editor and creative consultant, whether that's in print or online or in advertising/marketing, but to maintain an outlet for my personal point of view. I am much happier creating content behind the scenes; the medium is not important. What keeps me going in that respect is a deep love of fashion, culture, the industry, creativity and observing and analyzing the changes. But I very much value having the insider access, so my ambition is to maintain that.

Celebrity endorsements and what they can do for a fashion brand

As noted in Chapter 2, the idea of a celebrity opinion leader is quite ancient. Queen Elizabeth I, Napoleon and Queen Victoria – just to name a few – were political leaders of the global West who strategically shaped and influenced the opinions of their people (followers) and fashion. In fact, being affiliated with a royal "celebrity" was a fantastic promotional tool for merchants and artisans of that era. Cope and Maloney (2016) believe that the Royal Warrant, which was first introduced in the UK in the twelfth century, was one way to help highly skilled artisans grow their businesses. This included tailors, cobblers and dressmakers who might still have the warrant to this day.

In nineteenth-century France, Empress Eugenie was an avid fashion leader and endorsed her couturier Charles Frederick Worth, who is said to have been the first designer to put a name (and a brand) on his lavish creations. Associating with royals, even today, is something designers and brands strive for. For instance, Elizabeth Emanuel and her husband were catapulted into stardom after they designed Princess Diana's wedding dress. Some decades later, Kate, the Princess of Wales , became an opinion leader and fashion celebrity herself, promoting British designers by wearing their creations. By choosing to mostly wear UK high-street brands, those dresses were instantly sold out in stores and online, so much so that this was dubbed "the Kate effect". (Richardson, 2020)

Now let's see who else apart from royals could be considered a celebrity in the twenty-first century. Is it a famous actor or athlete? A singer? Is it a reality TV star, scientist or activist? Perhaps it is an iconic designer, another brand or a model. For the needs of today's fashion, it can be any of those and many more, but there has to be a common denominator.

In this context, celebrities have three things in common which are attractive to brands: they are instantly recognizable, they have millions of fans and they love to collaborate with brands. Celebrities can be used for both advertising and PR communication strategies. This is why the PR department might try to send gifts to celebrities or offer to give them a dazzling outfit for a night out on the red carpet, ensuring that their product gets seen and talked about.

In the case of advertising, the celebrities are featured in campaigns and actively endorse a brand.

How to establish a brand match between celebrity and consumer

Psychological studies (Amos, Holmes and Strutton, 2008) have shown that celebrities have a significant and positive effect on consumers, which benefits the brand.

1. Consumers want to emulate the celebrity.
2. Consumers believe the testimonial by the celebrity.
3. Consumers can memorize the advertisement much better when there is a celebrity.
4. Consumers associate the positive traits of the celebrity with the product (but when it backfires, they will also associate the negative traits with the product).

How is a celebrity interesting to a fashion brand? Here is a list of characteristics a fashion brand might be looking for when it wants to do business with a celebrity:

- Celebrity career: Has the celebrity had a shining career with great achievements?
- Celebrity scandals: Has the celebrity been involved in any scandal that generated negative press? If so, consumers might associate the advertised product with the negativity of the celebrity.
- Celebrity validity: Would consumers trust this celebrity as an opinion leader on the particular product?
- Celebrity authority: Is the celebrity an opinion leader or considered an expert in this area?
- Celebrity looks: In a world where good looks can sell a product, it is important that the celebrity is considered to be attractive among the target customers.

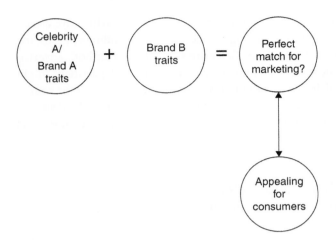

Figure 5.4 Compatibility model for celebrity and brand. Author's original illustration.

- Celebrity recognition: Will consumers easily recognize the celebrity?
- Celebrity/product harmony: Is the celebrity the right fit to endorse a product? Will they be in harmony?
- Celebrity endorsement portfolio: Does the celebrity endorse other brands? If so, would they be a competitor? Is the celebrity endorsing too many brands so that the impact is diffused?

Figure 5.4 is a basic compatibility model that can help establish a perfect match for collaboration.

> **Case example: Tod's or the living dead**
>
> One interesting way brands use celebrity endorsement is when they work with a famous person who has passed away a long time ago. Nobody would be surprised to see famous icons and movie stars such as Marilyn Monroe, Audrey Hepburn, Frank Sinatra or Einstein.
>
> What are the brand benefits? All the aforementioned positive effects can be triggered, as global consumers will recognize a star who is still an opinion leader and someone to emulate due to their legendary life. The celebrity shines a positive aura on the product.
>
> Tod's is a brand that played with this type of endorsement back in the 1990s, then known as J.P. Tod's. It featured Audrey Hepburn, the Kennedys,

Brigitte Bardot with Jacques Charrier and Grace Kelly in its print campaigns. The celebrities were shown in a black-and-white original photo that was positioned above a pair of Tod's loafers at the bottom of the page. The consumers were led to believe that these celebrities all wore Tod's loafers.

However, only Hepburn and Grace Kelly were wearing loafers in those photos; the Kennedys were barefoot. But that was not even the problem. The problem was simply a matter of chronology, which might only occur to people who know that Tod's was founded in 1978, very much in contrast to the celebrity photos. The photo of Audrey Hepburn is from her film *Funny Face* from 1957, John F. Kennedy only lived until 1963 and Grace Kelly's photo is from a promotional shot from the 1950s film *To Catch a Thief and Brigitte Bardot's snapshot with Jacques Charrier was from 1959*. To put it another way: during their lifetime, none of these celebrities could have possibly worn Tod's loafers from the future, and the loafers that they wore in the photos were, of course, from a different brand. In fact, Audrey Hepburn wore loafers by Salvatore Ferragamo in *Funny Face*, and Grace Kelly wore Weejuns Penny Loafers by G.H. Bass & Co., which first came onto the American market in 1936.

In this case, the celebrity endorses a product without his or her consent, and the public is led to believe that the brand was truly worn by them. Is it legal? It can be if all legal aspects are cleared.

What is the downside to this? According to *Ad Age*, "dealing with estates of departed icons and the parties related to their image and product – movie studios, music license holders and the like – can be fraught with complexity that sometimes ends in litigation" (Muratore, 2014).

Most poignantly, Tod's misled the public through the ad campaigns, creating the impression that the brand was prized and worn by various celebrities and that it is an older heritage brand which in itself is an ethical dilemma.

The Korean Wave: Hallyu and KOLs

Celebrity influence is highly prominent in Asia, where it has become a necessity for brand communications. The term used is not "influencer" but "key opinion leader", or KOL for short, which can include famous celebrities, industry experts and pure KOLs. The most popular ones are actors or reality TV stars, musicians and singers, internet influencers, and specifically in China, fashion designers as well asmake-up artists (Von Kameke, 2023).

South Korea has been associated with the term "Hallyu" or Korean Wave (referred to as Hanryu in South Korea), creating its own very unique KOLs and influencing not only adjacent Asian countries but now the entire world.

It was approximately from the mid-1990s and during the next decade when South Korean TV dramas and music became increasingly popular in close neighbouring countries such as Japan and China. China's major state broadcaster (CCTV) aired a Korean TV drama titled *What Is Love* in 1997, which ranked second in China's all-time imported video content (Korean Cultural Centre UK, n.d.).

From this moment on, the Korean Wave was born. It swept over Japan next, when in 2003, the KBS TV drama series *Winter Sonata* was aired via the state channel NHK. In Japan, the series resonated especially with "middle-aged women, mainly because of the drama's depiction of pure love, its overall aesthetic and poetic beauty, its portrayal of characters with traditional values".

By 2006, countries such as Japan, Taiwan, the People's Republic of China, Hong Kong, Thailand, Malaysia, Vietnam, Mongolia and Uzbekistan had been affected by Hanryu (Onishi, 2005, as cited in Hanaki et al., 2007).

From the mid-2000s to the early 2010s, the spread of the global Korean Wave was mainly led by Korean pop music boy groups and girl groups, but when in 2020, the film *Parasite* won four leading awards at the 92nd Academy Awards and became popular around the world, South Korean cinema also reached global fame. With this, Bong Joon-ho became the first Korean director to win the Palme d'Or at the Cannes Film Festival. Soon after, the global success of *Squid Game* firmly added to the rising popularity of Korean television fandom.

Over the last years, the number of Hallyu-related organizations has seen an increase of 7 per cent every year, and the number of members by 36 per cent. As of 2020, the total number of members who have joined Hallyu-related organizations in all countries around the world has reached nearly 100 million, which is a five-fold increase over five years.

The majority of them consist of K-pop fan clubs such as ARMY, BTS's global official fan club, and BLINK, BLACKPINK's official fan club. In a survey conducted in 26 countries in 2023, close to 50 per cent of respondents stated that the genre K-pop was popular in their country and over 70% found it generally popular(Statista, 2024).

Of course, there are many other organizations which are active in various fields, such as South Korean food and tourism (Korean Cultural Centre UK, n.d.). Korean beauty and skincare products are another incredibly popular category in neighbouring Asian countries and are now being exported worldwide.

Naturally, fashion brands have used the international popularity of Korean stars for brand promotion. Gucci collaborated with Kai of the K-pop band Exo; K-pop boy band BTS partnered with Louis Vuitton for a campaign; and BLACKPINK's Jennie, Rosé, Lisa and Jisoo appeared in a campaign for

Givenchy and were individually chosen to promote Chanel, Saint Laurent, Celine and Dior, respectively.

In 2024, Jing Daily reported that Korean stars such as rapper-singer Karina and singer-songwriter-actress Lee Ji-eun dominated Milan Men's Fashion Week and collectively saw more than $55.2 million in earned media value. The top 10 stars were collaborating with brands such as Gucci, Prada, Dolce & Gabbana and Zegna, and also included Thai KOLs such as actor Norawit Titicharoenrak (Ryder, 2024).

Interview with Kyungmi Lim

Figure 5.5 Kyungmi Lim. With kind permission from Kyungmi Lim.

Kyungmi Lim has been working as a fashion magazine editor in Seoul, Korea, for the past 20 years. Currently, she is in charge of celebrity fashion photography, interviews and casting for various luxury brand fashion shows. Since 2019, Kyungmi has lived in London and worked with K-pop stars in Europe. Her Instagram profile is @editork_work.

Q: Which fashion publications do you work for?

KL: Recently, I joined the fashion business journal *WWD Korea* to shoot and interview celebrities for covers, and I also contributed articles to *Vogue Korea* and *Marie Claire Korea*.

Q: What kind of preparation goes into the editorials?

KL: First, I check the schedule of celebrities and decide where to shoot and with which concept. If it's set overseas, I look for a sponsor from luxury brands who will cover all the expenses needed to shoot. Then I try to find the right fashion magazine and arrange a photo shoot. A column is created when the needs of celebrities, luxury brands and fashion media align. When I'm ready, I choose the right location and staff, take photos and conduct an interview.

Q: Is there anything in particular that you need to pay attention to when you start work on an editorial?

KL: As I mentioned earlier, my job is to meet the needs of celebrities, luxury brands and fashion magazines alike. It's very delicate and challenging. Working with celebrities requires coordinating sensitive processes at every stage, and luxury brands want to see their money well spent. In between, I have a big role to play in reconciling the various needs.

Q: How is a particular celebrity or influencer selected for the shoot?

KL: I usually shoot K-pop singers, and they are mostly ambassadors for each luxury brand. However, apart from these cases, celebrities who have a lot of followers on social media and are highly interesting to the public are the priority.

Q: Can you describe a typical day of shooting the editorial?

KL: I complete all the preparations until the day before shooting and constantly rehearse them in my head. It is important to keep to the timetable when working with celebrities. I also need to prepare various options because there can be some mid-shot variables. For example, if we're shooting on the street, I prepare various options for situations (e.g. the weather) where it is impossible. In Korea, finishing quality tasks flexibly and quickly is considered one of the important abilities of an editor.

Q: Who was your favourite star or influencer and why?

KL: I have been working with a celebrity for more than 10 years with whom I was once in a relationship. I love to share in their growth and feel rewarded. I mainly worked with Girls' Generation, SHINee and Red Velvet, and I also went to the New York Fashion Week Coach Fashion Show with Jisoo and Rosé in 2018. Particularly with the members of SHINee and Red Velvet, I have conducted photo shoots and fashion shows for more than 10 years. I will also attend the COS S/S 24 fashion show in Rome on 25 March with SHINee member Minho.

Q: How do you see the importance and growth of Korean culture (K-pop, K-beauty, K-drama) in the global fashion landscape?

KL: With the global success of BTS and BLACKPINK, I think K-pop is now recognized for its popularity in the global market, and not exclusively for enthusiasts. Its recognition has also made a big impact on the fashion and beauty sector thanks to the development of social media. Also, the success of the movies *Parasite* and *Minari* and the TV drama *Squid Game* has led to global success despite being productions with subtitles, and this has contributed to the growth of Korean content. Koreans have a high perspective and strict standards, so they continue to raise the level of content made in Korea. Korea is more trendy than anywhere else, and people in the cultural industry are making works with greater dedication than anyone else. While it was difficult to enter the international market, I think Korean content, which has already broken down barriers, will continue to grow.

Q: What power do Korean celebrities and influencers have these days? Can you give an example?

KL: Several K-pop stars were included in the 2023 Best Fashion Influencer rankings selected by the overseas marketing platform Lyst: No. 1 Kim Kardashian, No. 2 BLACKPINK Jennie, No. 3 BTS V, No. 4 BLACKPINK Rosé, No. 5 BLACKPINK Jisoo, and No. 7 BLACKPINK Lisa. This indicates that the status of K-pop artists in the global fashion world is increasing daily. In addition, in the recently announced "Top 10 brand AW24 Media Value (EMV)", BLACKPINK Jisoo topped the list with Dior, and Saint Laurent's Rosé ranked third, making for more than five K-pop stars in the top 10. Even more encouraging, however, is that in Korea, many girl groups, including AESPA and NewJeans, have already debuted and continue to be as popular as BLACKPINK.

Q: How should international brands prepare themselves for the near future if they want to tap into the Korean influencer market?

KL: Koreans are very sensitive to fashion and very trendy. Also, Korea's domestic fashion market has developed so much that it needs price competitiveness. In addition, with the development of internet technology, social media has developed more than anything else, and digital marketing is essential to capture them. It would be good to consider pop-up stores in fashionable areas in Seoul, such as Seongsu-dong. Koreans tend to be very interested in and admire celebrities' styles, so collaboration with celebrities and their brand identity is also essential.

Q: What advice would you give to anyone who wishes to embark on a career like yours?

KL: I think an overall interest in and passion for fashion and popular culture will be the most important. Since this is work, especially with celebrities, discretion, quick judgement and flexible ability to cope with various situations are also essential. To work in the media these days, not only writing but also various photography skills are useful, so it would be helpful if you are interested in taking pictures. In that sense, studying for a master's degree in fashion business management at the University of Westminster in London helped me a lot.

Q: Who would you like to work with in the future and why?

KL: I am constantly watching K-pop rookie groups that are likely to debut in Korea. RIIZE is the most interesting these days. Their potential has already been recognized by being named Louis Vuitton's Korean Ambassador on their debut.

Ethical considerations

How can consumers distinguish between influencer's real opinion and an endorsed or sponsored opinion? Should consumers have a clear understanding of the difference?

Working with selected influencers (opinion leaders) who are groomed by brands to endorse a certain product or service leaves many questions open: Are consumers aware that the opinion leader is being paid for the promotion? When is the opinion leader actually expressing a true personal opinion as opposed to a paid-for opinion that is likely not genuine? It is therefore very important to make this distinction clear to the consumer so that the consumer can make an informed decision.

The same is true for celebrity endorsement. There are many cases where a celebrity endorsed a brand, but it later became evident that the celebrity had completely different values, and the ethics of the brand and celebrity did not match. Although this might work at first for marketing measures, once the consumer realizes that the celebrity has a different opinion, this can create disbelief, a break of trust and frustration.

The regulations and laws on this are generally vague and provide opportunities to mislead the consumer.

The other question is whether an opinion leader or celebrity carries any responsibility for the effects of their endorsement, just like advertisers do. Could their endorsement be potentially harmful to the masses? Would it diminish their self-esteem and self-perception? What if children follow the celebrity through social media and, as a vulnerable group, are exposed to the same messages? These and more questions need to be considered when approaching marketing through the means of endorsements, influencers and opinion leaders.

Another aspect of celebrity culture is our obsession with it and the arguably unhealthy implications for our psychological and emotional well-being, our self-perception and self-confidence. Clinical psychologist Michael S. Levy (2015) suggests that we have become addicted in a way similar to how someone becomes addicted to drugs or alcohol. If this is true, then a brand which cooperates with celebrities and uses them for endorsements is actually fuelling the addiction and causing harm to society.

For instance, with the incredibly beautiful and near-perfect K-Wave celebrities, comes increasing social pressure for perfect appearance and high beauty standards, prompting many young women (and men) to use plastic surgery. South Korea now has the highest rate of plastic surgery worldwide and also one of the highest suicide rates worldwide. Women who did not agree with the immense pressure on their appearance founded a feminist movement called Tal Corset around 2018: 탈코 (tal-ko), short for 탈주 코르셋 (tal-ju co-reu-set) – "escape the corset" in English – that aims to allow women to free themselves from the strict patriarchal views dictating how Korean women should present themselves.

The movement gained global attention through a video on YouTube titled "나는 예쁘지 않습니다." ("I am not pretty."). The woman behind the video, Lina Bae, is a prominent beauty influencer who decided to use her platform to share her experiences of the South Korean beauty standard (Sharp, 2019).

Further reading

Bartlett, D. (2013) *Fashion Media: Past and Present*. London: Bloomsbury Academic.

Briggs, M. (2016) *Journalism Next: A Practical Guide to Digital Reporting and Publishing*. 3rd revised edn. Thousand Oaks and London: Sage Publications Inc.

Church Gibson, P. (2011) *Fashion and Celebrity Culture*. Oxford: Berg Publishers.

Cope, J. and Maloney, D. (2016) *Fashion Promotion in Practice*. London: Bloomsbury.

Elihu, K. and Lazarsfeld, P. F. (2005) *Personal Influence: The Part Played by People in the Flow of Mass Communications*. London: Routledge.

Ferragni, C. (2013) *The Blonde Salad. Consigli di stile dalla fashion blogger più seguita del web* [Italian]. Mondadori.

Fuchs, C. (2013) *Social Media: A Critical Introduction*. London: Sage.

Gelardi, P. and Barberich, C. (2014) *Refinery29: Style Stalking*. Kindle edition.

Houghton, R. (2012) *Blogging for Creatives*. London: Ilex Press.

Katz, E., Lazarsfeld, P. F. and Roper, E. (Foreword) (2005) *Personal Influence: The Part Played by People in the Flow of Mass Communications*. New York: Free Press.

Lazarsfeld, P. F., Berelson, B. and Gaudet, H. (1944) *The People's Choice: How the Voter Makes Up His Mind in a Presidential Campaign*. New York: Columbia University Press.

Levy, M. S. (2015) *Celebrity and Entertainment Obsession: Understanding Our Addiction*. Lanham, MD: Rowman & Littlefield Publishers.

Pringle, H. (2004) *Celebrity Sells*. Chichester: Wiley.

Richardson, T. (2020) The Kate Effect: The Duchess of Cambridge is asking 5 Big Questions about early years. University of Northampton (online) Available at: https://www.northampton.ac.uk/news/the-kate-effect-what-will-the-duchess-of-cambridges-survey-tell-us-about-early-years/

Schuman, S. (2009) *The Sartorialist*. Harmondsworth, UK: Penguin.

Sharp, A. (2019) Escape the Corset: #탈코. *Leeds Human Rights Journal* [Online]. University of Leeds. Available at: https://hrj.leeds.ac.uk/2019/11/29/escape-the-corset-%ED%83%88%EC%BD%94/

Tungate, M. (2012) *Fashion Brands: Branding Style from Armani to Zara*. London: Kogan Page.

Van Dijck, J. (2013) *The Culture of Connectivity: A Critical History of Social Media*. Oxford: Oxford University Press.

Digital marketing **6**

Chapter topics

A brief history of the internet

The first step of the digital landscape that we find ourselves in today was the internet, which was made available to the public in the 1990s. Prior to that, it had existed for several decades but was reserved for the military and scientific research. It was an innovation in part due to the Cold War and the space race between the United States and the USSR. The USSR successfully launched Sputnik (a satellite) into orbit in 1957, which was able to transmit signals back to Earth. This technological advance prompted a response from the US, which instructed major universities to work on a data transmission and communication project, while the USSR did the same. The US succeeded in setting up the computer network ARPANET in 1965, while the Soviet Union established the VNIIPAS institute sometime later.

Over the following decades, both countries succeeded in developing functioning internet infrastructure, including a secret joint one: the San Francisco

DOI: 10.4324/9781003449157-6

Moscow Teleport (SFMT), later known as the Soviet–American Teleport. In 1983, VNIIPAS, Joel Schatz, Don Carlson, Michael Kleeman, Chet Watson, and financier George Soros brought the teleport to life. For a brief moment, said Schatz,

> American and Soviet scientists, film makers, publishers, designers, teachers and others (met) on-line on a regular basis to exchange information and produce joint projects. The result is an electronic community that (reached) across space and time and also (spanned) the political gap.
>
> (Zweig, 1987)

According to Adrian Athique (2013), the first encounter with the internet and digital media for the general public was indeed coupled with a war. The Gulf War of 1990 became a spectacle of virtual imagery, very different from how people had experienced wars before. Images were accessible 24 hours a day, seven days per week, showing "computerized animations of battlefield situations" which seemed hyper-realistic or even incredulous. This led the famous sociologist Baudrillard to highlight the disconnect between reality and the depiction by electronic media and call it a *simulacrum* (something that replaces reality or "something that looks like or represents something else" if you were to consult the *Cambridge Dictionary*).

At first, the internet available to the general public was clumsy and not user-friendly because it relied on dial-up technology and blocked the telephone line when in use. It was slow, and the software was rather unspectacular. However, in 1993 there was the first browser, and within the next five years, global users could access material on the World Wide Web as well as publish their own content, chat and communicate via email (Athique, 2013).

This revolutionized many things, including how people socialize, how information is spread or obtained, and how goods and services are consumed. In 1994, the first internet banner appeared for AT&T, and in 1995 an online bookstore called Amazon was launched and became one of the first examples of e-commerce. By the turn of the millennium, most companies wanted to be represented on the World Wide Web with their own website, even though not all of the websites would have been transactional at that time (Charlesworth, 2014) In 1998, PayPal was launched as one of the first e-commerce payment platforms, and in another ten years, e-commerce morphed into s-commerce when the first smartphones arrived in 2007. By 2011, an astounding 2 billion people were using the internet around the world (Athique, 2013).

However, often forgotten in the mention of pre-internet development is the French phenomenon known as "Minitel" – a telephonic terminal that was established in the early 1980s and rolled out across France by the end of the 1980s, free of charge to households (but at a charge for services accessed through it). It looked like a miniature computer monitor or mini TV with a keyboard and was connected to the phoneline, allowing access to many services such as telephone book entries, banking, mail-order from retailers, news, purchase of transport tickets and text-based dating. An estimated 25 million people used Minitel by the year 2000 (O'Brien, 2022) Frequently, on the readio or on TV, audiences would be prompted to find out more by typing in a number on their Minitel. In 2012, Minitel was sadly discontinued despite having nearly 1 million users in France.

With the internet boom, fashion brands also embraced e-commerce with high-street and fast-fashion brands taking the first steps and mail-order catalogue businesses seizing the opportunity. ASOS launched its online business in 2000 with the name "As Seen on Screen" (originally selling clothing that looked similar to what celebrities were seen wearing) and is now one of the largest pure players in Europe along with its younger rival Zalando. In the UK, the retailer Net-a-Porter and the Italian company Yoox were established as pure play retailers by 2005 (Hines and Bruce, 2007).

In 2005, there was still a lot of mystery around what type of consumer would want to shop online rather than in a physical store or via a mail-order catalogue. Mintel reported on the willingness of UK consumers to shop online in the following way:

> Certainly catalogue retailers have been proactive in terms of developing e-tail initiatives exploiting the fact that customers with experience of well-established catalogue retailers may be less wary of buying online. Undoubtedly, at this current stage in the development of e-tailing, familiarity and trust are key factors in deciding with whom to shop with online as along with catalogue retailers, high street retailers such as Argos, Next Plc and John Lewis are also exploiting their brand awareness to a competitive advantage.

Whatever the true reason, internet shopping had overtaken catalogue shopping by 2005 (Hines and Bruce, 2007).

Digital marketing and the PEO framework

With the digital landscape rapidly becoming a place for brands to establish a presence, it also challenges their ability to adapt their marketing strategies to a new virtual marketplace. Essentially, digital marketing is similar to traditional marketing but uses digital platforms and has the added benefit that user data can be obtained almost instantly, and the success of marketing efforts can be measured. It can also transcend time and space, reaching customers anywhere in the world very quickly.

The other difference from traditional marketing is that customers might seek information on the brand on their own initiative. However, of course, digital marketing also captures the public's attention on digital platforms through advertising, banners and sponsored content, just like traditional marketing can do with posters, billboards, magazine ads and newspaper ads.

For a majority of companies that are not pure players, there is a combination of a physical presence and digital presence, and it is thus important for brands to think of omni-channel marketing, using both the digital landscape and their traditional media options.

Generally, a brand might consider investing in its wholly owned online presence and have a website in place that allows e-commerce, social media accounts and its own apps, possibly adapting these to different countries and languages. These particular activities would be supported by marketing and communications activities that can be launched through the brand's own channels or by placing content on third-party platforms (just like traditional brands would buy advertising space in a magazine, they can buy advertising space in an online magazine). If the marketing activities are effective and gain traction, the brand can earn favourable digital media mentions and interactions that they did not pay for or control.

This is the principle of the PEO framework, which combines these three categories into one and was published by Gini Dietrich around 2014. The acronym stands for paid, earned and owned media.

Owned

This digital content that the brand sets up can include the following:

Brand-owned website and e-commerce site
Brand-owned social media channels
Brand-owned apps
Brand-owned emails and newsletters
Brand-owned games for gamification

These particular digital options would be classified as "owned media" meaning that they are orchestrated and controlled by the brand.

Paid

The next category of what a brand can do online is to pay for specific media, which would be classified as "paid media" and includes the following options:

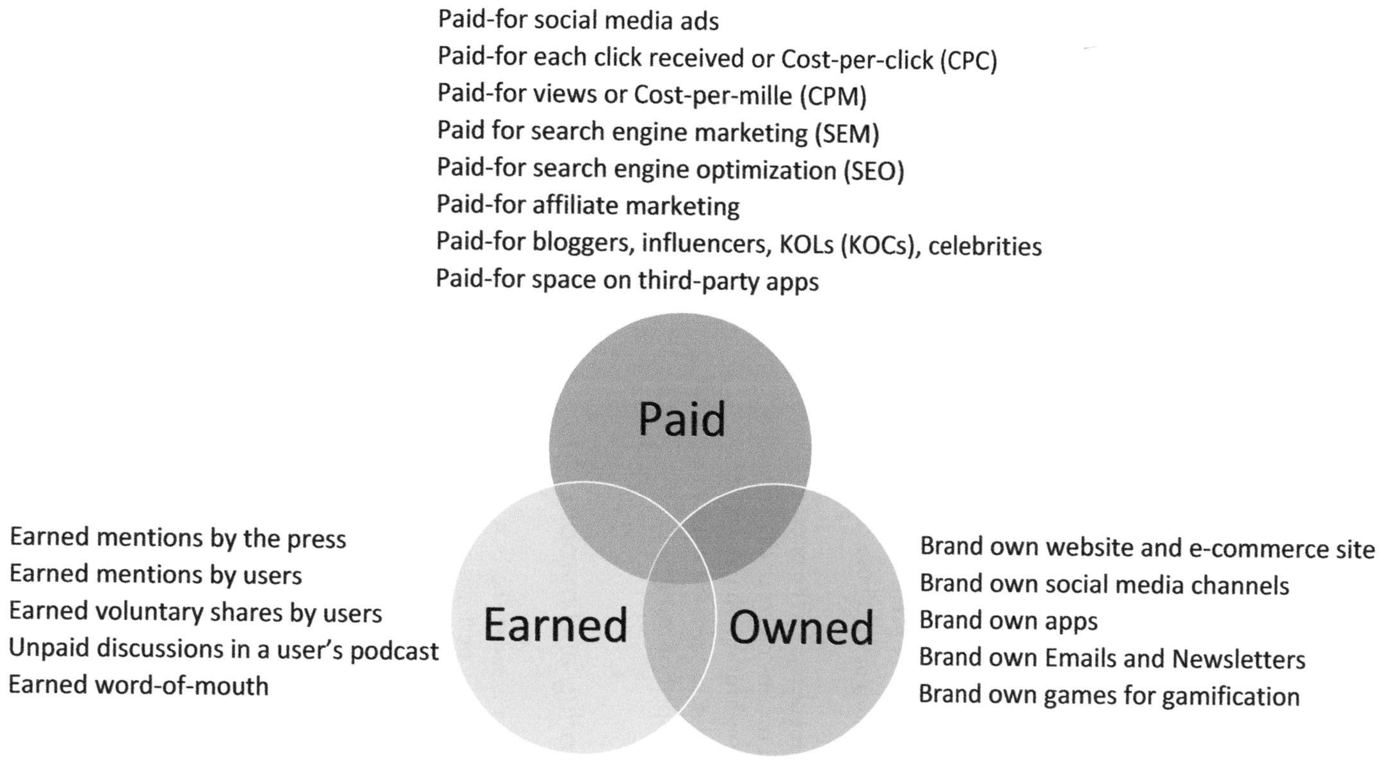

Paid-for social media ads

Paid-for each click received or Cost-per-click (CPC)

Paid-for views or Cost-per-mille (CPM)

Paid for search engine marketing (SEM)

Paid-for search engine optimization (SEO)

Paid-for affiliate marketing

Paid-for bloggers, influencers, KOLs (KOCs), celebrities

Paid-for space on third-party apps

Brand own website and e-commerce site

Brand own social media channels

Brand own apps

Brand own Emails and Newsletters

Brand own games for gamification

Paid

Owned

Earned

Earned mentions by the press

Earned mentions by users

Earned voluntary shares by users

Unpaid discussions in a user's podcast

Earned word-of-mouth

Figure 6.1 The PEO framework.

Paid-for social media ads
Paid-for clicks received or cost-per-click (CPC)
Paid-for views or cost-per-mille (CPM)
Paid-for search engine marketing (SEM)
Paid-for search engine optimization (SEO)
Paid-for affiliate marketing
Paid-for bloggers, influencers, KOLs (KOCs), celebrities
Paid-for space on third-party apps

Earned

The third category is classified as "earned media", which is perhaps the most valuable one to brands. Here, brands do not directly pay or put any specific efforts in place but reap the rewards from having worked hard on the owned and paid categories. These rewards can include the following:

Earned mentions by the press
Earned mentions by users
Earned voluntary shares by users
Unpaid discussions on a user's podcast
Earned word-of-mouth

Monitoring and mapping the customer journey

In order to achieve the best results with digital marketing channels, brands need to set key performance indicators (KPIs) and then monitor and measure the achievements. These KPIs can include brand awareness, social reach (followers, subscribers, impressions), engagement (likes, comments, sentiment, shares, mentions, reposts), media mentions, website traffic and more. For specific campaigns, the KPIs can measure the direct response, such as sales/conversions, conversion value, leads, sign-ups, downloads and click-through rates.

The digital landscape has the benefit of easy access to such metrics, and thus a return on investment (ROI) can be calculated for any digital marketing activity. With almost instant access to metrics, the digital marketing plan can be adjusted to achieve the best possible outcomes.

Data and metrics also help to optimize customer relations management (e-CRM) and clienteling, which includes customer selection, acquisition, retention and extension (Chaffey, 2009). Here, data on consumer behaviour on the brand's owned and paid-for channels is vital.

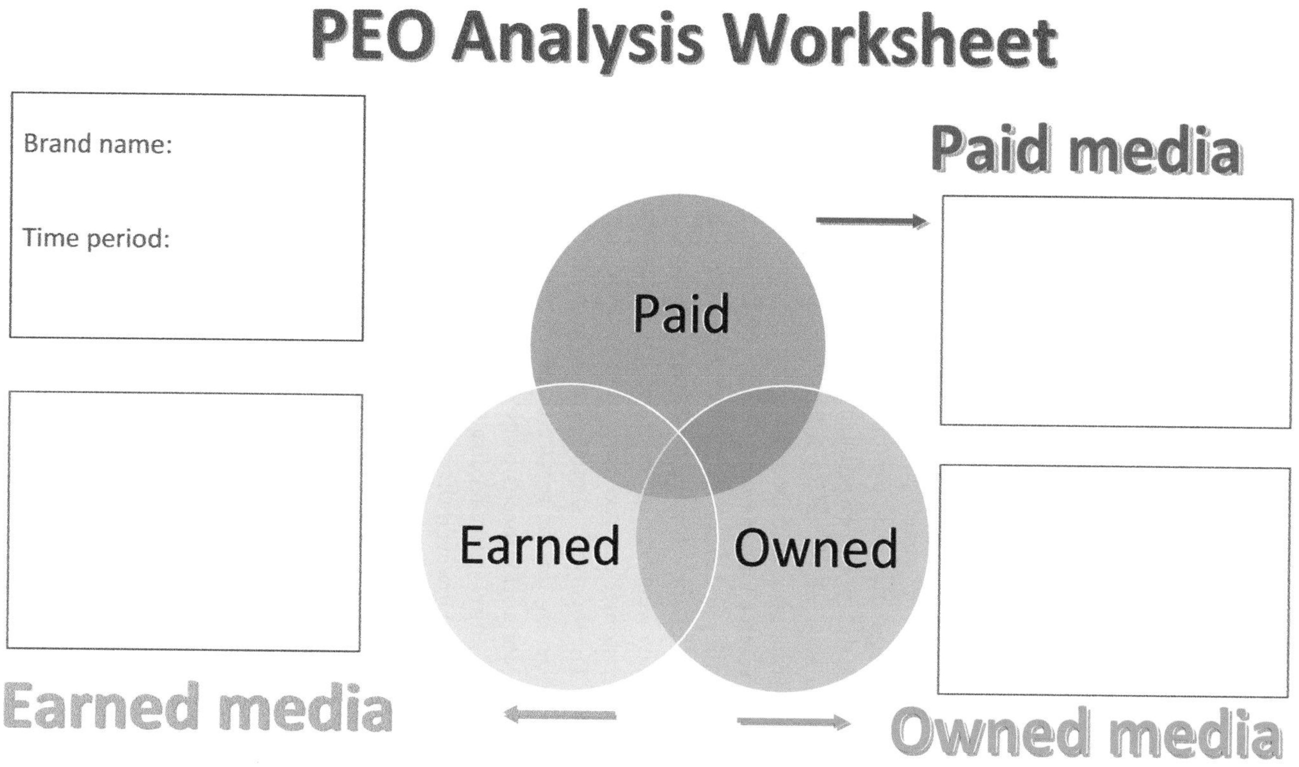

PEO Analysis Worksheet

Paid media

Owned media

Earned media

Paid

Owned

Earned

Brand name:

Time period:

Figure 6.2 PEO analysis worksheet: you can use this worksheet to conduct a PEO analysis for a brand's existing communication activities or map out a plan for future ones.

Mapping the customer journey

For an optimal end-to-end customer brand experience both online and offline, a brand can map out the touchpoints that a customer would encounter while getting to know the brand, considering a purchase, making the purchase, and their satisfaction and willingness to advocate for the brand or repeat a purchase in the future.

An ideal way to visualize this is by plotting the different brand touchpoints along a pathway, thus creating a customer journey map. Specific marketing activities can then be implemented to increase the effectiveness of each touchpoint and the entire route the customer takes.

For the purpose of creating awareness and retention, digital marketing activities can include welcome letters and newsletters, last-item reminders, updates on shipping status, prompts to see a new campaign or the latest video, offers to help with the choice of a product, tailored and personalized discounts, renewals and renewal offers, and the infamous "sorry to see you go" messages for those who wish to unsubscribe.

Advocacy is worth a lot to a brand and can make part of the earned media. According to Chaffey and Smith (2017), a checklist can help in ensuring digital marketing is set up to allow for and encourage advocacy.

For example, any website, page or brand app should have an option embedded where the customer can recommend or forward the content to a friend, share and like. The customer should also be given the opportunity to leave a comment and rating for the service or product and make suggestions for improvements. Monitoring needs to be implemented so that the brand can respond rapidly to any negative feedback and mitigate the damage an unhappy customer can cause. However, this does not mean that the brand should gaslight an unhappy experience with the brand but rather take it on board and improve its performance.

However, according to some experts such as Sharon N. Hughes, the customer journey has evolved, particularly as social media, e-commerce and s-commerce have evolved and become more cyclical. In this case, the brand touchpoints should be mapped out in a circle to represent the end-to-beginning customer journey.

Digital acceleration and digital assets

Although digital marketing and e-commerce have been developing rapidly since the late 1990s, a significant and unexpected moment of acceleration occurred during the global Covid-19 pandemic when physical stores were shut

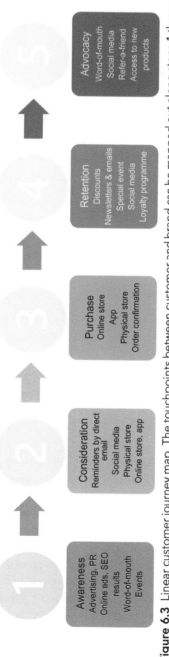

Figure 6.3 Linear customer journey map. The touchpoints between customer and brand can be mapped out along steps 1 through 5.

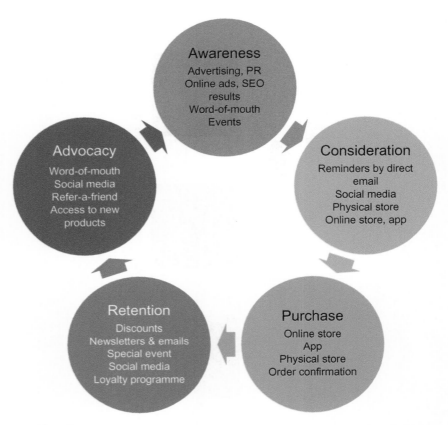

Figure 6.4 Cyclical customer journey map. The touchpoints between customer and brand can be mapped out and reconnected to the starting point of "awareness".

for long periods of time. Brands that already had a strong online presence were relatively safe from losing business, but other brands had to adapt very quickly and switch to digital commerce or expand whatever they had in place. It was a decisive point for luxury brands in particular, which up to that moment had refused to trade their exclusive products on the internet for fear that the brand identity would be harmed and their luxury status (and scarcity) would be tainted. Nevertheless, in their desperation, most of the reluctant luxury brands took the plunge into the unknown and were positively surprised. E-commerce went better than anticipated, and profits proved that it was working to their advantage. This is one of the reasons that the largest luxury conglomerate, LVMH, managed to increase its revenue during the pandemic and emerge with a new digital presence.

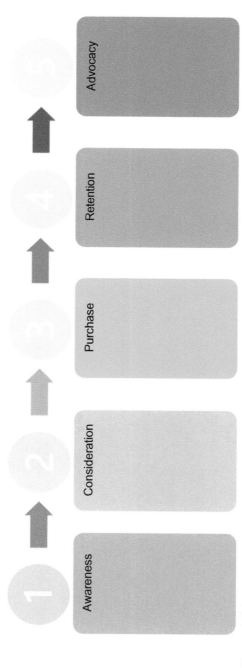

Figure 6.5 Linear customer journey map analysis worksheet: you can use this worksheet to conduct a customer journey map analysis for a brand's existing activities or map out a plan for future ones.

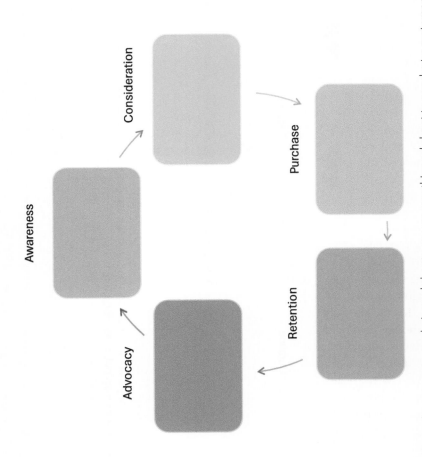

Figure 6.6 Cyclical customer journey map analysis worksheet: you can use this worksheet to conduct a customer journey map analysis for a brand's existing activities or map out a plan for future ones.

As the digital world develops further into a "metaverse", it also presents consumers with fully digital products that have no physical version. The metaverse is an "architecture with the integration of digital worlds and the human and physical worlds", which means that there is a cross-over of physical humans encountering completely digital offerings that are accessible through physical hardware, such as computers or mobile devices. According to Jaber (2022), the metaverse components are humans (who are at the core of the metaverse), the physical infrastructures (the real/physical world); the interconnected virtual worlds (named the sub-metaverse), the metaverse engine (whose functioning is fed through the use of blockchain, artificial intelligence, interactivity and digital twin technologies), the in-world information flow (the technologies permanently update the virtual world through inputs from the real world) and the flow of information across physical and virtual worlds (Jaber, 2022 in Sá and Serpa, 2023, pp. 7–8).

An example specific to the fashion industry is NFTs, which have been mildly popular and stand for non-fungible tokens – assets that have been tokenized via a blockchain.

The lluxury brand Gucci collaborated with Superplastic (creator of vinyl figures and digital collectibles) resulting in SUPERGUCCI NFTs, co-created by Gucci's Creative Director Alessandro Michele and synthetic artists Janky & Guggimon. Karl Lagerfeld was offering his miniature self in the form of NFT collectibles, which had the lucky number of 777 digital figurines sold for the price of €77, and a wardrobe that users would later be able to digitally change through subsequent digital drops. Meanwhile, as of 2024, Hermes is in an ongoing lawsuit facing artist Mason Rothschild over the digital Metabirkin NFTs that the artist had created and sold for a high price.

Although the popularity of NFTs has peaked and died down in the fashion industry, it is not entirely clear whether this is a transitional phase and new opportunities for digital offerings will arise from this, such as real world assets (RWAs). RWAs are able to transform tangible assets into digital tokens, which means that physical assets such as real estate, art, stocks, clothing and more become tokenized. When an NFT is used, it can become inimitable proof of ownership for the physical item (NFT Stars, 2023).

Case example: livestreaming in China

In China, digital marketing is very advanced and already offers all of the options that have been introduced in this chapter. One new digital advancement that has been on the rise for a few years in China is livestream commerce. It was launched by Alibaba's Taobao and JD.com during the pandemic lockdowns when regular shopping was not available to house-bound customers (Qin, 2021).

Although livestream commerce has been available in other global markets, China is by far the most mature one. A study by McKinsey confirmed that by 2023, 57 per cent of live-commerce users in China had used the shopping format for more than three years. But in Europe, Latin America, and the United States, there were just 5 to 7 per cent of live-commerce users (Becdach et al., 2023).

The way Chinese livestreaming works is simple: There is a livestream host who selects, showcases, and sells clothing and other products on their live show after an arrangement has been made with the respective brands that want their products to be showcased. It is a case of paid media that is using an affiliate and a third-party app (there are also options in which the livestream is on the brand's channel). Oftentimes, the arrangements are made through agencies that manage the livestreamers and liaise with the brands.

The possibility of doing effective livestreams is dependent on digital and technological advances and the creation of supporting apps that fully facilitate customers with the livestream on their devices and making purchases without having to switch away from it. The technology allows customers to minimize the video with the livestreamer and complete the purchase. In contrast to the Western media world, there are completely diffetrent platforms used in China and Asia and include Weibo, WeChat, Xiahongshu, Douyin, Taobao and Bilibili (DigitalCrew, 2024).

A 2023 survey reported that influencer endorsements worked particularly well in promoting fashion and beauty goods. Over half of Chinese respondents had purchased recommended cosmetics and clothing items, and a third bought promoted consumer electronics. In another 2022 survey, 67 per cent of consumers ordered the endorsed products with the desire to mimic the KOL's style. KOLs are key opinion leaders – popular individuals with many followers, who might be actors, singers, fashion experts, etc., and whose opinions are trusted by a huge audience of followers. Such stars can charge more than GBP1 million (more than 10 million RMB) for just a simple post, and are remunerated for the minutes they spend in a live video accordingly.

But in the case of China's livestreaming boom, a nobody can also become a successful livestreamer and is called a KOC, a key opinion consumer. KOC generally refers to the influence of their friends, followers and consumer behaviour of the consumer leader. Compared with a KOL, a

KOC has fewer followers and less influence, but they are more direct and cheaper. As followers accumulate, a KOC will eventually become a KOL.

Therefore, it comes as no surprise that brands in China have prioritized KOL and KOC promotion in their marketing plans. There are various advantages to collaborating with opinion leaders, such as accurate positioning, increasing brand exposure and stimulating purchase intention.

For instance, HLA, a clothing brand in China, adjusted quickly to the new and restrictive shopping situation at the beginning of the Covid-19 outbreak. The brand managed to quickly adjust its marketing strategies by focusing fully on e-commerce options. The result was remarkable: The HLA special livestreaming conducted by Lieer, a Chinese influencer with about 2.5 million fans on Taobao, sold nearly RMB 13.34 million on March 18, 2022 (Xin et al., 2023).

The audience for livestreaming is tens of millions of people who evidently trust the recommendations of these live streamers and can make thousands of orders from just one livestream session, where there is a chance to ask the host questions or communicate with other participants in the audience. The livestream hosts are matched closely to the type of audience that might watch them, present products that have been carefully selected, and tries them on or describes particular features that the target audience wants to know about. (It can loosely be compared to the American home-shopping channel QVC with live presentations of a myriad of products.)

The sector was estimated to be worth about 100 billion yuan in 2021, and the entire influencer economy could swell to almost seven trillion yuan by 2025 (Thomala, 2023) With this, an entire support network of businesses has emerged that supports or manages every aspect of livestream commerce, and some are concentrated in specific cities.

Beixiazhu Village in Eastern China's Zhejiang Province is one such city that is dedicated to livestreaming e-commerce, with many aspiring streamers (KOCs) moving there in search of success. Supporting businesses include schools offering intensive training courses or agents who recruit and train livestreamers, offer fully-equipped studios to work from and liaise with client brands (NHK World, 2023) In 2020, more than 10,000 e-commerce practitioners from outside the village were employed, with more than 1,200 stores involving 7,400 merchants, generating an average of 600,000 orders that were being sent out every day (Huaxia, 2020).

Xin et al. (2023) recently studied livestreaming commerce and introduced a framework for brands to optimize their digital activities. The framework offers two pathways that a brand can take: either livestream on their own platform or employ the services of a livestreamer. In the latter case, the process is more complicated and more expensive, as the brand needs to liaise and has less control over the conduct and outcome of the livestream.

Western luxury brands have slowly experimented with livestreaming e-commerce in China, including Gucci, Dior,Burberry and Armani.

On Tmall, Burberry showcased a mother-and-child livestream where the hosts were mothers who introduced the British brand's children's range with credibility. This is because livestream shoppers want to hear the true opinions and appraisals of the hosts and can ask questions directly (a feature that the technology permits). Burberry also offered a one-on-one livestream session on the digital platform Tmall Luxury Pavilion and its digital flagship store (Wu, 2022).

Ethical considerations

With digital marketing, the success of a brand still depends on the quality of its products and the service that ships the product to the consumer and facilitates a smooth return. If the physical products and services are not of the expected quality, no digital campaign can save the brand.

There is also an altered reality that is presented through digital media, which can offer manipulated images, unrealistic scenarios, and the simulacra that Baudrillard associates with the virtual and digital world – a substitute for reality. It can therefore be another problem for consumers' emotional and mental health, manipulated by imagery and dissatisfied with one's appearance in the mirror.

Furthermore, on digital platforms, consumers' interactions can become stages for cyberbullying and body shaming.

Finally, there is the question of how consumer data is collected, stored and kept safe by those who collect it. Very little transparency or accountability is provided by the majority of brands for the consumers. On the other side, the risk is equally big for brands which can become victims of cyberattacks, data hacking and simple data loss that can be detrimental to their business.

Further reading

Athique, A. (2013) *Digital Media and Society: An Introduction.* Cambridge: Polity.

Bendoni, W. K. (2017) *Social Media for Fashion Marketing: Storytelling in a Digital World.* London: Bloomsbury.

Chaffey, D. (2009) *E-Business and E-Commerce Management.* 4th edn. Harlow: Prentice Hall.

Chaffey, D. and Smith, P. R. (2017) *Digital Marketing Excellence: Planning, Optimizing and Integrating Online Marketing.* 5th edn. Abingdon: Routledge.

Charlesworth, A. (2022) *Digital Marketing: A Practical Approach.* 4th edn. Abingdon: Routledge.

Hines, T. and Bruce, M. (2007). *Fashion Marketing.* 2nd edn. Abingdon: Routledge.

Moriarty, S. et al. (2019) *Advertising & IMC: Principles & Practice.* 11th ed. Harlow: Pearson.

Ryan, D. and Jones, C. (2016) *Understanding Digital Marketing: Marketing Strategies for Engaging the Digital Generation.* 4th edn. London: Kogan Page.

Smith, P. R. and Zook, Z. E. (2016) *Marketing Communications: Offline and Online Integration, Engagement and Analytics.* 6th edn. London: Kogan Page.

Wu, W. (2022) Is Luxury Ready to Master Livestreaming in China? Jing Daily. Available at: https://jingdaily.com/posts/taobao-report-livestream-beauty

Target market and segmentation

7

Chapter topics

Do you need a target market?

If you take any fashion brand and pick out its core product, think about who the brand should sell it to.

The entire world? A few continents? One country? Perhaps the customers are young, single and affluent people who live in metropolitan cities? Or perhaps the product is suitable for the countryside and only for consumers over 50? The constellations are endless, and a brand essentially has two choices: mass marketing or target marketing.

With mass marketing, no effort needs to be made to figure out which people might or might not buy the product, and the brand's communication approach is to tailor one message to all. This can work especially well with staple products such as basic socks, basic underwear, and cotton T-shirts (think Hanes, Fruit of the Loom or Marks & Spencer) because – one might argue – a majority of people will need these items in their lives, no matter who they

DOI: 10.4324/9781003449157-7

are. In this case, to boost a bland staple product, differentiate the brand from its competitors and reach a mass market, collaborations between brands can be very useful, as was done in the case of H&M that collaborated with David Beckham for its underwear.

With target marketing, a brand makes an effort to narrow down and pinpoint its customer. This requires market research and segmentation of the market but promises to be less wasteful in terms of resources and more profitable if done correctly.

According to Jackson and Shaw (2009, p. 53), "Understanding how a market is segmented makes it easier to plan marketing strategies, to target consumers and position products more accurately".

What that means in reality is that segmentation is a powerful tool which gives a brand a competitive advantage over others and is the first stepping stone in the STP approach: segment, target, position the brand. In terms of marketing planning, brands are then able to predict consumer behaviour and "develop marketing campaigns and pricing strategies to extract maximum value from both high- and low-profit customers" (Rigby, 2015).

Thus, once the segmentation has taken place, the brand is aware of its target market or markets and can approach them directly in a way that works best. This is highly important for creating the correct marketing mix (be it the original 4 Ps or the New Marketing Mix with 4 Ds) and targeted brand communication in the form of advertising and public relations. A brand can only reach its consumer successfully if it speaks their language in terms of interests, preferences, attitudes and other significant factors.

Case example: Victoria's Secret and Agent Provocateur

Both Victoria's Secret and Agent Provocateur are brands that sell underwear, both online and offline, but their target consumers are very different. It is interesting to see how the brands also both failed to adapt to the changes in their target market, prompting critique.

Victoria's Secret was founded in 1977 by Roy and Gaye Raymond in the USA as a counterweight to conservative lingerie, selling fun but relatively low-quality clothing, paired with an affordable price. Victoria's Secret quickly grew to become the largest lingerie retailer in the US, with sales of more than $1 billion by the early 1990s (Hanbury et al., 2023). From that point on, the brand that had 350 stores nationally, went to global international success, moving into the UK in 2012.

The *Guardian* described the customer types one might have encountered in Central London's Bond Street flagship store of Victoria's Secret when it opened in 2012: "The shoppers are a mix of teenage girls with Topshop bags and tourists having their photos taken" (Cartner-Morley, 2012).

In terms of brand communication and marketing, the Victoria's Secret Angels were an integral part of the brand's DNA. Their appearance was very important: slim models of the famous runway carnival-like show were all in their 20s, except for an occasional few in their 30s, and most Victoria's Secret promotional campaigns were youthful, playful and showed seemingly happy girls. In the last years, there has been much controversy surrounding the well-being of the VS Angels who walk in the shows, and whether the brand has failed to embrace diversity and inclusion. An attempt to steer away from its usual aesthetic and model type during and after the pandemic, unfortunately, was a disaster and disappointing to consumers. The target market is predominantly still that of young women; however, their interests, lifestyles and values have changed, and there has been no proper adaptation to their needs.

Meanwhile, luxury lingerie label Agent Provocateur, which was founded in London by the son of Vivienne Westwood and his wife in 1994, is a brand that "is confident, sensual and irreverent. [Known] for [...] craftmanship, fit, our use of beautiful fabrics and our playfulness" (AP blog). Over the years, Agent Provocateur has grown from one small shop in London's raunchy Soho to a global presence. In 2015, the brand used Naomi Campbell in its promotional campaign at the age of 44, in glamorous pictures of a dark nature with a femme fatale set in crime scenes reminiscent of David Lynch's *The Lost Highway* and Brian De Palma's *Body Double*. It was targeted at a far kinkier, luxurious and perhaps more mature customer.

According to Martin Bartle, global communications and e-commerce director of Agent Provocateur, there was an in-house data warehouse which automatically flaged customers by value segment, recency, frequency and type of interaction. This information was later used to determine communication strategies with the customers (DynamicAction, 2015). Agent Provocateur's problem to date is that it was too focused on its original target consumers who had aged with the brand. Agent Provocateur did not offer much to appeal to younger consumers and has been struggling financially but attempted to launch a diffusion line in 2013.

It is probable that a typical Agent Provocateur customer would not purchase Victoria's Secret lingerie and vice versa, but both brands need to understand how their customers think and target them accordingly so that they remain relevant and profitable.

How to segment a market

Generally speaking, there are many ways in which a market can be segmented, and for the purpose of this book, the standard approaches are discussed along with rarer ones which are all relevant to the fashion industry. In order to segment a market, first, quantitative and qualitative market research data have to be collected and evaluated. This includes precise information on the demographics, geography, psychographics and purchase behaviour of customers as well as distribution, time, price and media. Sources for this information can be obtained from government census data, consumer surveys, questionnaires or focus groups, observations, data from the point of sale at the stores, e-commerce and online behavioural data, customer feedback, and more.

Demographic segmentation

What is demography? According to *Merriam-Webster*, it is "the statistical study of human populations especially with reference to size and density, distribution, and vital statistics".

This is a standard way of segmenting the market when people are grouped together based on their age, income, education level, housing type and sometimes their ethnicity. Consumers are also grouped by their gender, and in the fashion world of the twenty-first century, the topic of gender can be of particular interest. With transgender models on the catwalks and genderless fashion brands, this can be an effective segmentation tool all by itself.

In 2015, London's Selfridges department store cleverly used the topic of genderless fashion when it opened pop-up areas on its shop floors which offered unisex clothing by leading designers such as Nicola Formichetti's Nicopanda or Ann Demeulemeester. As the Mailonline reported, the space was "devised by renowned designer Faye Toogood, [and] is an environment in which shoppers are given the freedom to transcend notions of 'his' and 'hers', as you simply find your most desired item by colour, fit and style" (London, 2015).

Popular terminology used in segmenting is generational segmentation, which includes the terms Generation X, Y and Z, Millennials and several more (Figure 7.1). Consumers grouped by generation are given attributes which supposedly apply to all of them to the same degree. Although this type of segmentation is popular in marketing and featured in every marketing book, it must be critically noted that it is not a scientific way of

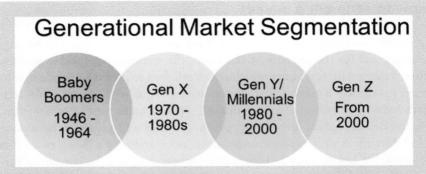

Figure 7.1 Generational segmentation. Author's original illustration.

segmenting people. The terms themselves were often coined by journalists or invented by Americans such as researchers Strauss and Howe, who mostly focused on the USA and invented the Strauss–Howe generational theory. Thus, these marketing generations are often criticized by academics for a lack of extensive empirical evidence, for generalizing and being inaccurate.

The generations are as follows:

- Lost Generation – born approximately between 1883 and 1900, participated in WWI.
- G.I. Generation (or WWII Generation) – born approximately between 1900 and the late 1920s, participated in WWII.
- The Silent Generation – born approximately between the late 1920s and before 1946.
- Baby Boomers – born approximately between 1946 and 1964, part of the post-war baby boom.
- Gen X – born approximately between 1970 and the early 1980s.
- Gen Y – born between 1981 and 2000. Often referred to as Millennials, they have many other names such as Generation Me, Echo Boomers and iGen, and are a promising new breed of consumers for marketers. The term "Generation Y" was first used in the magazine *AdAge* in the early 1990s.
- Gen Z – born from the turn of the millennium (2000) and 2010, although some sources go beyond this cut-off, overlapping with Gen Alpha.
- Gen Alpha – born after 2010 until 2025 with a special nickname: Glass Generation. This is in reference to children who are fragile, burdened with information overload and used to gadgets since early childhood. Those who were born in 2020 and 2021 do not have any experience of life before the pandemic. (Amies, 2023)

Geographic segmentation

What is geography? Geography is "a science that deals with the description, distribution, and interaction of the diverse physical, biological, and cultural features of the earth's surface" (*Merriam-Webster*).

Geographic segmentation thus means that people are segmented by continents, hemispheres, countries and cities; or urban, suburban and rural areas; north versus south; or coast versus inland. For fashion brands, this can have high importance because there is a great difference in the fashions worn globally based on location, climate, cultural, religious, political and ethical factors.

The dictionary's definition mentions culture, which is an element inadvertently connected to geography, as regions even within the same country can have clear differences.

For example, urban areas tend to be more extravagant when it comes to experimentation with fashion in comparison with conservative rural areas. An interesting example is how Western fashion brands market to Muslim countries by advertising the same clothing (often shot during the same campaign) but covering up the models. In China, Zara's clothes are associated with Western luxury fashion and reportedly cost up to 90 per cent more than in Spain, while in Japan, Western premium and luxury fashion brands and leather goods have a considerable mark-up, partly due to high import tariffs and positioning strategies.

In Japan, a consumer gets charged a 30 per cent duty on a pair of boots and then burdened again with a consumption tax of 8 per cent, giving a grand total of 38 per cent on a product. "Tariffs such as this imposed on leather items are imposed to make them more expensive than domestically-made leather items" (Higgins, 2015). This is because of Japan's own small leather industry which due to several historical reasons and scarcety of grazing land for cattle, cannot compete with cheap imported leather and thus import taxes intend to harmonize low-priced imports with domestic producers.

A brand might sometimes choose to change the name of the same product when it is sold in different regions, such as car manufacturer Mazda's MX5 Miata, which also sported the names Mazda Miata, Mazda MX-5, Eunos Roadster and Mazda Roadster around the world.

And when it comes to language, the same item of clothing might be called by a different name, such as pants in the USA and trousers in the UK (unless you are speaking of underwear).

Geodemographic segmentation is a further development of the regional categorization of consumers, for example, matching customers' postcodes with their profiles and ACORN is an example of that.

The ACORN classification system is widely used in the UK,stands for "A Classification Of Residential Neighbourhoods" and was developed by CACI Ltd. (Jackson and Shaw, 2009)

According to the ACORN user guide, it segments households, post-codes and neighbourhoods into 5 categories, 17 groups and 59 types. "By analysing demographic data, social factors, population and consumer behaviour Acorn provides an understanding of different types of people and places." (CACI, 2020)

1.   Affluent Achievers – A Lavish Lifestyles, B Executive Wealth, C Mature Money
2.   Rising Prosperity – D City Sophisticates, E Career Climbers
3.   Comfortable Communities – F Countryside Communities, G Successful Suburbs, H Steady Neighbourhoods, I Comfortable Seniors, J Starting Out
4.   Financially Stretched – K Student Life, L Modest Means, M Striving Families, N Poorer Pensioners
5.   Urban Adversity – O Young Hardship, P Struggling Estates, Q Difficult Circumstances

As an example, let's look at the large category number 3 - the Comfortable Communities - with 27% of the UK's population: ACORN states that most have a mortgage or own their property outright, and around 50% like to shop online. . However category number 4 - the Financially Stretched - makes up a close number of 23% of the UK population. Here ACORN reports a mix of traditional areas of Britain, including social housing developments specifically for the elderly. The people are living in 1 to 3 bedroom dwellings that are privately or socially rented and none are mortgaged. Together with category number 5 - Urban Adversity - of 17%, this makes up 40% of the UK's population that are not well off. (CACI, 2020)

Psychographic/lifestyle segmentation

First, let's find out what the term "psychographic" actually means.

According to the Cambridge Dictionary, it is "the way that a company divides its customers into groups based on their opinions, interests, and emotions". And if mixed together with their values, attitudes and lifestyle you get quite a life-like portrait of your customer. In fact, "psychographic" and "lifestyle" are terms which are often interchangeable.

In order to assess the opinions, interests and attitudes of consumers and then categorize them, qualitative research is conducted by interviewing individuals or groups (focus groups) and paying close attention to the interests, opinions and attitudes voiced. The more customers are questioned, the more accurate and representative the results are. The qualitative research can be conducted in person or via telephone, email/internet or even via snail mail.

For research in fashion, qualitative analysis can be varied and include straightforward product-based research as well as cultural or sociological elements.

Over the last decades, many marketing research companies have offered their help in customer segmentation by developing unique segmentation tools and marketing them enthusistically. They have some similarities to the ACORN classification described above. One of the oldest is the VALS tool, which was launched in 1978 by SRI International, now owned by Strategic Business Insights. VALS stands for "values and lifestyles" and currently covers the USA, China, the Dominican Republic, Japan, Nigeria, the United Kingdom and Venezuela.

Another large market segmentation service is called PRIZM by Claritas (formerly Nielsen), which looks at the US and stands for "Potential Rating Index for Zip Markets". There are 68 different segments to choose from, which group people into categories by using quirky names and adding engaging stories. For instance, category number 7 is called "Money & Brains" and groups together people with "high incomes, advanced degrees, and sophisticated tastes to match their credentials". They are described as married couples and city dwellers "with few children who live in fashionable homes on small, manicured lots with expensive cars in the driveway. These environmentally conscious individuals like to donate to political causes, the arts, and public radio" (Claritas, 2024a). There are 1,763,757 households across the US that match this category.

In stark contrast to this, there is category number 44 titled "Country Strong", which groups together 4,187,375 households across the US. They are described as middle-class families in rural America who concentrate on their families and like to go hunting, listen to country music and refrain from the latest technology. They own a Chevrolet and their preferred TV network is the Discovery Channel (Claritas, 2024b).

In Europe, Germany has the Sinus-Institut which produces the Sinus Milieus. It has a category called the "Adaptive Pragmatist Milieu", which is "the ambitious young core of society with a markedly pragmatic outlook on life and sense of expedience: success oriented and prepared to compromise, hedonistic and conventional, flexible and security oriented" (SINUS Markt- und Sozialforschung GmbH, 2015). However, it is intrinsically discriminatory because it groups pure Germans into one category and Germans with a migrational background into a completely separate category. The migrational background is bestowed upon any person who was born as a non-German or has at least one parent or grand-parent who was born with a non-German nationality. Even if all three generations presently hold German passports, they will still be classified as migrants. (More on this topic is available in the "Ethical considerations" section at the end of the chapter.)

Scholars and critics often voice their concerns about these segmentation tools for several reasons. The tool is usually trademarked and is aggressively marketed like any other product. This means that it is biased by the wish for financial gain by the proprietors. Second, most marketing research companies do not lay open their method of data collection or evaluation, which makes it unscientific in any academic circles. Third, consumer groups tend to change their attitudes, which can make the tools outdated. Finally, they are prone to stereotyping humans in a negative way through categories such as race and ethnicity. Sinus Milieus, for example, offers a separate psychographic category chart for pure Germans (both parents must be of German descent) and another one for all other Germans with a "migration background" (the person, or at least one parent, is not of ethnic German descent and migrated to the country after 1949), the latter of which makes up about 20 per cent of the country's population. Or to put it in other words, every third person with a migration background has lived in Germany since his or her birth but is to be treated differently in marketing terms. Although market segmentation tools can be very helpful, it is vital to question their ethics and remain critically observant of how one treats fellow humans.

One typology tool which fashion brands like to use is the so-called pen portrait. The pen portrait uses a fictional person and gives a profile of the person's appearance, lifestyle and attitudes. It will also give specific facts or hard variables such as age, income and social status. Ideally, primary research and qualitative gathering of data will inform the pen portrait and make it more accurate. Pen portraits can be circulated internally and used to plan marketing activities, design collections or stage events.

There is a closer look at pen portraits later in the "Media" segmentation section.

Purchasing behaviour

This area of customer segmentation groups people according to the occasion, benefits sought, usage rate, brand loyalty level, readiness and reason to purchase. Furthermore, the user status can be differentiated: potential, first-time, regular, etc.

Holidays and events often stimulate purchases. For example, a customer might regularly purchase staples such as underwear and socks and will be loyal to a brand that has provided products with the benefits sought, such as comfort, style and price. Whereas the acquisition of an expensive designer handbag might be tied to an occasion such as a birthday or a promotion and will require high involvement in terms of the purchase decision and the careful selection is tied to an anticipated status symbol.

Distribution

Here we look at the distribution channels of a product. For example, some premium or luxury designer brands in Europe, such as Bally, choose to sell in their flagship stores, at the airport in the duty-free sections as well as in outlet stores – each time at different price points. Other brands are more selective about their distribution. For example Chanel will never discount its products to more than 30 per cent off during sales. Also, its products are strictly available in its own stores as well as a few selected luxury retailers.

With the increasing importance of online channels, many brands are also distributed via e-commerce. Other brands develop their own apps for mobile devices and advertise in third-party apps.

For luxury brands, the distribution channel is strictly controlled to ensure scarcity, and e-commerce might be restricted or sometimes not available at all. At this price segment, the prestigious store and retail experience are part of the exclusive price that is being paid. In contrast, the fast-fashion accessories brands can be found in lots of busy locations such as train stations, concession shops within department stores and as stand-alone stores on high streets.

Customer segmentation worksheet

Fill in data on your target consumer to create a profile:

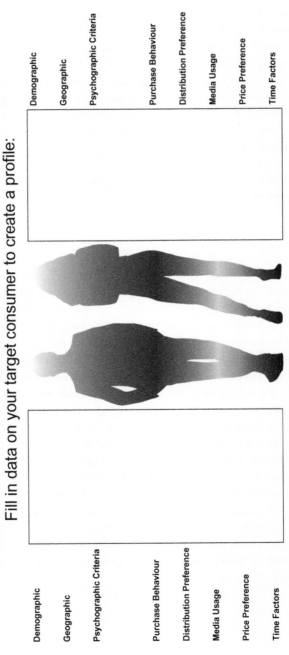

Demographic

Geographic

Psychographic Criteria

Purchase Behaviour

Distribution Preference

Media Usage

Price Preference

Time Factors

Demographic

Geographic

Psychographic Criteria

Purchase Behaviour

Distribution Preference

Media Usage

Price Preference

Time Factors

Figure 7.2 Customer segmentation worksheet.

Media

Media is crucial for the marketing communications strategy: Which media does the target market turn to and how engaged are they?

Consumers can be reached through a variety of media channels, so it is important to segment them by the media they use. For instance, according to Petrosyan (2023), the penetration of internet usage in the UK is 93 per cent but it is 99.7 per cent in Kuwait (Citra, 2024)

As mentioned previously, media data that magazines and papers provide can be very helpful for matching up the consumer and the preferred media.

For example, *Grazia UK* has a description (like a pen portrait) of its typical reader, who is a woman between the ages of 25–45 and caters to more AB profile readers than *Vogue* and *Elle*.

> She's a savvy, affluent, confident, busy and modern woman who actively participates in the world around her. She comes to *Grazia* for edited choice – on everything from the news she needs an opinion on that week to issues she wants to be moved by to simply discovering which heels will instantly make her wardrobe rock. She happily admits she's "addicted" to *Grazia*'s unique mix of news, views and shoes.

In 2024, this pen portrait is still considered relevant by the Bauer Media Group, which owns Grazia. According to Jackson and Shaw (2019), retailers might use pen portrait descriptions of their typical customers to help their design team as well as their retail buyers better understand and target the consumer.

Note the "AB profile readers", which is based on the National Readership Survey (NRS) social grades system, a classification used in the UK. Originating from the world of media and the National Readership Survey to classify readers, this grading is now often used for general marketing and has become a staple in Britain since its invention in the 1950s. It classifies social grade based on occupation and is similar to ACORN.

The National Readership Survey (2015) classification of social grade is as follows:

A Higher managerial, administrative and professional – (4% of population)

B Intermediate managerial, administrative and professional – (23% of population)

C1   Supervisory, clerical and junior managerial, administrative and profes-
     sional – (27% of population)
C2   Skilled manual workers – (21% of population)
D   Semi-skilled and unskilled manual workers – (16% of population)
E   State pensioners, casual and lowest grade workers, unemployed with
     state benefits only – (9% of population)

(Grazia, 2018)

Time

Time segmentation is rare but might be highly effective for certain brands
and markets. This is the case for products that are marketed along with the
changing seasons, holidays and special events. In the UK, you can look
at all the royal paraphernalia for each royal lifetime event, such as special
biscuit tins to commemorate the birth of Prince George, the passing of the
Queen or the coronation of the King. In terms of department stores, time
segmentation can relate to increased opening hours and scheduling of in-
store promotions.

Price

Although income levels are determined when the demographics are evaluated, a pricing strategy on its own can help a brand to better reach its
target market. In fact, when a brand is looking to expand its target market,
such as in the case of TAG Heuer, it might include cheaper products in its
range and thus facilitate entry-level products for its new target customers.
The brand will be discussed further on in this chapter.

Primary, secondary and tertiary target markets

After segmenting the market, suitable consumers can be grouped together,
and a brand can determine its primary, secondary and tertiary target markets.

The primary market consists of 60 to 70 per cent of the total target market,
the secondary market consists of 15 to 20 per cent of the total target market
and the tertiary market consists of the remaining 5 to 10 per cent (Bickle, 2010)
(see Figure 7.3).

Table 7.1 Overview of most important segmentation criteria and how a company might access it

Demographic Data source: Includes all facts about a person which might also be available from census data.	Age: From 0 to 100, as this depends on brand Generation: Baby- Boomers, Gen X, Y, Z etc. Sex: Female, Male, and in fashion gender- neutral, transgender, non-binary etc.
	Family size: from 1 to open end
	Family life stage young, single, married, no children, youngest child younger than 6, youngest child older than 6, married, separated, widowed, divorced, etc.
	Income: Personal income, household income, for children: caretakers' income, gross income or net income, disposable income, etc.
	Occupation: Working, unemployed, self- employed etc.
	Education: No formal education (this can also apply to children), school, high- school, some college, university (BA/MA), PhD; apprenticeship
	Social class: lower class, middle class, upper class; possible use of terms such as working class, bourgeoisie, aristocracy, etc.
Geographic: Data source: All data available on geographic region and its natural as well as cultural factors.	Region: Segmented by continent, hemisphere, country or union of states (i.e. EU, CIS), Inhabitants, population density Inhabitants, etc.
	Population density: Often classified as urban, suburban or rural (or rural vs. metropolitan) and segmented by location and population density.
	Climate: Segmented by impact of climate on population such as seasons (four seasons, opposite seasons, no seasons; Mediterranean, Temperate, Sub- Tropical, Tropical, Polar, etc.
Psychographic: Data source: Qualitative data on consumer, obtained through a form of survey or questionnaire.	Lifestyle Personality Activities Interests Opinions
Purchase behaviour: Data source: Qualitative data as well as quantitative data (for example collected through sales data) on a person's purchase patterns.	Benefits sought Usage rate Brand loyalty User status: potential, first- time, regular, etc. Readiness to buy Occasions: usual purchase or special occasion (such as holidays, festivals, cultural events etc.)

(Continued)

Table 7.1 Overview of most important segmentation criteria and how a company might access it (*Continued*)

Distribution Data source: Usually company-internal data evaluating best possible options.	Flagship Stand-alone-store or directly-operated-store (DOS) Concession Department store Pop-up store E-commerce platform Mail-order
Media Data source: Qualitative data as well as quantitative data which includes digital analytics data and media monitoring.	Media type, frequency of use, engagement: Printed media Digital media Mobile media
Time Data source: Usually company-internal data evaluating best possible options.	Political and social occasion Country-wide events such as Olympics, a royal wedding or a predetermined sales day such as Single's Day, Black Friday etc.
Price Data source: Usually company-internal data evaluating best possible options	Pricing strategy Premium and Luxury Special offers Promotions Discounts

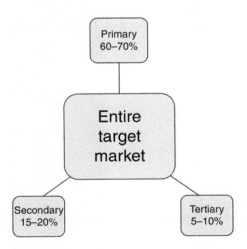

Figure 7.3 Primary, secondary and tertiary target markets. Based on Bickle (2010).

Encoding and decoding the brand's message

Once the segmentation has been successfully completed and the target market has been identified, the brand's marketing strategy and communication can be tailored to it. In terms of advertising and PR, this means communicating the right message through the right channels to the target audience.

There should be a clear understanding of who it is targeting with its message and how it wants the existing and potential consumers to react to it. As a brand develops the intended message, can it be sure that the message will be understood?

The theory of message encoding and decoding, first developed by Stuart Hall in the early 1970s, states that the sender encodes the message, sends it through media channels, and the recipient has to decode it or interpret it. Of course, the ability to interpret a message is influenced by an individual's culture, background and environment, personal experiences, language and social valances.

Only when the process of decoding has successfully taken place has the message been truly received. Thus, when creating brand communication, one must ensure that the message is readable for the target recipients.

Whatever the intended message is that the brand has sent, it has no meaning until the recipient has clearly understood it. This sounds very simple and logical, but science reveals that it is not always so obvious. In Figure 7.4, the communication model shows how the meaning of a message is created: The sender, for example a fashion brand, intends to send a message to their target customers. They use a combination of visual, verbal and non-verbal codes that are supposed to represent their message. The message is then sent through a media channel (for example ATL, BTL or influenc) and arrives at the consumer. The consumer then must be able to decode the cues and finally "gets" the intended message. Only at this very last step will the message actually have created meaning. Fashion, in particular, is built on visual culture, which

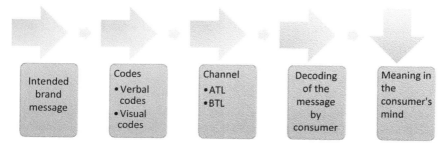

Figure 7.4 Communication model "coding and decoding of messages". Based on Scheier and Held (2012).

makes fashion imagery a language of its own. Fashion consumers expect to see messages that use visual language in fashion communication and have learned to decode them over the decades.

> ### Case example: TAG Heuer's "Don't crack under pressure" campaign
>
> As an example, let's look at watchmaker TAG Heuer, which, for nearly a decade now, has been trying to target younger customers such as Millennials (and older Gen Zs) to consider TAG watches and find them cool and desirable. The strategy included looking at the price, product, promotion and place with each element being revised. Over the years, new entry-level products were added to the offering at affordable luxury prices. The many points-of-sale were reduced to create directly-operated stores only, and the promotional campaigns were specifically designed with the target consumer in mind.
>
> TAG Heuer started to lower the price for entry-level watches to lure new target consumers. For example, in 2024, the TAG Heuer Formula 1 Date started at GBP 1300. Today, even payments in instalments are possible, which makes this truly accessible luxury.
>
> Furthermore, to launch its attack on the new target market, TAG aligned itself with a range of celebrities and launched the "Don't crack under pressure" campaign to sell the Carrera watch, which LVMH (the parent company) described in the following way:
>
> > (T)he new "Don't Crack Under Pressure" campaign was unveiled with an exciting, fast-moving video posted on the official TAG Heuer website, along with special window displays in its Paris flagship stores. The rollout was followed closely by a film featuring TAG Heuer brand ambassadors.
> >
> > (LVMH, 2014)
>
> In 2015, TAG Heuer added another popular brand ambassador, who at the time of the campaign had 30 million followers worldwide: the British supermodel Cara Delevingne. Together with the campaign, TAG released a limited "Carrera 'Cara Delevingne' Special Edition" watch.
>
> The advertising campaign used visual and verbal codes to encode this particular message by featuring Cara Delevingne – looking standoffish into the camera and showing her wrist with the watch – and the copy text "Don't crack under pressure". The imagery was printed as a classic ATL campaign in fashion magazines seen by consumers, along with social media campaigns, events and other promotions.

Could the target market interpret the intended message correctly? A millennial should have been around the same age as Cara in 2015 and know that she is a star model with a unique personality, described as "the most disruptive It Girl of the moment" (Karolini, 2015).

Furthermore, Cara is a celebrity and trendsetter, so by means of psychology, the recipient would automatically trust Cara's choice of watch. Finally, the verbal cue revealed the added benefit of having such a watch: It helps not to crack under pressure, making you stronger, cooler and more successful (emulation of the star) in any tricky situation.

Behind the scenes, Jean-Claude Biver, who at that time served as president of LVMH Watches and TAG Heuer CEO, stated that Cara "matches the brand" and that presently they sell between 35 and 37 per cent of watches to women, aiming for 50 per cent. "The watch is associated with success. [...] And success is 'don't crack under pressure'. If you crack under pressure, you will never be successful".

On its website, TAG Heuer describes the brand ambassador:

> From jetsetting off to Paris for a shoot to taking in long hours on film sets, Cara never stops, never settles and fights the constant pressures of being in the spotlight 24/7. This 'it' girl's never dainty, but always sparkling personality was the inspiration for our TAG Heuer Cara Delevingne special edition Carrera 41 MM that's elegant on the outside and unique on the inside with a feminine touch and a killer edge.
>
> She's beauty and the beast all rolled into one exciting package and we can't wait to watch her exciting life unfold.
>
> (Tag Heuer, 2019)

How about the technical features of this watch? Do the recipients care about what the Carrera 41 MM model does? Imagine TAG Heuer had sent out a different message instead of #DontCrackUnderPressure, describing the physical features in detail: *Calibre 5 is a self-winding movement with a balance frequency of 28,800 vph (4Hz) and a power reserve of 40 to 50 hours. It has push buttons with a black line at 2 o'clock and a black line at 4 o'clock.*

This copy text coupled with a beautiful close-up of the watch itself, but without Cara? Could the target audience interpret the intended message correctly? This excerpt from the technical specs would probably not mean much to Millennials (unless they happened to be watch collectors). However, an emotive campaign with the right slogan, a respected celebrity and a visually powerful ad can create the desired response in the targeted audience, leading to attention, desire and ultimately sales. The physical features of the watch would likely be a secondary reason for the purchase.

Ethical considerations

Segmentation has been used in marketing for many decades and remains a popular tool today. However, there is a main concern in segmentation, which is the risk of stereotyping, discrimination and stigmatization because segmentation primarily aims to group people based on predetermined characteristics and variables, judging them and predicting their behaviour.

The British ACORN and NRS Social Grade classification system equates occupation to social class, so immediately anyone who works in manual labour is "demoted" to a low social class status without verifying whether this is true. Similarly, the Sinus Milieus, which hails from Germany, deliberately excludes people who are migrants or the offspring of migrants in Germany (including third-generation migrants). They are not considered to be part of regular society and, in fact, have a separate classification chart.

Sinus declares on its website: "In 2008, SINUS was the first institute to systematically research the lifeworlds and lifestyles of people with different migration backgrounds in Germany. In 2018, the resulting Sinus Migrant Milieus model was empirically updated" (Sinus-Milieus, 2024). How can this approach be ethical?

As history has shown on numerous occasions, any classification of humans is intrinsically flawed and deprives individuals of their dignity and identity, giving way to social injustice. Furthermore, stereotyping encourages prejudice and aggression and can even incite violence.

Classification can be more accurate with the use of big data collection, but this system is also highly flawed and potentially dangerous. One main concern of big data is the collection, use, storage and deletion of it. Website traffic, social networks, mobile applications, forums, blogs and other digital platforms can collect and provide sensitive and detailed information about each individual and their online behaviour. For consumers, there is generally very little transparency in the processing and analysis as well as use and transmission of personal data. The ethical question is how data can be collected and processed when it is done so without people's conscious consent (in fact, they might not even be aware of this), but at the same time meet legal obligations. If it is artificial intelligence and machines that are used to collect the data, then who programmes and controls them? Finally, what harm can be done with this information, such as targeted discrimination or political and social exclusion? It may be that our technological advances have happened so fast that people have not caught up with its implications and are lagging behind in regulating it.

For brands however, the rist is that they wrongly segment their market and alienate consumers if they are not careful. The Abercrombie & Fitch case study in Chapter 3 demonstrates what can go wrong when delibarate exclusion of certain demographics is part of a brand's strategy.

Further reading

ACORN (n.d.) acorn.caci.co.uk

Amies, N. (2023) 'Glass Generation' struggling with information overload, psychologists warn. The Brussels Times (online). Available at: https://www.brusselstimes.com/433926/glass-generation-struggling-with-information-overload-psychologists-warn

Bickle, M. C. (2010) *Fashion Marketing: Theory, Principles, & Practice*. New York: Fairchild.

Citra (2024) Kuwait National ICT Figures. Citra Communication & Information Technology Regulation Authority. Available at: https://citra.gov.kw/sites/en/Pages/ict_indicators.aspx

Claritas (2024) Segment Details. Available at: https://claritas360.claritas.com/mybestsegments/#segDetails.

Claritas (2024a) Money & Brains. Claritas 360. Available at: https://claritas360.claritas.com/mybestsegments/#segDetail/PZP/07

Claritas (2024b) Country Strong. Claritas 360. Available at: https://claritas360.claritas.com/mybestsegments/#segDetail/PZP/44

Dubois, B. (2000) *Understanding the Consumer: A European Perspective*. New York: Prentice Hall.

Hooley, G. et al. (2020) *Marketing Strategy and Competitive Positioning*. Harlow: Pearson.

Jackson, T. and Shaw, D. (2009) *Mastering Fashion Marketing*. Basingstoke: Palgrave Macmillan.

Kawamura, Y. (2011) *Fashion-Ology: An Introduction to Fashion Studies*. New York: Berg.

McDonald, M. (2012) *Market Segmentation: How to Do It and How to Profit from It*. Revised 4th edn. John Wiley & Sons.

National Readership Survey: https://nrs.co.uk/

Posner, H. (2011) *Marketing Fashion*. London: Laurence King Publishing.

Sinus-Milieus (2024) Sinus Migrant Milieus. Sinus Institut [Online] Available at: https://www.sinus-institut.de/en/sinus-milieus/sinus-migrant-milieus

Smith, P. R. and Zook, Z. (2016) *Marketing Communications: Offline and Online Integration, Engagement and Analytics*. 6th edn. London: Kogan Page.

Strategic Business Insights (2024) VALS. Available at: https://www.strategicbusinessinsights.com/vals/

Solomon, M. R. (2020) *Consumer Behavior: Buying, Having, and Being*. 13th edn. London: Pearson.

United Nations (2017) World Population Projected to Reach 9.8 Billion in 2050, and 11.2 Billion in 2100. UN DESA: Department of Economic and Social Affairs. Available at: www.un.org/development/desa/news/population/world-population-prospects-2017.html

Target marketing and the international consumer
Coding and decoding brand messages

8

Chapter topics

A different approach for an international market

We live in a global, interconnected world, and many fashion brands expand beyond the domestic market while looking for further opportunities for growth and profit. Whether a brand is trying to reach customers in a neighbouring country or is a global player, it will have to consider the many differences in cultures and recognize that they will not interpret a brand's message in the same way. What works in the national market might backfire when a brand expands beyond its borders, which means that the international market needs to be researched and observed carefully prior to any marketing activity. Believing that your own cultural or ethnic group is superior to that of another – also called ethnocentricity – and relying on consumer behaviour in

DOI: 10.4324/9781003449157-8

the brand's native country can lead to crucial mistakes, yet oftentimes marketers do just that.

The most common challenges are barriers of language, culture and politics that need to be taken into account. A brand has to appraise whether people will understand the message in the same way at all and whether the reaction will even be a favourable one. Encoding and decoding messages becomes a very different task when advertising in foreign cultures.

Intercultural studies, in particular those by Geert Hofstede and Marieke de Mooij, have shown that there is a significant difference in how people perceive individualism versus collectivism, motivation towards achievement and success, tendency to avoid uncertainties, national or ethnic identity versus global identity, religion, and many other cultural factors (Müller and Gelbrich, 2015). There may be quite a lot of variation in the cultural understanding and perception of a myriad of things.

Geert Hofstede (1928–2020) was a social psychologist from the Netherlands who created the six-dimensions model of national culture based on his study of various cultures across the world, now known as the Hofstede Insights. The 6 Ds stand for the six dimensions of culture. Each of them has been expressed on a scale that runs roughly from 0 to 100 and is important to a culture's social function. Countries of the world can be grouped with others that are similar to them. For example, South America, Eastern Europe and Asia are mostly collectivist countries, whereas Western Europe and North America are individualist countries. This is important to know in brand management because, ultimately, consumption is connected to culture. The dimensions can be easily compared in the Hofstede comparison tool (www.hofstede-insights.com/country-comparison/) which gives an overview of many countries' characteristics. However, there is a natural element of generalization and it is not a substitute for thorough research as well as understanding culture, nations and behaviour.

Marieke de Mooij, an author and consultant who has worked in cross-cultural communications and taught globally, looks at advertising and media data which have revealed the stark international differences that brands must pay attention to. For example, multinational corporations might choose to standardize their advertising across different markets, but since one size does not fit all, this can have a negative effect on their return on investment. "When developing programs for global markets, marketers must – but more often do not – realize that programs reflecting their own values are likely to be less effective in markets where people have different values" (De Mooij, 2010, p. 306). It sounds rather banal, but it does occur frequently that management, marketing or both forget this simple rule of international trade (Mitterfellner, 2023) (Table 8.1).

Table 8.1 Hofstede's Six Dimensions of National Culture

Power Distance Index (PDI)	• To which degree do less powerful members of a society accept and expect that power is distributed unequally? The fundamental issue here is how a society handles inequalities among people.
	• People in societies exhibiting a large degree of Power Distance accept a hierarchical order in which everybody has a place and which needs no further justification. In societies with low Power Distance, people strive to equalize the distribution of power and demand justification for inequalities of power.
Individualism versus Collectivism (IDV)	• To which degree is there a preference for a loosely-knit social framework in which individuals are expected to take care of only themselves and their immediate families? The high side of this dimension, called Individualism, can be defined as a preference for individualism.
	• Its opposite, Collectivism, represents a preference for a tightly-knit framework in society in which individuals can expect their relatives or members of a particular in-group to look after them in exchange for unquestioning loyalty. A society's position on this dimension is reflected in whether people's self-image is defined in terms of "I" or "we".
Motivation towards Achievement and Success (MAS) (previously Masculinity versus Femininity)	• Does this society prefer achievement, heroism, assertiveness and materialistic rewards? If yes, then this would be classified as a masculine society, which is rather competitive.
	• Or does this society have a preference for cooperation, modesty, caring for the weak and quality of life? This would be a feminine society and is more consensus-oriented.
	• Most recently, this dimension has been renamed "Motivation towards Achievement and Success".
Uncertainty Avoidance Index (UAI)	• How uncomfortable do members of a society feel about the uncertainty of tomorrow? The fundamental issue here is how a society deals with the fact that the future is ambiguous. Do they try to control the future or just let it happen?
	• Countries exhibiting strong UAI maintain rigid codes of belief and behaviour, and have little tolerance for unorthodox ideas and behaviour.
	• Weak UAI societies maintain a more relaxed attitude in which practice counts more than principles. They are not too worried about an unexpected tomorrow.

(Continued)

Table 8.1 Hofstede's Six Dimensions of National Culture *(Continued)*

Long-Term Orientation versus Short-Term Normative Orientation (LTO)	• How does a society maintain links with its own past while dealing with the challenges of the present and the future? Societies will prioritize these two existential goals differently. • Societies that score low on this dimension, for example, prefer to maintain long-established traditions and norms. They will approach societal change with suspicion. • Those with a culture which scores high, on the other hand, take a more pragmatic approach: they encourage thrift and efforts in modern education as a way to prepare for the future.
Indulgence versus Restraint (IVR)	• How much indulgence and free gratification of basic and natural human drives does a society allow? Do people like to enjoy life and have fun? In this case the culture is indulgent. • A society that is strict and limits or suppresses gratification of needs and regulates it by means of strict social norms would be considered restrained.

Source: Adapted from Hofstede's Six Dimensions of National Culture. Kindly provided by Hofstede Insights and first featured in Mitterfellner (2023).

Example of gender equality

For example, American audiences might be offended by ads which show only men in a stereotypically male situation, expecting political correctness and gender equality. Chinese or Japanese audiences might feel offended by ads that show too much affection between opposite genders, whereas in some Muslim countries, women must not be shown publicly at all, although depictions in advertising might generally be permitted depending on the strictness of the country. When IKEA published its 2012 catalogue in Saudi Arabia, the deliberate omission of all visible women led to a small scandal – not in Saudi Arabia but in the brand's home country of Sweden. IKEA had gone to the lengths of airbrushing all the women out of the catalogue, which made government officials in IKEA's native Sweden concerned about the message the company was sending regarding women's rights. IKEA later issued an apology stating: "We should have reacted and realized that excluding women from the Saudi Arabian version of the catalogue is in conflict with the Ikea Group values" (Cullers, 2012).

Example of smells and tastes

In Japan, people dislike strong perfumes, especially in public places, and you will notice that many cosmetics and body care products have no scent or are very lightly perfumed. Some workplaces and religious places even ban the use of perfumes, and consumers generally prefer light fragrances to heavy ones. But, in Japan there is a great love for green tea flavour and scent which is prevalent in many foods or beverages, which is why you will find Western confectioneries such as green-tea flavoured Kit Kats, Oreos or Häagen-Dazs in the supermarket, alongside a myriad of Japanese sweets and snacks. Green tea is also in more serious settings and is connected to spirituality, such as in the tea ceremony.

Example of geography

In Russia, people accept that the country's geography is a challenge for logistics of e-commerce: there are 11 time zones and the infrastructure for "next-day delivery" across 17,098,242 sq km of land can be tricky. Despite that, Russia has one of the major e-commerce markets worldwide with online retailers Wildberries and Ozon making up over 80 per cent of total deliveries of e-commerce in 2022 (Melkadze, 2023). People accept that in the capital Moscow the quickest delivery time will be roughly 3 days but this can take 5 days for Yekaterinburg, which is further east, and 5.5 days for Novosibirsk, which is even further out to the East (Melkadze, 2022).

Example of language

In China, the language is based on the system of logograms rather than sounds (phonetical language), and each Chinese character represents a monosyllabic Chinese word or morpheme. There are more than 20,000 characters in a Chinese dictionary.

The CCPIT Patent and Trademark Law Office explains the challenges for brands venturing into China:

> When entering the Chinese market, a foreign company, besides application for the registration of its Latin trademark in China, needs to design the corresponding Chinese trademark and apply for its registration […] Due to the complexity of Chinese language, many foreign companies

may have doubts in translating their Latin trademarks into corresponding Chinese trademarks and protecting the Chinese trademarks.

(Wang, 2016)

Western brands have the choice of either translating the brand name into Chinese (this keeps the meaning of the brand name), using transliteration (stays close to the original phonetic pronunciation but does not necessarily keep the meaning) or using their Western name and logo in the hope that it will gain recognition. The ideal version is when brands create a new brand name which sounds like the original and retains the original meaning (Müller and Gelbrich, 2015).

For example, in terms of favourable transliteration, "Armani" has become 阿玛尼 ("A MA NI"), "Chanel" was changed to 香奈儿 ("XIANG NAI ER") and "Lancome" to 兰蔻 ("LAN KOU"). "All the selected Chinese characters are related to beauty, elegance, poetry, flowers, perfume, etc., similar to the Latin trademarks in pronunciation, and easy to read. At the same time, these characters, as a whole, are not ready words or phrases with specific meaning in the dictionary" (Wang, 2016).

Mercedes-Benz is a company which achieved the creation of a brand name with a suitable meaning, sound and phonetical length when it translated its name to "ben-chi" (奔驰). This quite suitably means to gallop (or run faster) and thus offers a near-literal translation of the brand and what it represents. However, before it invented "ben-chi," it reportedly had a translation glitch when it used "ben-si", which has a negative and morbid connotation.

Furthermore, the Chinese culture dates back some 4,000 years and permeates modern-day citizens. This is evident in the mixed significance attributed to conforming with tradition and becoming more "Western". Brands which understand this as a fundamental need of the Chinese consumer have a greater chance of winning their support.

Case example: The Pretenders: a look at pseudo-international brand names

Superdry is a fashion brand with a logo that features Roman letters and the Japanese Kana and Kanji alphabets – they are two of the three alphabets commonly used in the Japanese language. Therefore, many consumers assume that it is a brand that originates in Japan.

Yes, the three Superdry founders really have been to Japan (so this part is true) at some point in the past, but they never lived there. They are not from Japan, and they do not even speak "Nihongo" (Japanese language in

Japanese). They did, however, fall in love with things like the Asahi Super Dry beer and many other products which claim to be "super"-something. This led the founders to start a fashion label based in the small British town of Cheltenham.

In Europe and the USA, the brand Superdry has gained immense popularity with its Japanese-inspired printed clothing and brand name. But what exactly does this Japanese combination of letters mean? When you read Superdry's famous graphics 極度乾燥(しなさい) you hear "Kyokudo Kanso (shinasai)", which can be translated to something like "Extremely dry (do it now)" – and it is not a polite request at all, but rather an order which parents might give to children.

Even though the founders of the brand admitted to the nonsense wording in 2011, the brand continues to grow and has not deterred its fans in the slightest. This is because in the West Japanese-made goods are considered superior, cool and different, and the typeset is a powerful USP which is instantly recognizable. The *Branding Journal* reasons:

> Research has shown that European consumers aspire and exhibit inclination towards Japanese brands and this is reflected in their purchase decisions. Moreover, packaging/products scripted in Japanese tend to exude a certain degree of quality and 'wow' factor in the customer's perception.
>
> (Ryan, 2016)

To put it briefly: European consumers cannot decode the writing literally, but more importantly, they decode it as cool.

Interestingly, or perhaps logically, there is not one Superdry store in Japan (last updated in 2024). This is, however, a strategic step by the brand, as Japanese people would not know what they are supposed to think of the phrase of "Jinglish" – a mix of Japanese and English. In fact, in Japan, popular items are T-shirts with English or French prints and fashion brands which sound Western – the exact opposite of Superdry's appeal in the West – because Japanese consumers love brand names that sound Western, regardless of whether they are imports or domestic ones. You will find many brand names that are made out of a combination of Japanese and English. They sound almost authentic, these supposedly Western brands, which are called Dainy by JURIANOJURRIE, YUMMY MART by PEACH JOHN, Delyle NOIR as well as Ober Tashe. These are just some of the labels which are on offer in one of the most famous department stores in Tokyo, Shibuya 109 – or "Ichi-Maru-Kyu" as the locals call it by spelling out the number. This is a fashion mecca for lovers of J-Fashion where young and fashion-conscious people flock in search of fashion styles like "Kawaii" (super cute), "Gyaru" (super girly) or "oshare" (highly fashionable).

And just like the exotic names of the aforementioned fashion brands, customers also love T-shirts with prints in Jinglish: "World Difference Execute", "Trusting To Luck", "Everything is in your hand" or "Much Like Hold" they read. The English-inspired prints are not limited to shirts nor to Tokyo, but you can find them on all sorts of products (chocolate, cosmetics, bath essences, etc.) and all over the country.

As in the case of Superdry, the attraction of an imported and superior brand is conveyed by means of a foreign name on the product. The customer transfers these characteristics onto the pretend-brand – irrespective of its true qualities. This smart marketing move can work well for selected brands.

Working with unfamiliar territories

First, working with unfamiliar territories and unpredictable customer responses calls for an extension of the communication model of coding and decoding of messages to six steps and a feedback loop, thus turning a one-way communication model into a two-way communication model (Figure 8.1).

If you compare this with the earlier communication model of coding and decoding brand messages, you will see a few differences: The codes are not

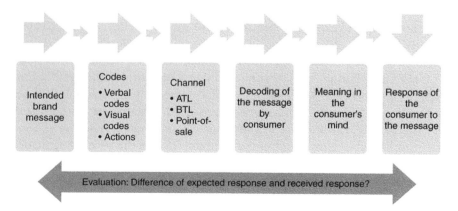

Figure 8.1 Two-way communication model for international markets. Based on Scheier and Held (2012) and Castro and Lewis (2011).

only verbal and visual codes but also actions taken by the brand. This can be PR, advertising or opening of stores as well as simply entering a new market by placing the products on the shelves of other retailers. This is why the point of sale is added to the channels in step 3. After the consumer has decoded the message and the meaning of the intended message has emerged in his mind, a crucial step follows, which is the response of the consumer to the said message. On international turf, this response is so vital for a brand to "make it or break it". In familiar markets, the worst that can happen is that a consumer only partially understands the message or is simply disinterested. But in foreign markets, the consumer might be repulsed or angered by a brand, and he or she will then refuse to accept it. The response of the consumer is critical for the brand, and it must evaluate if there is any difference between the response expected and the response received.

This theory of comparing the expected response to the intended response is actually used in the aviation industry, where communication is the key to a successful and safe flight operation. For example, in the cockpit, there are constant verbal exchanges and confirmations between the pilot and co-pilot, as well as air traffic control. In order to ensure that the intended message is received and understood correctly, a system of repetition, verification and control is employed. Oftentimes, when aviation accidents happened and the flight deck recording was later examined, there was miscommunication present and thus a human factor responsible for a less than desirable event. According to Airbus (2004), a survey by NASA found 80 per cent of all accidents to have occurred due to incorrect communication, with 45 per cent attributed to listening.

For this reason, the so-called cockpit and crew resource management is a recurring training factor for aviation professionals. All businesses on the ground can learn from aviation by not only listening to responses from their consumers but also expecting that the response might not be the intended one. (Internal business communication can also benefit from CRM applied to interpersonal communication, leadership and smooth decision making).

If the brand fails to consider the cultural and linguistic intricacies of a foreign culture, there can be several detrimental consequences, such as in the case of Dolce and Gabbana in China when a provocative campaign was launched in 2018.D&G is known for provocative ads which certainly made some people uncomfortable. However, this is a common trade of the advertising industry and most certainly the fashion industry. Sex, drama and weird innuendos receive attention in a media message overloaded world. Fashion in particular, has a close relationship with pushing and crossing all boundaries of social decency.In fact, there is a history of many provocative ads by the D&G brand and it has become somewhat of their signature style. In the past, D&G showed stereotypes of the Sicilian Mafia, clergy and women (or mothers), had shown stereotypical tourists in Venice – but equally all on the home territory of the designers. However, this is not acceptable for all cultures and becomes even more of an issue when outsiders mock a culture. In the case of the campaign targeting China, the imagery, voice-over and inuendo appeared to be racist, playing with stereotypes, derogatory and insulting. An Asian-looking woman, in a cliché Asian setting, in a stereotypical dress was trying to eat equally stereotypical and oversized Italian food clumsily with chopsticks, whilst being talked to by an invisible male spectator, making her feel incompetent. There were several episodes of the ad: one with oversized cannoli, a pizza and an immense bowl of pasta and each one was considered to be worse than the last. Chinese netizens were outraged and so was the fashion scene. The upcoming fashion show was cancelled, models swore to never walk for D&G again and consumers vowed to boycott the brand. The scandal reached its climax when D&G's Stefano Gabbana posted derogatory social media messages accusing the Chinese of eating dogs. This is not the only scandal, and many more examples persist to appear around the world. Some of them are appropriating culture and others are disrespecting it – but they could all be easily avoided with respectful studies of foreign culture and the employment of cultural consultants. (Mitterfellner 2023)

In terms of segmentation, a different approach is also needed for an international market.

Wind and Douglas (2001) have suggested that international markets need to be segmented in two steps: first the country in terms of the macro environment has to be evaluated and then the customer characteristics.

In detail, the recommended segmentation criteria of the macro environment include:

General country characteristics
Geographic location
Demography
Level of socioeconomic development
Cultural characteristics
Political factors
Economic and legal constraints
Market conditions
Product-bound culture and lifestyle characteristics

The customer characteristics are based on the same principles as the segmentation mentioned at the beginning of this chapter, including demographics, psychographics and lifestyle data.

Adapting the marketing message for international communication

One way for brands to work with their international communication strategy is to consider adapting the message or the product. This can be done at any stage, either before entering a foreign market (this is the ideal option) or as a follow-up to improve the customers' understanding of the brand message.

In both scenarios, the brand can choose whether it wants to implement any changes to its communications strategy and/or the product, or it might even choose to create a completely new product (aligned with brand identity and image) for the foreign market.

According to Kotler et al. (2008), there are five basic options for a brand that considers adaptation (Figure 8.2):

1. Straight product extension: New market, same product. No extra costs are involved for product development.
2. Product adaptation: New market, modified product. Intended to meet specific needs of the foreign market.
3. Product invention: New market, new product. Same communication.
4. Communication adaptation: Change the message and campaign to suit the foreign market.
5. Dual adaptation: New market, new product, new communication strategy.

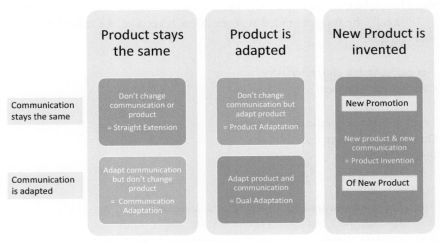

Adapted from Kotler et Al (2008) Principles of Marketing

Figure 8.2 Options for international product and promotion adaptation according to Kotler et al. (2008).

Case example: Cadbury Dairy Milk in India

Here is an example of the Western brand Cadbury, which cleverly used the knowledge of a foreign market to advertise chocolate. It used fashion as a common denominator of self-consciousness to get the audience interested but ultimately sells chocolate. The product was not adapted, but the brand communication is unique to Indian culture and a local advertising agency was hired to create the campaign.

> Imagine a tricky social situation, such as a woman in her 50s wearing a pair of jeans for the first time and being too scared to leave her home because her neighbours (and mother-in-law) will judge her negatively. Her husband hands her a small piece of chocolate and this gives her the confidence she needs to step outside her door. Once she does, her neighbours praise her new jeans and all is well.

Most likely, this scenario makes little sense to you unless you are familiar with Indian culture. Why would a woman in her 50s not wear jeans? Why would neighbours have any right to comment? And why would a small piece of chocolate solve this mysterious emotional trouble?

The answer lies in a commercial that was launched in 2010 by Cadbury Dairy Milk (CDM) and the infamous advertising agency Ogilvy & Mather. This campaign, under the name of "Shubh Aarambh" is based on the concept of the Indian tradition of having something sweet before every auspicious occasion, with the belief that it leads to a favourable outcome.

There are several commercials in the series, and Abhijit Avasthi, national creative director, Ogilvy & Mather India, said:

> While unfolding the "Shubh Aarambh" theme, we were consciously looking for situations which have universal appeal, though they might connect a little better with certain age profiles. [...] "Jeans" might work a little harder with the adults. Other themes that follow will be equally surprising yet real.

> (Rao, 2010)

Has Cadbury managed to create a brand message that can be decoded by the consumers of that particular culture? This campaign is said to be extremely successful, having replaced traditional Indian sweets with Cadbury Dairy Milk chocolate at home.

If we were to check the Hofstede Cultural Dimensions for insights on India, we would see that it scores 77 on Power Distance. This means that there is an acceptance of hierarchy and a top-down structure in society and organizations. India scores relatively low regarding individualism at 24 points, which means that the actions of the individual are influenced by the opinion of one's family, extended family, neighbours, work group and other such wider social networks that one has some affiliation toward. Rejection by one's peers feels terrible for someone from a collectivist society (Hofstede Insights India, 2024). These two dimensions out of six already give a clear picture of how the story of the ad connects perfectly well with the local culture.

Furthermore, Ogilvy & Mather made sure that the campaign would be suitable for television – a very popular medium in India amongst advertisers. In fact, Asia Pacific has been growing and is the second-largest regional advertising market in the world, with advertising spending in the region reaching a total of US$240 billion in 2024 , with India being one of the fastest-growing advertising markets in Asia. (Navarro, 2024)

The potential of international markets

With all the challenges given, is it still worth venturing out into the international market? Consider the forecast for the future: The EU and USA are mostly saturated markets with little growth prospects and currently battling a fine line of falling into recession. However, there are high hopes for the emerging economies of the BRICS countries: Brazil, Russia, India, China and South Africa, as well as the new additions as of 2024 – Egypt, Ethiopia, Iran, Saudi Arabia and the United Arab Emirates (UAE).

China had the highest GDP growth of any of the BRICS countries over the last two decades, until India overtook China in the mid-2010s and is predicted to have the highest growth in the 2020s (O'Neill, 2023), According to Credit Suisse, the number of dollar-millionaires residing in China is estimated to be 6.2 million individuals, ranking second after the United States. This is a steep rise since 2021 when there were 4.07 million millionaires in China (Mitterfellner, 2023).

Russia's gross domestic product (GDP) was estimated to have increased by 4.6 per cent in 2024 (Interfax in Statista, 2024). It is estimated that there were 408,000 millionaires in Russia in 2022, while the number of ultra-high-net-worth individuals worth over $50 million had increased by nearly 4,500 (Glover, 2023).

Figure 8.3 Nevsky Prospekt/Невский Проспект in St Petersburg, Russia, is a part of the UNESCO World Heritage list. The street houses cultural landmarks, many shops and churches, and offers entertainment for day and night. Image source: Pixabay by mobinovyc.

A further 83 Russian individuals were classified as billionaires by Forbes's list of the world's billionaires, and 539 Chinese individuals have the same financial ranking. The US, India, Germany, Hong Kong, Canada, Brazil, Taiwan, South Korea, Japan, Thailand and Indonesia are also featured on the top 20 list for 2022, giving a good indication as to where brands might see international demand (Chang, 2022).

South-East Asia as a whole, excluding South Korea and Japan, is rapidly gaining momentum. Indonesia is one example of a nation rapidly accelerating in production capacity and GDP increase.

How will demographics develop globally?

Africa has been forecast to experience the most population growth in the next 80 years. The most populous locations will be Asia and Africa, respectively, whilst Europe will experience a decline (Dyvik, 2024). By 2100, Africa's overall population is predicted to rise to nearly 4 billion, slightly behind Asia (Figure 8.5). This information correlates with Iqbal (2021), who stated that the BRICS countries are significant to the world economy in terms of

Figure 8.4 The Special Capital Region of Jakarta is Indonesia's largest city and has around 11 million inhabitants. Jakarta is an economic, cultural, political and administrative centre of Indonesia. Image source: Pixabay by katon765.

population (40%), GDP (25% nominal and US$16.039 trillion), land coverage (30%), world trade (18%) and global forex (US$4 trillion). Since 2001 and till the end of 2010, the BRICS as a group worked on sectoral cooperation in many areas, namely science and technology, trade promotion and facilitation, energy, health, education, innovation, and the fight against transnational crime (Mitterfellner, 2023).

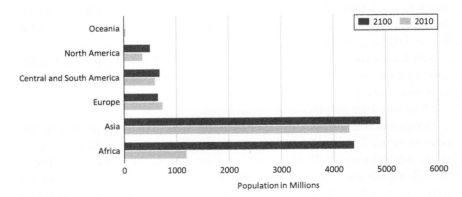

Figure 8.5 Global population growth with a forecast up to the year 2100, by continents, in millions. Data from the United Nations and Statista.

Additionally, there is a new form of global economy on the rise: e-commerce. It can reach consumers around the world and tap into their financial wealth and spending power without having to invest in a retail location abroad. This is supported by the numbers, as retail e-commerce sales are estimated to exceed US$6.3 trillion worldwide, with further growth expected in the future (Van Gelder, 2024).

One key factor to successful international marketing for brands is to remain flexible. As Euromonitor reported in 2015: "As in all emerging markets, success is based on knowledge – an understanding of the market, but also the economy, consumers, competitors and suppliers, which have been successful in China have managed". This remains true in 2024 and beyond.

Domestic ethnic advertising

Lastly, there are different ethnicities within one country or region that call for ethnic marketing. This is usually targeted at ethnic minorities who might respond better to being addressed in their native language, with brand communication that understands their values and needs.

Such is the case with fashion and lifestyle magazines which cater to African-American audiences in the USA, or brands such as Khushbu Fashions, a UK-based fashion brand which sells Indian clothing and Pakistani fashion online.

Ethnic marketing is well developed in the USA and the UK, but it is in its early stages in continental Europe. It is, however, a lucrative market in countries where there is a high percentage of ethnicities. In Germany, about 20 per cent of inhabitants have a non-German background, and ethnic marketing has been tried. However, this might prove unlucrative in Japan, where around 2 per cent of the population is non-Japanese, making it a highly homogeneous market by comparison.

Ethical considerations

Intercultural awareness and sensitivity are indispensable when designing a brand message for a consumer group outside our own comfort zone. The comfort zone might be the domestic market or specific cultures and countries which the fashion brand is well aware of and knows what is considered acceptable and what will offend consumers.

However, outside this zone, the brand can tread in dangerous waters of miscommunication which can easily backfire and even destroy a business, as many have seen with the Dolce & Gabbana case in 2018 in China when an ad was labelled everything from "provocative" to "racist" to simply "incomprehensible".

One take on a faux pas such as the one by D&G is ethnocentricity.

Any country can be accused of ethnocentricity. It means "believing that the people, customs, and traditions of your own race or nationality are better than those of other races", but it is not necessarily racist. Ethnocentric behaviour is therefore not the same as racism or patriotism, although it's often found alongside both of these. Ethnocentricity compares people to outsiders by using the cultural norms of their own group, so one can believe that but not act out the sentiment.

However, this can become an instant problem if this is your business's attitude. As we see quite clearly in such cases as D&G's ad for the Chinese consumers, when you are trying to break into a foreign market and appeal to foreign consumers, not researching their mentality meticulously and not respecting their cultural norms can become a massive problem. D&G's creative team continued to use the same European, ethnocentric, tongue-in-cheek approach to advertising and brand communication in a very different market, a very different cultural setting, resulting in a big outcry and negative social media storm.

Further reading

Briggs, P. (ed.) (September 2016) The State of Broadband 2016: Broadband Catalyzing Sustainable Development. *Broadband Commission for Sustainable Development*. Available at: www.broadbandcommission.org/Documents/reports/bb-annualreport2016.pdf

De Mooij, M. (2010) *Consumer Behavior and Culture: Consequences for Global Marketing and Advertising*. 2nd edn. Sage Publications.

Dyvik, E.H. (2024) Forecast of the world population in 2022 and 2100, by continent. Statista. Available at: https://www.statista.com/statistics/272789/world-population-by-continent/

Hofstede, G. (2023) The 6-D Model of National Culture. Available at: https://geerthofstede.com/culture-geert-hofstede-gert-jan-hofstede/6d-model-of-national-culture/

Iqbal, B. A. (2021) BRICS as a Driver of Global Economic Growth and Development. *Global Journal of Emerging Market Economies* 14(1), 7–8. https://doi.org/10.1177/09749101211067096. Article first published online: December 21, 2021; Issue published: January 1, 2022. Available at: https://journals.sagepub.com/doi/full/10.1177/09749101211067096

Kotler, P. et al. (2008). *International Product and Promotion. Principles of Marketing*. 5th edn. Financial Times/Prentice Hall.

Matharu, S. (2011) *Advertising Fashion Brands to the UK Ethnic Market: How Ethnic Models influence Ethnic Consumer Purchase Behaviour*. Verlag, Germany: VDM.

Mitterfellner, O. (2023) Luxury Fashion Brand Management: Unifying Fashion with Sustainability. Abingdon: Routledge

Navarro, J.G. (2024) Advertising worldwide – statistics & facts. Statista. Available at: https://www.statista.com/topics/990/global-advertising-market/#topicOverview

Solomon, M. R. (2020) *Consumer Behavior: Buying, Having, and Being*. 13th edn. London: Pearson.

Wind, Dr. Yoram and Douglas, Susan P. (2001). *International Market Segmentation*. Wharton School, University of Pennsylvania and CESA. Available at: https://faculty.wharton.upenn.edu/wp-content/uploads/2012/04/7213_International_Market_Segmentation.pdf

Brand communication at the point of sale 9
Sensory branding

Chapter topics

Sensory branding

Sensory marketing and sensory branding try to appeal to all the senses in relation to the brand. Brands use the senses to relate with customers on an emotional level and increase brand awareness. Sensory brand immersion also creates an emotional sense of place and promotes brand loyalty. "The term *emotional sense of place* describes the sum of human feelings, which can be evoked by a certain physical location [...] The feelings are based on personal experiences, memories and symbolic meanings which are all connected to the location" (Bischoff, 2006).

Our five senses are made up of visual, auditory, olfactory, gustative and tactile senses, and there are various studies that indicate which sense can pick up the most information. One version states that the visual sense – our eyes

DOI: 10.4324/9781003449157-9

Table 9.1 Information transition rates of the senses

Sensory system	Bits per second
Eyes	10,000,000
Skin	1,000,000
Ears	100,000
Smell	100,000
Taste	1,000

– is the strongest, followed by the tactile sense of our skin, the ears, smell and finally taste. Each of the senses absorbs around 11 million bits of information per second, which directly feed into our subconscious. This is because our conscious mind is only able to process 40 bits of information per second. It is assumed that due to this, up to 95 per cent of our purchases are triggered by our subconsciousness.

Furthermore, when activated alone, or together in combinations, the effect on our brain and lasting emotional memory can be quite strong. This is due to the fact that sensory perceptions are processed in the limbic system of our brain.

One of the oldest examples of sensory branding for commercial purposes is Singapore Airlines appealing to our olfactory sense. The airline started spraying its signature "Stefan Floridian Waters", a mélange of rose, lavender and citrus, on its hot towels more than 30 years ago. The company recently tried applications of the same perfume in a Singapore ticket office. Passengers fondly spoke of a typical Singapore Airlines smell when entering the plane and had pleasant memories of the in-flight experience.

Burberry on Regent Street in London appeals to our sense of taste (and smell) by offering a gustatory experience in its Thomas's Café. The menu features everything from eggs benedict to lobster and from Japanese tea from Kyoto to champagne.

Armani has a more Italian approach, which certainly is aligned with the brand's ethos: the Armani caffés and restaurants in Milan, Paris, Cannes, Munich, London, Doha, Dubai, Hong Kong, New York and Tokyo. Armani's Dubai location in the Burj Khalifa even offers a choice of restaurants, such as Italian, Indian, Japanese and European. One such restaurant states: "the essence of Italy is brought to life through an inspired pairing of the finest ingredients and exquisite flavour combinations in a stunningly designed location."'' (Armani Hotel Dubai, 2024).

The food's luxury description is almost interchangeable with the description of Armani's luxury fashion and thus is a sensory experience that will make the brand most memorable in the subconscious, probably influencing the next purchase decision.

Confectionery is another popular item: Gucci has Gucci chocolates, and Hermès had created an edible Birkin bag also made from chocolate. In China, an emerging economy that is continuously important for the fashion and luxury business, brands are in a race to offer the most beautiful and tasty moon cakes for the mid-autumn festival. This round pastry is a traditional sweet which luxury houses such as Louis Vuitton, Tiffany, Tod's, Gucci, Armani, Kenzo and Fendi send to high-profile customers and KOLs, or key opinion leaders, in beautiful boxes with traditional greatings.

Communication buildings

"A good building must do two things, firstly it must shelter us, secondly it must speak to us", said Peter Stutchbury (2016), an award-winning Australian architect.

A directly operated store, and a flagship store especially, can serve as a point of brand immersion and communication with the customer. For such projects, company budgets often invest millions.

One such exemplary communication building is not from the fashion industry but from the automotive industry. The BMW Welt, which means "BMW World" in German, is an impressive building and interactive space set over 25,000 sqm, which was commissioned by the car manufacturer and opened in 2007. It sits on the outskirts of Munich and attracts up to 25,000 visitors on some days. According to the architectural firm HimmelB(l)au, the space is

> where the corporation goes into dialogue with its customers, friends and visitors from all over the world – a place of meeting and of change (...) This means: To see, feel, hear, smell, taste the brands – in brief: To experience the world of the brands of BMW Group with all senses.

In fact, the sensory experience is triggered by a modern, bright and vast space, carefully designed to feature interactive exhibitions, tours, food and drink, as well as a dramatic sales platform where new cars are handed over to customers in an emotionally charged ritual (customers report crying when seeing their car for the first time during the ritual). If you describe the space with adjectives and describe the BMW brand with adjectives, you would likely have interchangeable words which means that the translation of the brand's attributes into a physical space has been done correctly.

This is a successful example of a communication building from another industry. Can fashion create such spaces, too?

Case example: Hugo Boss flagship store in Tokyo

The menswear flagship store of Hugo Boss in Tokyo is such an architectural and sensory marvel, partly because award-winning architect Norihiko Dan had the task of squeezing it onto a small plot of land directly within the

Figure 9.1 The Hugo Boss Keyaki building (flagship store) in central Tokyo, Japan, which is taller than the L-shaped Tod's flagship store immediately surrounding it. Image kindly provided by Hugo Boss.

Figure 9.2 Inside the Hugo Boss Keyaki building (flagship store) in central Tokyo, Japan. Image kindly provided by Hugo Boss.

L-shaped embrace of the concrete flagship store of Tod's that was already standing there. Also known as the Keyaki building, Hugo Boss opened the flagship in 2013 which features a structure composed of multiple leaf-shaped columns made from steel-reinforced concrete. The concrete columns have a surprising woodlike texture (visible when close), which was developed by pouring concrete into a wooden mould.

The concrete construction stands in the upmarket shopping district of Omotesando, where luxury shoppers seek to be entertained by brands. Within the Hugo Boss store, the use of materials such as concrete, wood, textiles, and light and smell (there is a Hugo Boss–scented candle) takes the shopper on a sensory immersion and into the world of Boss.

Within the space of a flagship store, the consumer can experience a brand with all his or her senses, and the more positive the experience is, the more positive memories will be created, which can lead to loyalty and brand preference.

Integrating digital technology at the point of sale

Currently, customers live in a fusion world of the digital and physical, expecting brands to reach them on all possible channels. Thus, it is only natural to offer both worlds inside the store too.

This creates a journey for the customer from the first digital contact on a personal device to the physical purchase experience in the store. According to a study by McKinsey & Company (Remy et al., 2015) on the digitalization of companies, customers have reported a dramatically better brand experience and engagement.

Some brands that have previously played with the idea of integrating a digital interface in their stores are:

Burberry – Interactive tables, video walls
Prada – Digital changing rooms
Tommy Hilfiger – Augmented reality fashion shows and changing rooms
Karl Lagerfeld – Interactive digital tables and mirrors
Zara – RFID technology
Gucci – Digital entertainment for children
Nike – Multi-touch, multi-user wall, smartphone interaction

Very early on, Karl Lagerfeld installed iPads inside the changing rooms in the flagship store in Munich, Germany, with the intention of inviting the customer to take selfies and upload them on social media, turning the shopper into a brand ambassador. This simple installation creates a buzz around the brand,

Figure 9.3 The iPad in the Karl Lagerfeld flagship store in Munich, Germany, invited customers to engage with it when spending time in the changing room.

reaches opinion leaders, helps interaction between customers and potential customers through social media, and ensures harmony of offline and online communication activities.

The iPad features a photo of Karl behind a camera, seemingly ready to snap your photo. In the new clothes, the customer takes pictures and edits them with frames and decorations. After that, the interface asks to upload the picture onto the Karl Lagerfeld Facebook page.

In summary, the benefits of using sensory branding at the point of sale and in brand communication are:

- Increase in in-store traffic
- Increase in the time spent in the store
- Increase in brand awareness
- Customers are connected to social networks
- Increase in sales and revenue
- Repeat sales

If the store uses technology for stock management, further benefits can be better merchandise and stock management, improved customer service and sales, as well as personalized service, including individualization and product adjustments directly in stores.

Sonic branding

How do you make a brand forever recognizable by a jingle? How does a song become a bestseller (perhaps for a second time)? You need to write brand-identifying sounds and put them into commercials, and the science behind this is sonic branding which builds on the idea of our auditory sense. Many brands have engraved themselves in our memory thanks to recognizable jingles or by using popular songs as their identity. Prime examples are the sound bites electronics and computer operating systems make when you start a device, which uses sound bites that last no more than a few seconds but are instantly recognizable. McDonald's famously aligned itself with Justin Timberlake's song and kept the jingle "I'm lovin' it" as its brand sound.

Case example: Levi's and Flat Eric

For fashion brands, it is more complex when it comes to creating consumer associations with sound, and a jingle hardly suffices.

Fashion brands use longer tracks of music in commercials, from short extracts of well-known songs to full-length compositions accompanying an entire film.

Music in fashion ads can even rise to fame, become a symbol of popular culture and become a hit single. Such was the case with Levi's when, in the late 1990s, the brand teamed up with a yellow furry puppet called Flat Eric. The ad agency Bartle Bogle Hegarty (BBH) was initially approached by Levi's with a simple brief to create a commercial that would target 16- to 24-year-olds in Europe, the Middle East and Africa, providing an opportunity for the target market to engage with the ethos of the Levi's brand (Springer, 2008) The genius behind the ad was advertising legend Sir John Hegarty, but not even Hegarty himself could predict the success of the commercial which seemed a bit odd to the brand's executives at first. It all began with a yellow puppet that was styled by the Creature Shop, which belonged to the creator of The Muppets: Jim Henson. The yellow puppet was first seen in the music video of a hit tune by the French electronic musician and filmmaker Quentin Dupieux, aka Mr Oizo. Hegarty's team used the puppet, Mr Oizo's hit tune and put them into a series of cheeky Levi's commercials where the puppet Flat Eric and his human friend were up to no good.

Interestingly, this campaign was one of the first to use the internet to engage with the target audience and create a viral sensation, in the days when young people were only learning how to sign up and have their own email. Flat Eric was sent around the internet in URLs, as email attachments and was featured on Levi's website before the ad was released. High school kids shared information about Flat Eric, and it became quite a movement.

Then the first ad was released, and instantly the popularity was of an explosive nature, with fans building fan sites dedicated to the puppet and requesting Flat Eric merchandise. The fictional character rose to cult status and created subcultural capital for the Levi's brand. Flat Eric was eventually released as a limited-edition physical toy, with the packaging branded by the Levi's brand and copy reading "the famous Levi's character" (Springer, 2008). The box also contained three of Mr Oizo's tracks on a CD. Any high schooler in Europe who could get a hold of the limited-edition puppet would place their Flat Eric puppet visibly in the car – a sign of being cool.

Levi's went on to make several more commercials with the yellow puppet, establishing a clear link between commercial fashion and popular culture (Caird, 2016). The Levi's ad series came to a close with the last ad when Flat Eric was captured by the authorities. In 2010, Flat Eric reappeared in a music video by Mr Oizo featuring Pharrell Williams, who was releasing the puppet from prison. Today, collectible Flat Eric puppets are sold on the internet and can fetch several hundred to several thousand euros.

Before Flat Eric, Levis had revived Dinah Washington's version of "Mad About the Boy", which she first sang in 1952. BBH had created a timeless commercial titled "Swimmer" in 1992, where a young man, clad in Levi's jeans, traversed multiple backyards by means of diving and swimming through their respective swimming pools and interrupting social gatherings. In the last backyard, he grabs a pretty young girl in a pink dress by the wrist and pulls her with him. The final scene shows both jumping off a tall platform into the water, with the young man unchanged in his Levi's but the girl now in a white bikini.

Susan Credle (2023), who is a creative advertising powerhouse, described the significance of this and other iconic ads by Levi's in the following way:

> These films held two truths. They were no doubt ads for a brand. They are also enduring art pieces celebrated by the public. They became a part of culture. They were inspired by art, and they introduced that art to a bigger audience through advertising.

In 2002, Levi's used classical music for the first time in its advertising, when with the help of BBH (again), the brand produced a highly expensive commercial using music by Handel. The arranger of the classical piece was John Altman, who has scored more than 4,000 TV commercials and is quite a celebrity in his industry.

Altman, an Emmy Award-winning composer, arranger and conductor, writes music for films and TV and has won every major creative award, including the inaugural MPA Music in Advertising Award. His compositions for Levi's and Renault won the Campaign Award for Best Soundtracks in 2003 and 2004. In 2022, he published his book *Hidden Man: My Many Musical Lives*, where he recounts his involvement in the music and film industry for over five decades. Altman's scores include such well-known film sequences as "Always Look on the Bright Side of Life" from *Life of Brian*, which he arranged, conducted and whistled; the tank chase through St Petersburg in the James Bond movie *Goldeneye*; and the ship sinking in *Titanic*, with the orchestra playing on deck.

Amongst Altman's commercials for famous fashion brands are Gucci, Wrangler and Prada to name just a few. He scored Ridley Scott's fashion film for Prada, which was released in 2005 at the Berlin Film Festival. It was timed with the launch of Prada's new fragrance, and Miuccia Prada asked film director Ridley Scott and his daughter Jordan Scott to create the film project. Jordan wrote the poem "Thunder Perfect Mind", which deals with the endless aspects of female psychology. At the same time, Altman composed the music for a classic Barbie campaign in the US.

Interview with John Altman

Q: How did you start writing music for TV, film and advertising?

> JA: I was in a group called Hot Chocolate, played saxophone, and they weren't happy with the musical arrangements that had been done for them. So I said: "I'll do some if you like". They liked what I wrote and suddenly I was an arranger. And in those days, in the mid-1970s, a lot of the TV arrangers were ex-dance band musicians who looked down on genres like reggae, country & western funk and although I liked all popular music, from the turn of the century almost, I was also conversant with all the other forms of music because I was a young guy. So they would pass it on to me – if they had to do a variety show – any arrangements that were slightly more modern. I started writing for popular television variety shows and about the same time I had started arranging for commercials and records.

Figure 9.4 John Altman.

One day an advertising agency in the Netherlands wanted to use a Beatles song in their commercial, but in those days it was impossible to licence a Beatles track for advertising. So the director said, "Why don't you write something?" And well, I did and they loved it and that became the music for their campaign. And immediately I was a composer as well as an arranger. Then I started composing for BBC drama and arranging music for other composers in music and a similar thing happened. Somebody said, "Why don't we get you to write the music and cut out the middle man?" and I became a film composer. This was all happening simultaneously, while I still carried on my career as an arranger with lots of hit records to my credit and as a saxophone player with people like Van Morrison. I was firing on all cylinders!

Q: You have worked on many films such as *Titanic* and James Bond *GoldenEye*. Why is it that fashion brands have now turned to films, or rather short films, instead of advertising? Is there something they want to copy from the movies?

JA: Films are a unique combination of visual effects, emotional storylines and impactful music. When we watch a really strong film, it will create a lasting memory in our minds. So I think fashion brands want to tap into this powerful emotional connection with their audience.

The element of the script, or the storytelling if you want, is the same for both feature-length films and short films, which is exactly what brands today do – they tell compelling stories.

Q: How would you say this storytelling in the short fashion films differs from classic commercials, such as the Levi's one where you arranged Handel's music?

JA: The absolute luxury of commercials really is time. You have to tell everything immediately. When you think that the longest TV commercial is going to be 90 seconds and the shortest possibly 10 seconds, you really have to make maximum impact in the short time. With film, this gets stretched, so, for example, the film I did for Prada directed by Ridley Scott was 7 minutes long, which is ample time to create a vibe, a general atmosphere which can either focus on one product or many.

Q: With the Prada fashion film, what was the creative process when you wrote the music? How did you interpret the brand's message and how did you translate it into sound?

JA: It had to be stylish, mysterious, timeless and impactful yet fun and playful so in a way very much what the brand stands for. In terms of interpreting – the same process I would use for scoring a full-length feature film. The only difference being 7 minutes which is unusual for a feature film, unless it is for example a chase sequence.

Q: You used a live orchestra to record the soundtrack for the commercial. How do you feel this is more beneficial than using a synthesized track?

JA: The main benefit is the emotional impact you can make by using live musicians that you can't achieve by using machinery. For example, using a muted trumpet with crescendos and diminuendos broadens your emotional palette and also allows the music to breathe.

Q: Fashion films are often filled with a star cast of directors and actors. Who was involved in the Prada one?

JA: There were Jordan and Ridley and the French director of photography, Philippe Le Sourd.

Miuccia Prada had designed the clothes which the protagonist and supermodel Daria Werbowy wore, styled by Kym Barrett of Matrix. And then there was Tom Foden, who has worked with both Ridley and Jordan in the past and came on board as production designer. Blanca Li was the choreographer for the film.

The music was performed by a small jazz ensemble that included Frank Sinatra's bass player of choice, Chuck Berghofer; trumpeter Jeff Bunnell; percussionist Tiki Pasillas, who features with Marc Anthony (Jennifer Lopez's husband). The drummer is Bernie Dresel from the Brian Setzer Orchestra. It was recorded in LA.

Ethical considerations

Sonic branding and music, gustatory experiences and beautiful smells, even for commercial purposes, can enrich our lives in positive ways and become "enduring art pieces celebrated by the public" as pointed out by Credle (2023). However a factor to consider is the negative side effects of sensory branding. Sensory overload is an overstimulation of our senses, which can have detrimental effects on physical and psychological well-being. It is problematic for people who might have conditions such as a predisposition to seizures, autism and neurodiversity , as well as a sensitive nature to stimuli. (The idea of sensory overload is discussed in more detail in Chapter 10 which deals with the negative side of brand communication.)

In a race to impress the consumer with immersive experiences and take more of the market share, brands become indifferent to the effects of their marketing practices. A high-stimulation place with lots of digital interfaces might also be confusing and unsuitable for children and elderly people.

Buildings, flagship stores and shopping malls, which are the locations for many sensory brand experiences, can also be scruitinised. Gjoko Muratovski (2011 and 2013) argues that architecture has been used since ancient times as a means of political and religious propaganda, such as in ancient Greece, Rome or Egypt where buildings were commissioned to convey the power of the ruler or an empire. In more modern times, the USA, the ex-Soviet Union, Berlin and other capitals constructed monumental structures that were "architectural propaganda". Today, global cities want to promote themselves as desirable destinations to stakeholders such as investors, tourists, and prospective residents and create buildings for purposes of commerce and leisure.

However, when brands transform our landscape, what are they propagating? Our immediate environment is designed and curated by companies with strong commercial interests and in turn propagates unhealthy consumerism and the destruction of significant communities.

When cities no longer represent the fine arts, architecture and urban development but are a playground for the coolest, the loudest the tallest branded buildings, what *emotional sense of place* do we derive from our surroundings? A museum building, in contrast, is a cultural space that is often accessible to all people, of most ages and backgrounds (free or for a small fee). Are branded spaces equally inclusive and accessible without the prerequisite of making a purchase, and does it add to the cultural value of a place?

Brands thus become responsible for our cultural capital, the heritage of a city and the socio-cultural environment of present and future generations. However, this responsibility towards society is not necessarily compatible with business interests.

Furthermore, big brands and corporations have been known to fuel gentrification. They can drive out small businesses that add to the liveliness and authentic character of a city and might have a long-standing heritage. As Naomi Klein already wrote as we entered the twenty-first century, Starbucks had a strategy for taking over urban spaces: The company took over entire neighbourhoods by simultaneously opening several cafés, forcing small and long-established competitors to close. Nearly two decades later, the strategy still very much applies with no large global city left untouched. The downside of commercial gentrification is also true in the example of Tokyo's upscale shopping street Omotesando where all the luxury flagship stores line the street: Once there were the Dōjunkai Aoyama Apartments (built 1926–27) which housed small independent businesses, galleries, start-ups, and original residencies. In 2005, they were replaced by Omotesando Hills (designed by star architect Tadao Ando), depriving the area of "variety and vitality (...) in favour of corporate business and all the sterility and homogeneity that implies." (Barr, 2018). As beautiful as shopping streets can be, they permanently chain the social fabric of a location and its history and should be part of a larger debate.

Further reading

Altman, J. (2022) *Hidden Man: My Many Musical Lives.* Sheffield: Equinox.

Armani Hotel Dining (2024) Armani Hotel Dubai. Available at: https://www.armanihotels
.com/en/hotels/armani-hotel-dubai/dining/

Ferrari, P. and Rizzolatti, G. (eds.) (2015) *New Frontiers in Mirror Neurons Research.* Oxford: Oxford University Press.

Fiore, A. M. (2010) *Understanding Aesthetics for the Merchandising and Design Professional.* New York: Fairchild Books.

Gabay, J. (2015) *Brand Psychology: Consumer Perceptions, Corporate Reputations.* London: Kogan Page.

Hulten, B. (2009) *Sensory Marketing.* New York: Palgrave Macmillan.

Lewis, R. and Dart, M. (2014) *The New Rules of Retail.* 2nd edn. New York: Palgrave Macmillan.

Lindstrom, M. (2010) *Brand Sense: Sensory Secrets Behind the Stuff We Buy.* Revised, updated edn. New York: Free Press.

Minsky, L., Fahey, C. and Kotler, P. (2017) *Audio Branding: Using Sound to Build Your Brand.* London: Kogan Page.

Muratkovski, G. (2013) Urban Branding: The Politics of Architecture. Design Principles and Practices: An International Journal — Annual Review Volume 6, 2013. https://doi.org/10.18848/1833-1874/CGP/v06i01

Pelger, M. (2015) *Designing the Brand Identity in Retail Spaces.* New York: Fairchild Books.

Springer, P. (2008) *Ads to Icons: How Advertising Succeeds in a Multimedia Age.* London: Kogan Page.

A critical look at advertising

10

Brands selling hopes, dreams and objectification

Chapter topics

Why criticize advertising?

Advertising surrounds us everywhere; it informs us about products, entertains us and sometimes irritates us. We think that we know what it is all about and can consciously choose to ignore its influence if we wish to do so. Or do we? A fundamental problem with advertising has been pointed out by many critics, authors and academics: it causes more harm than good to society, it misinforms, it warps reality, it obviously tries to influence and manipulate consumers, and "by the sheer weight of exposure, advertising sets a social agenda of what is expected, what is fashionable, and what is tasteful" (Lane et al., 2008, p. 755). Advertising is more powerful and more harmful than we think.

DOI: 10.4324/9781003449157-10

The exposure to ads is inescapable because one cannot unsee or unhear an ad in most public and private surroundings. As individuals encounter ads, they inadvertently and often unconsciously form a psychological and emotional relationship with them.

Still, many people are in denial of the influences of advertising because "it is quick, cumulative and for the most part it's subconscious" (Kilbourne, 1999).

Advertising is even more harmful to children and adolescents who are easily influenced and might copy peers or role models they see. In some instances, advertising is blatantly disturbing, such as in the case with shock advertising.

However, there are regulations and watchdogs that can step in when advertising goes too far. Also, some places have consciously chosen to limit or eradicate advertising in public spaces (and beyond). In these places, the landscape changed dramatically due to the limit or absence of ads. What is it like to live in a place with no advertising? An interview with a former Soviet movie star gives answers to this question.

The relationship of the self with the ads: hopes, dreams and fears

To understand our relationship with advertising and the influence it has on us, we first have to look at the mutual relationship between the person and the ad. What exactly happens in our minds and which emotions appear when we look at an ad?

Sofia Coppola, who directed the ad for the Marc Jacobs fragrance "Daisy", inadvertently explains the mechanism in fashion advertising: "I guess with the fragrance, you imagine the woman you're going to be when you wear it. Part of the experience [...] is that you think about a life you're going to have. That's what fashion is too" (Blasberg, 2014).

There is a relationship that advertising forms with us. Sigmund Freud's disciples and successful marketers like Bernays or Dichter applied the then-new theories of the self and hidden desires as a clever marketing tool. They believed that each person has hidden dreams, hopes, fears and insecurities deep in their subconscious. They argued that people could be made much more aware of those deep emotions and offered a solution to the problem: buying things.

This worked very well in many instances because people did not realize that the emotions would not subside with the purchase and went shopping to feed their aspirations -again and again - perpetuating the scope of consumerism.

Modern-day neuroscience has confirmed what psychologist Ernest Dichter argued from the 1930s to the 1960s: purchase behaviour is not conscious. It is not even subconscious but unconscious. Dichter studied the theories of Freud in Vienna and fled the growing Nazi regime in the early 1930s. He came to

New York and began a new career in marketing, which was built on his knowledge of psychoanalysis. It revealed that for customers, objects had the meaning of sex, fear, rewards and prestige. He worked for many companies, including Chrysler and Ivory soap. Dichter infused his marketing and advertising messages with implied meanings. For example, he noticed that people paid close attention to their cleanliness and bathed before a romantic date. So Ivory soap was advertised with copy like "Romance can't be rationed – if you take Baby's Beauty tips!" giving hope to those individuals who were eager for romance. Brands like Ivory had to communicate to our insecure self, to the hopeful self.

Let's look at a technique that was used in the middle of the twentieth century: fear and social exclusion. Fennis and Stroebe (2010) recount a famous ad for Listerine which used the scary medical term "halitosis". Listerine, which was originally sold as a surgical disinfectant (for the body and floors), made bad breath a socially unacceptable trait and a catastrophe for all relationships even though, prior to the ad campaigns, people were not self-conscious about it and certainly did not see it as much of a problem. But the ad campaigns aimed at the very nerve of humans, which is social exclusion. Halitosis would leave women "Often a Bridesmaid ... never a bride" or lonely without any friend but a single bird in a cage. There were many terrifying examples like these in the ads, and they all offered a solution, which was the infamous mouthwash. When people watch such ads (and there are many of them even today, using fear as a motivator), they immediately empathize and identify with a person – at least for the duration of the commercial but often beyond. If the ad resonates with the inner self, the person will also try to imitate it to a certain degree.

This is something that neuroscience has supported recently when it found so-called mirror neurons, a type of neuron which is said to fire when a primate sees others in action or does the action itself. For the neuron, there is no difference whether the action was passive and just observed, or whether we imitated the action. Scientists have argued that this is the neurological function of empathy, and this very empathy is what we experience through advertising.

But even without a scientific explanation, we humans have the capacity to imagine ourselves in someone else's situation; we seem to "try on" someone else's shoes for a moment. But if an ad is cleverly made, it will not just make us empathize it will also stir strong emotions in us – strong enough to react impulsively and long enough to solve the insinuated issue with a purchase of the advertised product.

As Judith Williams (1978, p. 70) once pointed out:

> This – a Lifestyle Kit – is precisely what ads offer us. In buying products with certain 'images' we create ourselves, our personality, our qualities, even our past and future. [...] We are both product and consumer; we consume, buy the product, yet we *are* the product. Thus our lives become

our own creations, through buying; an identikit of different images of ourselves, created by different products.

And this patched-together, carefully created self often has a very unhealthy relationship with the ads we see.

So, how unhealthy can advertising be for us? Since advertising warps our self-perception and causes damaging insecurities, it can be lastingly unhealthy. Specifically, fashion advertising is especially skilled at warping self-perception because fashion is about being tall, beautiful, stylish, young, desirable, with a perfect and flawless body, dressed ideally for every situation and being socially a winner whilst having an extraordinarily lavish lifestyle. At this point, I would like to ask the reader to reflect and count how many people (and not any social media stars) he or she personally knows who fit this description. And now, please think about how many fashion ads and influencer posts you remember which fit this description. Even if you work at the top notch of the modelling industry, you will still see more idealistic and retouched ads than real people.

When you look through a fashion or lifestyle magazine the advertising overshadows any editorial content (Winship, 1987). On average, the content of a "September Issue" by American *Vogue* will feature two-thirds advertising, and the last third will be split between its own photography and a bit of actual writing. Just get yourself a copy and count each full advertising page per issue, and then count the editorial pages with actual text (not product descriptions next to a model wearing the items). In 1999, Vogue had 562 pages of ads in a 700-page September Issue (that's over 80 per cent of advertising content); ten years later in 2019, Vogue had reduced it to 356 ad pages inside a magazine totaling 596 pages, making the September Issue still a whopping 59 per cent advertising overall. Closely behind are Herper's Bazaar, Elle and InStyle whose September magazines sell 50 to 55 per cent to advertisers. (Hays, 2019)

Of course, it's a catch-22, since magazines are financially dependent on advertisers and will make space for as many ads as possible unless they firmly believe in a different business model. *Tank Magazine* was reportedly very cautious about whose ads it showed and how many of them, raising the price per issue.

However, it is not uncommon for advertisers to use their position of power and withhold advertising if they are waiting for confirmation of a favourable editorial piece or a negative piece on a competitor (Lane et al., 2008).

What is significant is that visual imagery, in colour especially, overshadows the written word. It has an immediate and rich impact the latter cannot inspire, while the associations of these colour images tend to stamp the firmest trace on magazine and reader's memory alike.

Winship (1987, p. 55)

The way we are used to consuming fashion, as this passage from the 1980s shows, is solely through visual representations of a make-believe world with make-believe people.

Erving Goffman (1976), one of the most influential sociologists of the twentieth century, would call it "commercial realism" when advertisers try to present the advertising world in ways which could be real. He compares the staging of reality in advertising to that of staging a play: The viewer engages in acknowledging a make-believe world, the simulation of reality, of how things could be.

> The standard transformation employed in contemporary ads, in which the scene is conceivable in all detail as one that could in theory have occurred as pictured, providing us with a simulated slice of life; but although the advertiser does not seem intent on passing the picture off as a caught one, the understanding seems to be that we will not press him too far to account for just what sort of reality the scene has.
>
> (Goffman, 1976, p. 15)

Knowing this, ads should appear strange to us, but most of the time they do not.

Warped self-perception and psychological implications of ads

Predominantly in fashion and beauty ads, an unrealistic standard of beauty is exaggerated and becomes a commercial reality when perfect people are depicted – already thin and beautiful to begin with – and touched up in Photoshop during post-production.

What message do women, men and children receive when they see such imagery everywhere, from fashion magazines to videos to posters for social media campaigns? Anthony Cortese (1999) claims that women start feeling dissatisfied with their bodies, lose self-esteem and can even develop psychological problems such as eating disorders – all because of the unrealistic body image that one is asked to aspire to (Figure 10.1).

It is in fact almost impossible to live up to beauty standards just as it is impossible to naturally have Barbie's body proportions. However, the secret desire to be model-perfect still permeates our society and darkens the psychological and physical (as well as financial) health of many women, men, girls and boys who grow up with self-hatred – a very serious topic which Jean Kilbourne uncovered as early as 1979 when she made the documentary film *Killing Us Softly*. (The documentary has been updated and currently has a fourth version.)

Figure 10.1 A childhood spent growing up in an inescapable hyper-real world, overshadowed by unrealistic beauty ads in the public space. Streetshot taken in 2003. With kind permission from photographer Aleks Budimir.

One activist group called Adbusters has made it its mission to subvert advertising messages, point out their dangerous "side effects" and raise the public's awareness. Because Adbusters uses the same codes and visual language in its subverted fashion ads, one can easily decode them and understand the social implications at a glance. For example, a series of spoof ads takes inspiration from Calvin Klein advertisements for the fragrance "Obsession", yet it depicts very different scenarios, such as a woman who is being sick above a toilet, already thin. The question arises whether she can ever be thin enough. Can she ever be happy with who she is? Is she perhaps similar to many other women?

The female body and its stereotypical thinness are presented to children at a very young age through dolls of unrealistic proportions. As women grow up, they are groomed by brands to become consumers fuelled by a myriad of self-doubts that they mistakenly try to resolve through consumption. Figure 10.2 depicts a critical take on this issue by asking whether the female consumer is in fact voluntarily and freely consuming or is a victim and consumed by modern marketing, advertising and brands. This is part of a photography series which was exhibited in the UK and in Europe by the author, using Barbie dolls to raise important questions and subvert the consumerist narrative.

Figure 10.2 Is the female consumer happily consuming or is she being happily consumed? Author's original photography.

Gender and the objectification of bodies in advertising

Men and women are targeted in different ways, which becomes evident when comparing ads in men's and women's fashion or lifestyle magazines. Have the traditional roles of men and women changed over the last decades, and can we see this evidence in advertising?

It is true that especially women have been objectified in advertising for several decades now and are shown to be bodies without power, submissive to men and without a voice (Cortese, 1999). their bodies are "chopped up", only showing parts such as their breasts, stomachs, behinds and legs. What's worse is that through these images of subjugation, it is made clear to men that the women are weak, there to be dominated by men, whether it be through sexual or violent actions (Kilbourne, 1999).

This becomes even more interesting if you consider that women in the US have never fully attained equal rights since the Equal Rights Amendment wasn't ratified (Kilbourne, 1999) despite attempts to do so in 1972. Far away in

Europe, Germany saw equal rights for women only in 1977 and the Swiss canton of Appenzell was one of the last to grant women the right to vote in 1991, making several Middle-Eastern, African and Asian countries far more progressive in comparison. Thus, the dominating male was in fact a Western cultural norm and continues to thrive in our western visual culture.

One ad that is representative of the objectification of women is the Weyenberg ad for Massagic Shoes from 1974. It shows a naked woman lying belly down on the floor, admiring a man's shoe. Her body is "chopped", as only her upper torso is shown and cut off from below her chest. She is happily smiling at the shoe, her eyes focused on the object and not the camera, and the copy reads: "Keep her where she belongs…" This was in the 1970s, but have ads changed since then? Look at any ad by Skyy Vodka in the 2000s, for example, and you will see similarly disturbing imagery.

Regarding the "lag between advertising and feminism", the *Atlantic* wrote in 2015:

> And many ads today—be they for underwear or footwear or baby-powder-scented body spray—are in their way as retrograde as these specimens from the '70s. They can assume that women's consumer decisions are based on conceptions of male desire. They can assume that the key decision-maker in a commercial transaction, regardless of who spends the money, is a man.
>
> We may well have come, in the words of Virginia Slims ads, "a long way, baby." But we still have far—very far—to go.
>
> (Garber, 2015)

Sexualization of children

Another aspect which needs to be looked at is the early sexualization of children and teens, which is now dominant in advertising.

According to Anthony Cortese (1999), women and men, as well as girls and boys, learn through advertising how they are expected to behave and what role they must play in society.

There are clear dangers in this advertising practice. An example is the viral video star Brendan Jordan, a 15-year-old self-proclaimed transgender boy who has been snapped up by American Apparel and extensively used in its campaign, highlighting his sexual orientation. American Apparel's ads were highly criticized by advertising watchdogs during the reign of CEO and founder Dov Charney. He used underage girls, put them in sexually suggestive positions and photographed them himself. Some of these girls and some employees sued AA for molestation. Charney's ad campaigns were banned in some countries by advertising watchdogs due to indecency. The campaign with Brendan Jordan was conceived after Charney was made to leave the company, under the supervision of CEO Paula Schneider. Schneider reportedly wanted to tone down the overtly sexualized imagery of the brand, but insisted that she wanted to stay true to the original image by keeping it sexy and edgy. Brendan Jordan was a boy whom the brand gave a voice to, being able to come out of the closet through the campaign, she said in an interview with the *Independent* (Akbeiran, 2015).

The problem here is not the sexual orientation or activity of teenagers but rather the ethical implications. Is it ethically viable to exploit their sexuality for the purpose of fashion advertising whilst being underage? They are not allowed to buy alcohol in some countries, yet a fashion company is allowed to use them in a very vulnerable way and expose their sexuality to the rest of the world, in exchange for sales and profit increase. The repercussions for the teen from social media, bullying and peers might be difficult to handle, as it is often a mix of praise and hate. How much will the brand protect the exposed and vulnerable teen after the campaign is finished whilst the individual has to continue dealing with social media issues?

These examples clearly show that advertising does not simply reflect changes in society but has its own influence on it. Because ads sell a dream and an enhanced or sometimes warped reality, gender is constructed within this "commercial reality", developing its very own meaning, which in turn influences society. And as soon as the imagery in advertising becomes visible to a large number of people, it can create a reaction and shape roles. If the imagery is viewed by consenting adults, they could arguably make an informed decision about the content. However, when the most vulnerable members of society see them, namely children and teens, great harm can be done. Studies by psychologists and psychiatrists have shown negative impacts on sexual behaviour, aggression, eating disorders in children and adolescents because they imitate (consciously and unconsciously) the role models presented to them, inhibiting their own healthy development. They engage in sexual actions and orientations before they are psychologically and emotionally ready, which can leave them in an unhealthy state for the rest of their lives (Villani, 2001).

Figure 10.3 Steetshot of a young child reading a magazine and being exposed to advertising, such as an age-inappropriate ad for beer on the back cover. With kind permission from Iona Mitterfellner.

Case example: shock advertising and the Benetton case

Shock advertising is advertising that "deliberately, rather than inadvertently, startles and offends its audience by violating norms for social values and personal ideals". It relies on so-called shock tactics to get a message across by using offensive and graphic imagery – sometimes in combination with copy – all serving to put the recipients in a state of disturbed shock, fear or repulsion, gaining immediate attention. Oftentimes, the imagery is full of cultural, religious, political or sexual taboos, loudly showing the sort of things that nobody wants to hear or see – yet it is inescapable due to being placed in the public sphere.

The origin of the terminology "shock advertising" is often attributed to the late 1980s and early 1990s due to Benetton's shocking fashion advertising imagery. The ads were criticized in many countries, and in Germany had to go through court, which decided that it is indeed possible to use shock advertising in public. The photographer Oliviero Toscani was the mastermind behind the ads, and his unique philosophy shaped the imagery. He showed a duck drenched in oil to make a point about human pollution of nature and the suffering of innocent animals; he showed David Kirby with AIDS on his deathbed; he showed child labour in a Third World country; he showed the blood-stained uniform of a fallen soldier from ex-Yugoslavia; he showed a newborn baby covered in all the natural vernix and blood, with the umbilical cord still attached; he played with religion, race, colour and ethnicities.

The images were criticized for deliberately manipulating people's emotions, exploiting human (and animal) misery for purely financial gain and for being indecent. However, for instance, in Germany the ads were permitted by court on the grounds of the freedom of expression and the freedom of the press. From then on, shock advertising was deemed permissible, as long as it does not offend human dignity (the depicted person is not ridiculed, mocked or humiliated).

As shock advertising became fashionable and legal, other companies followed suit, most notably Diesel, Calvin Klein, FCUK and The Body Shop, but also charities, non-profit organizations and human-rights activists in order to raise awareness.

One example of a highly controversial print advertisement is Barnardo's "Child poverty campaign" (2003) advertisement which was banned by the Advertising Standards Authority after receiving 330 complaints. The ad showed a baby with a seemingly live and large cockroach crawling out of its mouth, "which is seen as a metaphorical reference to the destitution of many children" (Noel, 2010).

Barnardo's apologized about the campaign.

If you were personally distressed or offended by the images then we apologize. Having said that, we feel it is our duty to ensure the issue of child poverty in this country is no longer neglected and that is the reason we have run such a hard-hitting campaign.

(Cozens, 2003)

The question here (and in most advertisements) is a purely ethical one: Is it worth disgusting the public with "hard-hitting" images to get attention, even if it is for a good cause? Is the good cause worth the harm its imagery causes in society? And can attention be obtained in a more responsible way?

Ill bodies and minds

Can fashion shock advertising support a good cause, too?

Fashion together has created a monster of self-doubt, a warped self-perception, eating disorders such as anorexia or bulimia, and a myriad of psychological issues. With the help of Oliviero Toscani, a fashion campaign tried to provide an antidote to the harm that it has caused.

Because Toscani is an artist, hhe believes that taboos should be broken, whether it is in art or in a fashion magazine. He wants to provoke people and test where the limits are. In an interview, he recalled his collaboration with Benetton, stating that most managers and decision-makers were offended or embarrassed but ultimately granted him freedom as an artist. Regarding anorexia, he said:

I'm interested in anorexia. It's about wanting to disappear, to become invisible, not wanting to be dependent. There are so many interesting implications in that illness. Initially, I did a short film on anorexia and, later on, I started to do portraits with anorexic people. At a certain point a clothing company contacted me.

Toscani shot a campaign in collaboration with the fashion brand Nolita, using Isabelle Caro, a sickly anorexic model, in order to raise awareness about the illness. The model made it her life's mission to raise awareness about her illness, which caused her to pass on at a very young age, and agreed to be part of ads. In the campaign, she was depicted nude with the words "No Anorexia" and the brand's logo. But when they put up billboards in Rome and Milan, it caused an outrage and the Institute for Advertising Self-Regulation (IAP) banned the campaign.

Toscani's work stands in contrast to the lawsuits that were filed against fast food chains, which have led to obesity in children and adults due to their high-fat, highly-processed and high-calorie menus, the dangers of which had been downplayed or omitted in ads. But both extremes of eating-related health issues are powered by advertising, whether it be through fashionable images of size zero models or all-you-can-eat menus.

Interview with Jean Kilbourne

Jean Kilbourne is internationally recognized for her ground-breaking work on the image of women in advertising and for her critical studies of alcohol and tobacco advertising. In the late 1960s, she began her exploration of the connection between advertising and several public health issues, including violence against women, eating disorders and addiction, and launched a movement to promote media literacy as a way to prevent these problems.

Figure 10.4 Jean Kilbourne.

A radical and original idea at the time, this approach is now mainstream and an integral part of most prevention programmes.

> Q: Fashion advertising and media communication in general show perfection: beautiful models, beautiful clothes, beautiful settings – a dream landscape. It includes women, men and children. How do you perceive the dream which is pushed on us by the fashion and advertising industry?

> JK: There is research that it is harmful, that it affects self-esteem. It's particularly damaging to women because, although men are objectified more than they used to be, there still isn't that kind of pressure on men to look a certain way, whereas for women there is. The advent of Photoshop has changed everything, as has the Internet, because now women and girls do this to ourselves. We put images out there, so the pressure is even more intense and more damaging, I would argue, than even in the past.

Many people feel that advertising is trivial and that therefore it doesn't really matter. My argument has always been that it is not trivial, that it affects us in fact very deeply and, in many ways, very negatively. I was the first one to speak about this way back in the late 1960s. I made the film *Killing Us Softly: Advertising's Image of Women* in 1979. Since then I have remade the movie three times, with the latest version being in 2010. I have been updating it all along and it is very widely used all around the world.

> Q: You have probably seen the most recent fashion imagery that shows imperfection. Fashion brands are using models who have a variety of body types, might have disabilities, pigmentation deviations, etc. Brands are selling it under the flag of being socially inclusive. Do you think fashion advertising has to demonstrate social exclusion in order to remain aspirational?

> JK: Two things: I think it is very important for ads to show a wide range of body types of women, because at the moment, there basically is still only one body type considered desirable. Even the "plus-size" models are still thinner than the average American woman. I think showing a wide range of bodies and colours is important and would make a difference.

I also think that most advertisers, of course, are doing this for public relations. They're doing this to demonstrate to their consumers that they are hip and open-minded, so I don't think necessarily that they are doing this out of the goodness of their hearts.

But I don't care because what's important is that we see a wide range of what's considered beautiful because up until now we've just had this one definition and it excludes most women and really does have an effect on how women and girls feel about ourselves. I think that it is the push to have advertising be more diverse, more inclusive, more representative of real people that is good.

It seems to me that people in the fashion industry would be interested in working with a variety of body types rather than to be stuck with such limited images. It is also an exciting opportunity for students to have a broader palette to work with.

Q: A really important topic: Children. Advertising has been for a long time and still is using children. It is sexualizing them, showing them in inappropriate settings. What is your take on using children in fashion campaigns, such as the controversial one by American Apparel, which used Brendan Jordan, a self-proclaimed transgender child (15 years old at the time of the campaign), in its campaign? What should the future advertising industry think about sexualizing children? What is your view on this?

JK: I talked about the sexualization of children in the original version of *Killing Us Softly* back in 1979 and I wrote a book about it called *So Sexy So Soon*. So I think this is a very big problem. For the most part I am not in favour of legislation and that sort of thing, but I think there should be tremendous pressure on advertisers not to do this, not to sexualize children, and there could be legal guidelines. But mostly, change will happen because of public pressure, through consumers protesting. Of course, this doesn't happen until enough people realize that this is a very bad thing to be doing.

People have to see it, take it seriously and realize that this is damaging to children. And the research is very clear that this is indeed damaging to children. On my website there is a resource list that includes an American Psychological Association report on the sexualization of girls in advertising and the harm that it does. Different countries have different regulations. In the United States it is extremely difficult to put any limitations on advertising due to free speech and treating corporations like people, etc., but in other countries it is more possible.

I think this is one of the most serious issues in advertising. What happens when children are sexualized? For one thing, sexualizing children is normalized, which encourages paedophilia and also encourages people to blame the victim. A few years ago, a little girl was sexually assaulted, and a judge here in the United States said that she was seductive. She was five years old. Sexualizing children also damages children because it encourages them to think of themselves as objects, which does an enormous amount of harm.

This issue is one of the most serious in fashion advertising. There needs to be a multi-pronged approach, including consumer education, guidelines insofar as they are possible, some legislation and, in general, many people saying, "This is not okay, this has got to stop".

Q: Let's talk about "shock advertising", which first entered the fashion scene with Oliviero Toscani's controversial campaigns for Benetton. On the one hand, he was really ahead of his time in terms of inclusivity – black and white and Asian models – he put everyone together. But at the same time, he was using very sensitive imagery, shocking things to sell multi-coloured sweaters.

JK: And that is the problem, really. The problem is not the images themselves, as they are often images we probably should see and should be aware of, but it is when they are attached to buying stuff. What does this have to do with each other, a dying AIDS patient with – like you said – multi-coloured sweaters? This to me just trivializes the whole issue and exploits our emotions in order to sell us something. It's not the images – it's the use of them in the service of selling us stuff that is the problem. If these images were used to solicit donations to charities or something like that, that would be a different thing, but this is trivializing, it's exploitive and ultimately it also can desensitize us to these issues. If we are surrounded by these images being used to sell us something, we can get used to them and they cease to shock and that becomes a problem.

Have you heard of the expression "compassion fatigue"? It's what happens as people are overwhelmed by images and then feel numb about them. It can happen not just with advertising but in general. When we harden our hearts to these realities, it is dangerous to our society.

Q: The visual communication of fashion advertising often shows weird, strange and bizarre images of women and sometimes men, with violence (like the highly sexual and controversial D&G ad from 2007, with four men standing over a woman on the ground) or chopped-up body parts. What do you think about ads where women are reduced to a few chopped-up body parts in ads, with no face, no voice and no power, withdrawn?

JK: Often these images are violent and that, of course, is a big problem. Using violent images like this, especially when violence is eroticized and made sexy, does a huge amount of harm. It normalizes violence against women, it perpetuates stereotypes and it also makes it more likely that people will blame the victim.

Q: My last question is about the future of fashion marketing professionals. They will be selling fashion, they might be creating ad campaigns, they will be in marketing and working with brands. Is there any message that you would like to convey to them? How can they make sure that they are doing their job, perhaps under pressure to meet certain business targets, but at the same time think about ethical issues, ensure their ethical integrity and have a clear conscience? What would you recommend to them?

JK: One thing that I recommend is that they find allies, that they find other people who share their wish to be ethical, because it's difficult to do this alone. This is why the 3% Project has been so important – because women and men in advertising agencies got together and said, "We don't want to do this anymore". So that is one thing. Also, having allies and being in groups like this can help refine one's own opinions.

Secondly, these issues should be brought up in fashion schools, in business schools, and there should be a strong ethical component in all schools where these questions are raised. I've often told my audiences: "Ask yourself these questions before you have a mortgage. Think about what you want to do before you are locked into a job where you can't afford to rock the boat". So raise these issues early on.

Back in the day when advertisers, or at least the ones with power, were almost entirely male, I would say things like "Put your mother's face, your daughter's face, your sister's face, your wife's face into this ad. How do you feel about that?" Now there are more women with power in the field (although still not enough!) but it is still important to ask oneself, "How would you feel if this was *your* daughter, *your* son?" Make it human, make it real and make it personal.

When I've addressed advertising audiences, I have often said, if the only way you can sell the product is to exploit and diminish people, what does that say about your product? It's important to think about what it is exactly that you are selling. In fashion, one thing that could happen that would be very good is not just a bigger range of models but a bigger range of fashion for different body types. Because at the moment fashion is designed for women who are very tall and thin and narrow. Let's redesign fashion to make all women and men feel more attractive. This opens the door to more creative possibilities for the fashion industry and for students.

Regulatory bodies

Advertising has come a long way since its early days, both in terms of regulations that limit it and social norms that it has pushed away. It is important to understand that brands and the forceful advertising industry do not have complete control over the messages they spread. Individuals have the right to complain, and there are many reasons why the authorities might take a complaint seriously and recall an ad. Advertising is viewed by different people, including children, and those people come from various ethnicities and religions with a wide range of sensitivity or tolerance towards advertising content. For the benefit of society, not everything can be shown openly.

Ads are often recalled for inappropriate content, the sexualization of children, the degradation of women, sexism and racism, indecency, and lies or false advertising. In the fashion industry, the latter often occurs when women are excessively photoshopped in order to promote a beauty product.

Who steps in, and what can be done?

First and foremost, there are laws which prohibit unlawful and illegal advertising. However, many ads can pass legal constraints but are nevertheless harmful to society, so in this case advertising watchdogs step in. For instance, in Europe, the European Advertising Standards Alliance (EASA) is the coordination point for the views of national advertising self-regulatory organizations throughout Europe. Under its umbrella, there are regulatory bodies for each country:

Austria – Österreichischer Werberat
Belgium – Jury d'Ethique Publicitaire
Czech Republic – Rada Pro Reklamu (RPR)
Denmark – ReklameForum
Finland – Liiketapalautakunta (LTL)
France – Bureau de Vérification de la Publicité (BVP)
Germany – Deutscher Werberat (DW)

Germany – Zentrale zur Bekämpfung unlauteren Wettbewerbs
Greece – Enossi Diafimistikon Etairion Ellados (EDEE)
Hungary – Önszabályozó Reklám Testület
Ireland – Advertising Standards Authority for Ireland (ASAI)
Italy – Istituto dell'Autodisciplina Pubblicitaria (IAP)
Lithuania – Lithuanian Advertising Bureau
Netherlands – Stichting Reclame Code (SRC)
Poland – Rada Reklamy (RR)
Portugal – Instituto Civil da Autodisciplina da Publicidade (ICAP)
Slovakia – Rada Pre Reklamu (RPR)
Slovenia – Slovenska Oglasevalska Zbornica (SOZ)
Switzerland – Commission   Suisse   pour   la   Loyauté / Schweizerische
        Lauterkeitskommission (CSL/SLK)
United Kingdom – Advertising Standards Authority (ASA)

The ASA in the UK, for example, takes action to protect consumers when complaints are made by businesses and individuals to ban ads which are misleading, harmful, offensive or irresponsible. In 2023 alone, the ASA received 39,034 complaints relating to just under 25,041 ads and a further 5,425 cases on its own initiative, with a total of 27,378 ads being either changed or removed (ASA, 2024). In relation to the topics raised in this chapter, the ASA held two round tables in 2023 to further examine potential harm arising from the use of digitally altered images in ads. One of the round tables was facilitated by a children's charity, to hear young people's own experiences and observations on the impact of digitally enhanced images in ads on body image. The ASA also took action against ads that trivialised the decision to have cosmetic surgery overseas, pressured consumers and omitted material information about pre-consultations and where they would take place.(ASA, 2024)

Sensory overload: ads are all-present

Rarely do fashion brands choose to opt out of advertising. Zara, the top fast fashion retailer, reportedly only spends 3 per cent of its revenue on advertising. So, how can Zara remain successful without ads? The retailer has a completely different strategy, which builds on the artificial limitation of goods, prime retail locations and beautiful interiors. Since Zara copies luxury fashion brands that extensively advertise, one can assume that Zara reaps the benefits by selling knock-off versions of the original garments at a fraction of the price. However, consumers will not feel bombarded by advertising from Zara, as they would from many other brands which surround us with an unhealthy amount of information, attacking our senses.

Raimund (2008) notes that the 10 Commandments only contain 279 words. Castro and Lewis (2011) add that Lincoln's Gettysburg Address contains only 266 words. Yet on a daily basis we are bombarded with thousands of advertising messages everywhere in public and equally in our private lives. Not only does this give room for psychological harm, which was discussed in this chapter, it also can have a direct negative effect on our well-being through the sheer volume of unnecessary information. Sensory overload is a term which is now well known and used by psychologists and doctors as a condition which leads to negative physical as well as psychological states such as increased heart rate, blood pressure and breathing; and anxiety, confusion, distress, aggression, sadness, agitation or erratic behaviour to the point of mental breakdowns, neurological problems and even seizures (in people with predispositions such as neurodivergency , these occurrences are even more likely to happen). In terms of marketing, when brands compete with each other to attract and reach the customer, they are either causing sensory harm through overload or, even worse, the consumer becomes indifferent to the multitude of messages, which is a psychological way of protecting oneself, rendering the marketing messages ineffective to a certain degree.

The question arises whether this bombardment by marketing and advertising signals is something we should accept or something we should amend. What would the streets of a city look like if suddenly there were no advertisements? How would people find out about products or trends? There are a few places which choose to amend the amount of sensory stimulation for the benefit of the people or due to political ideology.

Case example: ad-free places – Grenoble, São Paulo and North Korea

In some cases, governments and the mayors of cities step in to regulate advertising. Grenoble, France, and São Paulo, Brazil, have banned outdoor advertising for the benefit of their populations, and there have already been positive reactions from both inhabitants of the cities and business owners.

In São Paulo, a city of more than 11 million inhabitants, one can walk down the streets without being bombarded by advertising messages. In 2006, São Paulo's populist mayor, Gilberto Kassab, passed the "Clean City Law", outlawing the use of all outdoor advertisements, including on billboards, transit and in front of stores. A total of 15,000 outdoor ad spaces were taken down, being classified as "visual pollution" (Da Silva, 2020).

Figure 10.5 São Paulo, Brazil, by night without any billboards or notable ads, 2016. Image source: Pixabay by Zabarov.

This was not done without some hesitation, as local businesses and citizens feared that the ban would cause a revenue loss of $133 million and 20,000 job losses. However, since then São Paulo has been thriving with 70 per cent of city dwellers being in favour of the ban (Curtis, 2011) (Figure 10.5).

In Grenoble, France, Eric Piolle, the mayor of the city since 2014, is not only dreaming of a green and sustainable city of the future, he has also taken action against visual pollution. The city chose not to renew its advertising contract with giant JCDecaux, instead removing 326 billboards (Dejean, 2014) Under Piolle, Grenoble's green government cited that up to three-quarters of people in France think advertising has become invasive and that they must "put an end to this hyper-consumerism, where citizens are no longer viewed as people but as consumers" (Bamat, 2015) (Figure 10.6). Over the years, the city has become renowned for its progressive approach to sustainability and innovations, and has been named European Green Capital 2022 by the European Commission.

North Korea is an almost "ad-free" environment due to communist politics. The only types of advertising which are allowed are political propaganda (Figure 10.7).

Architect Philipp Meuser edited the first-ever architectural guide on Pyongyang in 2011. He shares his views on the ad-free streets:

Figure 10.6 Grenoble, France, is a city that has banned most outdoor advertising. Image source: Pixabay.

In those countries which are underpinned by a Communist system, architecture and urban planning can be experienced in unadulterated form – there are no advertising signs nor garish, neon-lit billboards. We are seeing design and construction carried out under laboratory conditions. No matter how fascinating such an untarnished city may be from the architectural standpoint, its very nakedness reveals a state which could scarcely be more totalitarian. Where there is no advertising there is no competition either. Billboards are replaced by propaganda posters which have been hand-painted and indeed call for considerable artistic expertise. Although very nice to look at, their content is anything but amusing, eg 'Our ideology, our fighting spirit, our way of life – let everything be as our forefathers decreed!', or 'A strong country – let us restore the glorious past of our forefathers!' These are calls-to-arms which in other countries would be attributed to radical political parties. And yet, because the streets are so densely hung with such morale-boosting slogans – in a similar manner to advertising signage in the West – we can only surmise and indeed hope that they scarcely register with the people fleetingly rushing past them.

(Meuser, 2012)

Figure 10.7 Pyongyang, North Korea. The sign reads: white words, "ideology / fight spirit / life style"; blue words, "all about above, we will follow Kim Jeongeun". Image credit: © Philipp Meuser. Image kindly provided by Philipp Meuser of DOM-Publishers, from the book *Pyongyang. Architectural and Cultural Guide* (2012).

Is there really no advertising in North Korea? "For the past decade or so the only evidence of advertising in Pyongyang had been the handful of billboards for Pyonghwa Motors, which borrow popular slogans from state propaganda campaigns" (Abrahamian, 2016).

But the country seems to be slowly awakening to the new discipline of consumerism, which they understand as propaganda for consumer products.

Interview with Evgeniya Sabelnikova

Evgeniya Sabelnikova (Евгения Сабельникова) was a famous Russian movie star in the 1970s and 1980s at the country's largest film studios, including Mosfilm, starring in more than 23 films and being the voice actress for many

Figure 10.8 Photo of Russian actress Evgeniya Sabelnikova in the 1970s.

more. She was also a model at Dom Modeley, the most famous fashion house of the former USSR.

Q: In the USSR, a country under communist rule, how was political propaganda perceived by the people?

ES: It was either not noticed at all or, if it was, then perceived with light and habitual repulsion. If it was written stupidly, people would laugh on the inside, but it was uncommon to do it publicly. The communist propaganda was like a restaurant which always serves bad food without fail. But in the 1970s, when the regime was not as strict as it was under Stalin, young people began to mock it verbally.

Q: Was there any advertising for consumer products?

ES: None on TV, none on the radio, none in the printed media. Zero in journals. There were very rare billboard ads: "Fly Aeroflot!" a poster would proclaim. But when Aeroflot is the only state airline in the entire country, what else would you fly with? And people used to joke about such ads. There were a few advertisements for holidays in Crimea or Sochi, sort of emulating other countries, but again, where else were people going to go on holiday but there?

But there was a magazine called *Rabotnica* [Работница], a journal for the interests of working women, founded in 1914, which had editorials with illustrations and photos of what to wear and what was fashionable at the moment. It also reported about the Soviet factories which were sewing the clothes, but everyone knew that they were awful!

Q: Apart from the journal, how did people know what was fashionable?

ES: There were three or four unofficial and unmentionable methods to find out. First, there were political TV shows – in the style of a documentary – reporting on the terrible life of people in capitalist countries with much critique and a political agenda. They showed thriving capitalist countries such as France, England and the USA, and there were 3- to 5-minute sequences showing the poor people who were suffering from capitalism, such as the unemployed on the streets of New York, etc. and everyone, especially women, watched the show. "Look at this jacket that unemployed guy is wearing on the street in New York! That is a nice jacket!" someone would exclaim. Or: "There, the women in the background in Paris – see the dress, see the cut? We can make this". Women watched the shows to find

Figure 10.9 From the personal archive of Evgeniya Sabelnikova: High-school ball in the 1960s, group photo, St Petersburg, Russia. The clothing would have been either purchased in stores or hand-made following the latest fashion trends, such as those found in the national magazine *Rabotnica*, which also supplied fashion patterns.

out what's in fashion and then they would copy the styles and sew them at home. Then one day, suddenly the journal *Burda* was available in a very limited number of copies. It was worth gold! If you had this magazine you were a queen! Not only did you get the images of what was in fashion but also the patterns to sew. And we had wonderful fabrics in stores, in abundance and not expensive. So women bought the fabrics and sewed themselves. This *Burda* became very popular. Another method was through friends, those rare people who got to go abroad and brought back mail-order catalogues. The catalogues were either resold for a very high price or kept at home where friends could come to visit and flip through the magazine the whole day long if they wished. There was not just fashion but interiors, too.

Q: You worked as a model in the famous Moscow Fashion House, the "Dom Modeley" [Общесоюзный дом моделей одежды (ОДМО)]. Can you tell a bit more about it?

Figure 10.10 From the personal archive of Evgeniya Sabelnikova: High-school ball in the 1960s, individual photo, St Petersburg, Russia.

ES: Yes, these were the centres of the USSR's fashion, in St Petersburg and Moscow only. It was Russia's way of competing with global fashion, of having something similar to the catwalk shows abroad, to show that we were as creative and prosperous as the capitalist countries. Often, foreigners would be invited to the catwalk presentations to see how beautiful our women were and how well they were dressed. Like in the West, normal people could not get in to see the shows. Other attendants were the political elite and the top elite from show business like actors, singers, etc. They were allowed to come and watch the shows but needed a special permit to order clothes. The clothes were great designs by very talented designers like Slava Zaitsev, who was the top couturier in the 1970s and is now world famous. But the communist party members were not allowed to purchase the clothes and had to come in the typical suits that were appropriate for political figures.

Further reading

ASA (2024) Annual Report 2023: Building our world-leading AI capability. Available at: https://www.asa.org.uk/news/annual-report-2023.html

Carter, C. and Steiner, L. (2004) *Critical Readings: Media and Gender.* Maidenhead: Open University Press (McGraw-Hill Education).

Chomsky, N. (1998) *Profit Over People: Neoliberalism and the Global Order.* New York: Seven Stories Press.

Cortese, A. J. (1999) *Provocateur: Images of Women and Minorities in Advertising.* Boston: Rowman & Littlefield.

Cull, N. J., Holbrook Culbert, D. and Welch, D. (2003) *Propaganda and Mass Persuasion: A Historical Encyclopedia, 1500 to the Present.* Santa Barbara: ABC-Clio Inc.

Ellis, N., Fitchett, J., Higgins, M., Jack, G., Lim, M., Saren, M. and Tadajewski, M. (2011) *Marketing: A Critical Textbook.* London: Sage Publications.

Goffman, E. (1976) *Gender Advertisements.* New York: Harper Torchbooks.

Hlynsky, D. and Langford, M. (2015) *Window-Shopping through the Iron Curtain.* London: Thames & Hudson.

Kelso, T. (2018) *The Social Impact of Advertising: Confessions of an (Ex-)Advertising Man.* Lanham, MD: Rowman & Littlefield Publishers.

Kilbourne, J. (1999) *Can't Buy ME Love: How Advertising Changes the Way We Think and Feel.* New York: Touchstone.

Klein, N. (2010) *No Logo.* 10th anniversary edn. London: Fourth Estate.

Levine, D. L. and Kilbourne, J. (2009) *So Sexy So Soon.* New York: Ballantine Books Inc.

Meuser, P. (ed.) (2012) *Architectural and Cultural Guide Pyongyang.* Berlin: DOM Publishers.

Miles, S. (1998) *Consumerism: As a Way of Life.* Thousand Oaks, CA: SAGE Publications.

Sheehan, K. (2013) *Controversies in Contemporary Advertising.* 2nd edn. Thousand Oaks, CA: SAGE Publications.

Taflinger, R. F. (2011) *Advantage: Consumer Psychology and Advertising.* 1st edn. Dubuque, IA: Kendall Hunt.

The United Nations of Photography. In Coversation: Oliviero Toscani. Available at: https://unitednationsofphotography.com/2016/01/25/in-conversation-oliviero-toscani/

Williamson, J. (1978) *Decoding Advertisements: Ideology and Meaning in Advertising.* London: Marion Boyars.

Winship, J. (1987) *Inside Womens's Magazines.* London: Pandora.

Sustainability and marketing

11

Chapter topics

What do we mean by sustainability?

In order to understand what fashion companies do wrong and how the ideal industrialized world should look, it is important to remind oneself of what "sustainability" actually means. Arguably, by now, most people have an instant understanding of something being unsustainable and likely think of overproduction, post-consumer textile waste, poisonous chemicals in clothing and Third World labour in dire conditions. Sustainability is also often equated

DOI: 10.4324/9781003449157-11

to ethics. If something is sustainable, it is also naturally ethical, but definitions of what ethical fashion specifically means can vary substantially so that the term can be applied incorrectly and used as part of public relations to greenwash consumers.

Sustainability is equally a much broader subject that encompasses aspects which a fashion consumer might not be immediately aware of. According to McGill University and the University of Alberta, there are three pillars of sustainability which summarize these important aspects.

1. Environmental sustainability: Ecological integrity is maintained, and all of Earth's environmental systems are kept in balance, while natural resources within them are consumed by humans at a rate where they are able to replenish themselves.
2. Economic sustainability: Human communities across the globe are able to maintain their independence and have access to the resources that they require, financial and otherwise, to meet their needs. Economic systems are intact, and activities are available to everyone, such as secure sources of livelihood.
3. Social sustainability: Universal human rights and basic necessities are attainable by all people, who have access to enough resources to keep their families and communities healthy and secure. Healthy communities have just leaders who ensure personal, labour and cultural rights are respected, and all people are protected from discrimination.

One of the main frameworks that underpin the understanding of sustainability is the Brundtland Report (WCED, 1987 in Ravago et al., 2015), which is credited with establishing sustainability as a critical part of economic development policy. Based on a notion that the United Nations issued in 1987, it defined sustainability as "development that meets the needs of the present without compromising the ability of future generations to meet their own needs".

Understanding the three pillars of sustainability as one theory model, they can now be applied to fashion businesses to highlight the many aspects that are unsustainable. For instance, environmental systems are not respected during raw-material procurement, production, shipping as well as consumption; and workers throughout the supply chain are exploited and unable to access health care, security or even basic financial remuneration to ensure livelihood. Furthermore, there is overproduction and pre-consumer waste at the factory level, as well as post-consumer waste when individuals discard fashion items. The origins of problems in the modern fashion industry can be traced back to the industrial revolution, which artificially increased production and with it the consumption of its many goods.

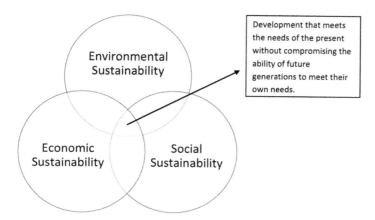

Development that meets the needs of the present without compromising the ability of future generations to meet their own needs.

Environmental Sustainability

Economic Sustainability

Social Sustainability

Figure 11.1 Adaptation of the Brundtland Report. The three pillars (3Ps) ultimately support the notion of what the United Nations issued in 1987 and what the Brundtland Report reiterated: "Sustainable development is development that meets the needs of the present without compromising the ability of future generations to meet their own needs" (WCED, 1987 in Ravago et al., 2015).

To quote McDonough and Braungart (2001, p. 142), products designed and made according to the principles of the industrial revolution

> put billions of pounds of toxic material into the air, water and soil every year; measure prosperity by activity, not legacy; require thousands of complex regulations to keep people and natural systems from being poisoned too quickly; produce materials so dangerous that they will require constant vigilance from future generations; result in enormous amounts of waste; place valuable materials in holes all over the planet, where they can never be retrieved and erode the diversity of biological species and cultural practices.

Certainly, with the ultra-fast supply chain and mass production in Third World countries, which enables the sale of clothing at very low prices, there is very little scope for sustainability. The constant demand for low-price clothing means that brands manufacture high volumes of garments, including synthetic petroleum-based garments (often polyester and nylon) in developing countries. This creates elevated levels of greenhouse gases (GHGs) and landfill waste with synthetic fabrics which are non-biodegradable and difficult to break down into raw components. Planned obsolescence is embedded into the life cycle of these garments, which is linear and not cyclical. This means that the end-of-life status of such a fast-fashion garment will be landfill, with no option for longevity through the quality of the textiles, repair or reuse built in. The goal is to sell large quantities of clothing frequently at an affordable price without considering the environmental impact, and recycling efforts by brands are often ineffective (Wren, 2022).

Addressing the consumers, in 2017 Greenpeace stated that in order to break our fast-fashion addiction, we have to embrace "true materialism". The group is referring to a book by Kate Fletcher, *Craft of Use*, which describes true materialism as "a switch from an idea of a consumer society where materials matter little, to a truly material society, where materials—and the world they rely on—are cherished". This means treasuring the materials we possess, not discarding them, and curbing new purchases. However, this cannot become the burden of the consumer alone but rather requires an ethical code of practice by the manufacturers, distributors and marketers of material goods, which the consumer can partake in.

Luxury and sustainability

It would then logically seem that luxury brands that use textiles of superior quality and produce timeless designs would be free of this problem. However, luxury fashion has its problems, too, but they are frequently ignored or untold because they would taint the perfect image. In fact, the recently launched BoF Sustainability Index (Kent, 2021) rated luxury conglomerates such as LVMH, Kering and Richemont similarly to fast-fashion brands in the components of transparency, emissions, water and chemicals, materials, workers' rights and waste. BoF's rating was most unfavourable.

This rating is despite a "robust sustainability strategy" which luxury conglomerate Kering has been implementing. In an interview in Jing Daily (2005), Marie-Claire Daveu, the chief sustainability officer and head of international institutional affairs for Kering, said:

> [Y]ou just need to look at our raw materials to understand our reliance on nature; cotton, silk, leather, cashmere, wool, and so on. As for our manufacturing processes, they depend on water and energy, amongst other resources. At Kering, like the entire fashion industry itself, our supply chains are complex and often stretch across multiple countries around the world. What we must also take into account is that the livelihoods of people and communities living in these regions rely on our supply chains. Running your supply chain in a resilient manner, which protects the environment, supports people, economic development and business growth, is no longer a luxury – it is a necessity. In our rapidly evolving and volatile world, a robust sustainability strategy can provide your business with the focus, knowledge, and solutions necessary to

address and adapt to the said resource constraints, to the changing needs of consumers, and to other unprecedented events.

(Flora, 2015)

For this purpose, Kering publishes the EP&L, or "environmental profit and loss", report.

Arguably, transparency might be the most important disclosure that a fashion business should aim to achieve. Transparency can include information about absolutely all sustainability aspects and would fully explain where luxury materials, such as cotton, linen, silk, leather, including exotic animal and fish skins, cashmere, sheep's wool, guanaco or vicuna wool, fur, lotus flower silk, shahtoosh and so on, are sourced and what the process from origin to shop floor entails. Ideally, there should also be an end-of-life provision, whether it is repairing, recycling or reselling.

However, in terms of transparency, BoF laments that Kering and Richemont did not publish a supplier list for any of their brands, although Kering claims that it can trace 88% of its materials back to at least the country level. Transparency would include the names of raw material farmers and yarn and textile producers; and those involved in textile embellishing and processing; tanning, dyeing and printing; as well as cutting, sewing and assembling. Sadly, there are only a handful of luxury fashion brands that can truly call themselves sustainable and transparent, while most other brands have serious issues. The well-known premium and luxury brands which are doing quite well include Stella McCartney, Loro Piana, Brunello Cucinelli, LOEWE, Marine Serre, Deploy, Patagonia and Pangaia. They might have achieved certifications by various bodies and organizations to verify their sustainable measures (i.e. Higg or B Corp) and disclose all relevant aspects of their business to the public.

Case example: LOEWE

LOEWE is a luxury fashion brand that has embedded sustainable practices into its business model, creating value for employees, stakeholders, animals and nature.

Originally, this brand dates back to 1846 when it was a cooperative of leather craftsmen and artisans based in Madrid, Spain. This makes LOEWE one of the oldest luxury fashion brands and it holds a royal warrant, granted as the Supplier to the Royal Court in 1905.

Since 1996, LOEWE has been under the ownership of the French luxury conglomerate LVMH, and in 2013, LOEWE appointed J.W. Anderson as its creative director. Under this new directive, LOEWE put measures in place to ensure sustainability and continuity.

LOEWE is known for its remarkable high-quality leather goods such as bags and accessories, which is due to the quality of Spain's lambskin. Lambs bred in the Cordero Entrefino region, high in the Spanish Pyrenees, produce incomparably soft and supple leather. To preserve this exceptional savoir faire and at the same time minimize the environmental impact of producing these skins, LOEWE works closely with its supply chain.

Since LOEWE stopped using exotic skins, it relies on the local lamb population for its skin as well as fur. The brand helps tanners enhance their environmental management, sharing best practices and carrying out audits and inspections to ensure the quality remains intact from the pastures to the tanneries. "The … lambskin materials that come out of these tanneries thus have a reduced environmental impact" (LOEWE , n.d.).

This falls in line with environmental improvement and worker safety as well as water and energy use at the tanneries. According to LOEWE, it works with

> high quality, low impact materials that are sourced and produced with our planet in mind. Factors such as traceability of origin, fair conditions for farmers, animal welfare and the protection of biodiversity closely inform the way we approach and procure raw materials.

These raw materials come from tanneries that are certified by an international organization called the Leather Working Group, which was founded in 2005 on a membership basis. It helps with responsible leather sourcing across the supply chain (LWG, 2023) and evaluates the environmental compliance and performance of the leather industry. LOEWE equally experiments with upcycled and recycled fabrics, organic cotton and other low-impact materials.

LOEWE takes care of local societal needs by training youth and investing in their future. This covers education, workforce skills and the community's economic development. LOEWE inaugurated the LOEWE School of Leather Craft (la Escuela Marroquinera de Loewe), which is located at its factory in Madrid. It equips a new generation of artisans and trainees with the particular craftsmanship which the luxury house has developed over 160 years. LOEWE ensures the hiring of skilled artisans, especially those trained at its school, to keep 75 per cent of production in-house. LOEWE, 2023)

Furthermore, LOEWE has invested in the preservation and celebration of cultural capital by establishing the LOEWE Foundation. One of the primary purposes of the foundation is to support design and craftsmanship.

The LOEWE Foundation was established as a private cultural foundation in 1988 by Enrique Loewe Lynch, a fourth-generation member of LOEWE's founding family. Today, under the direction of his daughter Sheila Loewe, the foundation continues to promote creativity, support educational programmes and safeguard heritage in the fields of poetry, dance, photography, art and craft. The foundation was awarded the Gold Medal for Merit in the Fine Arts, the highest honour granted by the Spanish government, in 2002.

Within the foundation, individual artisans and groups are invited to apply for an annual LOEWE Craft Prize, which offers a cash prize (€50,000 in 2023) and, of course, promotion through the LOEWE channels. The applicants must demonstrate their prowess in the applied arts such as ceramics, enamelwork, jewellery, lacquer, metal, furniture, leather, textiles, glass, paper, wood, bookbinding, weaving and many more which they make by hand. Their creations must demonstrate "superior aesthetic value". (LOEWE Foundation, 2023)

Most recently, LOEWE launched the Surplus Project in 2021, which advocates for rethinking and reusing surplus material from previous LOEWE collections in order to create something beautiful with low impact. The in-house artisans use high-quality leather remnants, for example, to create items such as the woven basket bag. (Hughes, 2021) Unfortunately, LOEWE does not include all its sustainability efforts in its marketing sufficiently to inform consumers and potential clients. It is knowledge that a limited number of consumers have, but it could have an impact on far more people in the future.

Mid-market and premium brands that are truly sustainable and transparent are rare, too. There is People Tree, which embeds sustainable practices and social responsibility into its entire supply chain. The small German label AA Gold manufactures directly in Europe and has a zero-waste policy that is achieved through ingenious pattern-cutting, which aims to use up all of the fabric during production. NAE Vegan Shoes is a long-established Portuguese shoe manufacturer that researches all sustainable leather substitutes very carefully and discloses the properties of each one on their communication channels. The shoes also come from certified and ethical factories in Portugal.

The Brazilian sneaker brand VEJA creates synthetic shoes using recycled plastic bottles or natural shoes from leather that is 100% traceable, starting at the slaughterhouse in Brazil and Uruguay to the sneaker manufacturer. Their chrome-free tanneries are certified gold by the Leather Working Group (Veja, 2024).

And then there is the Swiss company Freitag, which creates bags and accessories from discarded truck tarpaulins. Its unusual choice of material and approach to circularity is explored in the following case example.

Case example: Freitag

Figure 11.2 Freitag's concept was to take used truck tarpaulins and reuse them to make durable bags. In this image, the unique design of the bags becomes quite evident as no tarpaulin is the same and the section cut out for the bag will have a completely unique combination of colour and pattern. With kind permission from Freitag.

One remarkable brand is Freitag, which makes bags and other accessories from discarded truck tarpaulins. It was founded by Markus and Daniel Freitag in Zurich, Switzerland, in 1993 and started very simple, very small when the brothers experimented with leftover truck covers and made robust, one-of-a-kind messenger bags. The first one was the F13 TOP CAT messenger bag, which was popular with young people in Zurich and a little later all over Europe. It was a statement of subcultural coolness as the bags were difficult to obtain because you could only get them in Switzerland. The choice of design was dictated by what was in stock, and every bag was absolutely unique. In this way, the owner was expressing his or her uniqueness, ecological consciousness and ability to get a hold of a cult item.

Figure 11.3 The F11 Lassie messenger bag by Freitag has a comfortable shoulder strap, quick-release buckle for on-the-go adjustment, two-step extension with Velcro closure, and is robust and water-repellent. It was first launched in 1995 and currently retails for CHF 235. Image credit: Peter Würmli. With kind permission from Freitag.

Due to the main material used, by default, Freitag bags were never part of a seasonal trend as the collections depended on the leftover tarps available (and still do to this day). In turn, this made the products "long life classics" with an extended lifespan embedded from the design stage. The founding brothers were very clear about the functionality, quality and sustainability of their brand from the very beginning (Buergi and Spafford, 2010). Once you got a Freitag bag, it was durable and virtually indestructible.

The company has enjoyed remarkable growth since its launch in Zurich in the 1990s, and although several copycat brands have tried to offer a similar product, nobody could outdo the original, which increased in demand. Currently, there are 30 Freitag stores across Europe, Japan, South Korea, Thailand, China and Australia, and a further 300 sales partners in 23 countries and online stores based in Zurich-Oerlikon and Shanghai. The flagship store in Zurich is housed in an unusual industrial building made from recycled containers and referred to as The Bonsai Skyscraper.

To meet growing demands by global consumers, Freitag employs 250 people, producing around 500,000 bags and accessories for which they use about 340 tons of used truck tarps, 600 km of B-stock car safety belts, 30,000 B-stock bicycle inner tubes, 50,000 m² of recycled PET textile and 1,300 B-stock airbags.

Figure 11.4 The Bonsai Skyscraper is Freitag's flagship store located next to Zurich Hardbrücke, the very same place that inspired the Freitag brothers in 1993 to start making bags from used truck tarps. It has been there since 2006 and is a retail space that perfectly expresses Freitag's corporate philosophy. Instagram: @freitagflagship. Photo credit: Roland Tännler. With kind permission from Freitag.

Freitag calculated that the heavy-duty PVC tarps it uses first spend an average of six years on the road and then survive for many more years once turned into a durable Freitag bag or accessory. To keep their carbon footprint low, the recycled materials have short transport routes to the factory. Along Freitag's entire value chain, the company is actively working to further reduce its direct and indirect greenhouse gas emissions. The most recent calculations have shown that using old truck tarps instead of new material reduces Freitag's CO_2 emissions by 22 per cent. Freitag believes in honesty and transparency and now publishes a Freitag Impact Report about its sustainability measures (Freitag, 2024a).

The brand has also won dozens of sustainability and design awards over the last decades, including the 6th Zurich Entrepreneur Award for innovative, sustainable and commercially successful work in 2011 and the Circular Globe label (Level: Advanced). The brand is regularly assessed by the Circular Globe label, which is an assessment model developed by the Swiss Association for Quality and Management Systems (SQS) and Quality

Figure 11.5 Every year, 350 tons of used truck tarps are delivered to Freitag's factory. The Freitag Truck Spotters keep their eyes open for the most beautiful tarps all over Europe. With kind permission from Freitag.

Austria. Out of 1,000 available score points, Freitag has most recently achieved 600 and is aiming for 800 points by 2030. This is fully supported by its own circularity roadmap (Freitag, 2024b).

To achieve these targets, the company is also growing its sustainability offerings: To extend the life of its products, Freitag now provides repairs, product customization (F-Cut & FREITAG Yourself Stations), a free bag exchange platform (S.W.A.P.) and a take-back initiative.

These initiatives are detailed in the annual Impact Report, which was launched in 2021 and provides insights into how Freitag aligns its overall strategic goals, projects and daily work with its overarching purpose: "Intelligent design for a circular future" (Freitag Group, 2023).

When it comes to circular product design, the report details the following design concepts:

DESIGN FOR DURABILITY

We give our products a long life by selecting robust materials and a timeless design that increases the product's emotional value the older it gets.

DESIGN FOR DISASSEMBLY

We rely on modular design and reversible material connection, which simplify repairs, replacement, remanufacturing and recycling of the product. We enhance this by keeping the number of material groups to a minimum.

CHOOSE PURPOSEFUL MATERIALS

We select our materials in line with strict criteria. We rely on circular, recycled materials produced using environment-friendly methods, avoiding any that do not comply with our Restricted Substance List (RSL).

VALUE THE MATERIALS

We develop products that can be produced with minimal material waste, emphasize the unique character of products made from used truck tarps and declare the materials used on the products.

(Freitag Group, 2023)

Furthermore, Freitag details that its customers participate in the swap initiative or have their bags repaired by the thousands. A few years ago, Freitag deliberately closed its stores on Black Friday and instead encouraged consumers to swap their old bags as part of a anti-Black-Friday campaign. The brand wants to encourrage customers to think about circularity, which is why the campaign centred around a Tinder-style bag exchange between existing Freitag customers. Freitag's head of communication explained the rationale behind it:

"We didn't want to start talking about extending the life cycle of a product in a way that felt too educational – we believe a message can have more impact if you manage to do it in a fun and entertaining way. That's why the idea came up to create a dating app-style bag exchange that allowed customers to swipe and swap their bags with other Freitag bag owners." (Mclaughlin, 2020)

Consumers are also invited to observe the design and manufacturing process in the factory. In 2022, there were 98 guided tours with more than 1,900 participants at the factory located outside of Zurich in the Nœrd industrial complex.

Interestingly, due to their legacy, some vintage Freitag bags are appreciating in value and can fetch very high prices with Freitag fans. They are sold on Depop, Vestiaire Collective, Poshmark, eBay and other such websites around the world, extending their life span. Finally, to ensure circularity and a cradle-to-crade approach, when a product really has reached its usability limit and cannot be fixed by the brand's repair service, Freitag welcomes the return of products and recycles them responsibly.

The triple bottom line and greenwashing

Corporate social responsibility is a trendy term that is increasingly applied by many brands, including fashion brands. The trigger was that, at some point, brands were accused of aggressively looking for profit at the expense of society, nature and resources and not showing themselves as responsible members of society. Notably, in 1994, John Elkington devised the concept of the triple bottom line (TBL or 3BL), which is popular today but something he came to revisit and nearly recalled several decades later. To understand his change of heart, one must first understand what he had proposed with the TBL (Mitterfellner, 2023).

Table 11.1 The three Ps of the triple bottom line

People	Planet	Profit/prosperity
TBL considers how society can benefit whilst shareholders benefit. A positive impact on people can be achieved through the responsible consideration of the needs of all stakeholders, such as communities, individuals, employees, customers, future generations, etc. Goals can be set to combat unemployment, improve human rights and gender equality, offer education and healthcare, end poverty and hunger, etc.	Industrial and business activity can take a huge toll on the planet and environment. This means that TBL initiatives that can protect and preserve the planet must be considered. All inhabitants, animals, flora and fauna can benefit from positive initiatives. Fashion companies are renowned for their contribution to the destruction of the planet, so areas of the entire supply chain and product life cycle need to be considered. Setting of goals such as conscious and limited electricity consumption, waste management, land usage, safe work environments, animal welfare, raw material replenishment, reduction of hazardous substances, etc. and deadlines to achieve them.	A capitalist economy is driven by profit, but with TBL in mind, there has to be a higher purpose than that, bringing positive change to society. The TBL also has a connection to the Sustainable Development Goals (SDGs) of the UN. The 17 Sustainable Development Goals "recognize that ending poverty and other deprivations must go hand-in-hand with strategies that improve health and education, reduce inequality, and spur economic growth" (United Nations, n.d.). The profit a company generates must enhance everyone's life and livelihood.

Source: Adapted from Miller (2020).

The TBL is a business concept and business metrics framework that offers three categories – people, planet and prosperity (or profit) – and asks companies to commit to measuring their impact across these three parameters. Thus, it includes their social and environmental impact – in addition to their financial performance – rather than solely focusing on generating profit, or the standard economic "bottom line" (Miller, 2020). The three Ps of the TBL include the following elements and can be individually adapted to any business in order to change it into a responsible member of society. According to the TBL inventor, John Elkington, and a reflective article on the TBL published in the *Harvard Business Review* in 2018, the original idea was wider still, encouraging businesses to track and manage economic (not just financial), social, and environmental value added – or destroyed.

This idea infused platforms like the Global Reporting Initiative (GRI) and Dow Jones Sustainability Indexes (DJSI), influencing corporate accounting, stakeholder engagement and, increasingly, strategy. But the TBL wasn't designed to be just an accounting tool. It was supposed to provoke deeper thinking about capitalism and its future, but many early adopters understood the concept as a balancing act, adopting a trade-off mentality.

Decades later, Elkington is unsure whether people really understood the depth and breadth of his invention. He laments that

> [f]undamentally, we have a hard-wired cultural problem in business, finance and markets. Whereas CEOs, CFOs, and other corporate leaders move heaven and earth to ensure that they hit their profit targets, the same is very rarely true of their people and planet targets. Clearly, the Triple Bottom Line has failed to bury the single bottom line paradigm.
>
> (Elkington, 2018a)

Elkington sees many businesses using TBL on the surface whilst at the same time doing unethical business and wonders if it is up to governments to regulate companies, forcing them "to take people and planet as seriously as profit" (Elkington, 2018b).

However, Elkington thinks positively about the growth of B Corporations (or B Corps for short) with over 2,700 members worldwide. Apart from the designation of a B Corporation, there are others, including social purpose corporations and low-profit limited liability companies, which all steer businesses in the right direction of "system change". They try to implement the TBL philosophy and measure brands' performance according to it. Today, organizations know success is not just reflected in their profit-and-loss statements. Rather, to get an accurate, well-rounded perspective of their operations and relationships with the environment, community and economy, organizations

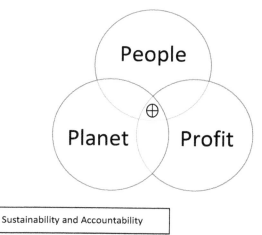

⊕ | Sustainability and Accountability

Figure 11.6 Triple bottom line framework: people, planet, profit can be illustrated as a Venn-diagram with the common denominator of sustainability and accountability.

must fully account for all costs associated with doing business by going beyond compliance. Certified B Corporations help the concept of the triple bottom line, as John Elkington designed it, come to life. B Corporations are a relatively new type of business, legally required to consider impacts on all stakeholders, including employees, customers, suppliers, the community and environment. Their mission is to become a community of leaders who drive a global movement of people using business as a force for good.

Despite this, when it comes to the fashion industry, of the 2,700-plus B Corps that exist today, only 250 are apparel companies. CSR is often misused in the fashion industry to mimic sustainability measures – also known as greenwashing, a term now widely known and originally attributed to environmentalist Jay Westerveld in 1986 (Orange and Cohen, 2010).

Greenwashing

Greenwashing describes the efforts made by businesses in promoting their sustainability endeavours rather than implementing actions that effectively minimize their environmental impact. This is a misleading method, manipulating trusting consumers who believe they are supporting truly sustainable businesses that care about bettering the world (Robinson, 2021). It is estimated that nearly 60 per cent of all sustainability claims by European and UK fashion brands are misleading and could be greenwashing, which is not always easy to spot (Rauturier, 2022).

Of the many incarnations of greenwashing, one is the proclamation of targets, manifestos and promises to be achieved in the future, which are never met and whose progress is shrouded in mystery. The target year can be moved forward again and again, dangling the carrot in front of an ethical consumer forever. There might be certifications, seals of approval or logos on the brand's channels, but it is not always indicative of sustainable practices, and without robust proof and transparency, it cannot be verified to be true. Thus, promises of sustainable measures or special collections (green ranges, sustainable capsule collections or eco-products) are often just eloquently described in promotional campaigns but have little impact on the actual supply chain and production methods (Rauturier, 2022).

If a consumer wants to find out specifics about the raw materials, workers' welfare and production sites, it is nearly impossible to find anything on the brand's platforms and channels. The brand cannot back up its claims with data and prove that its words are more than a superficial marketing trick. The danger is that consumers will find out about the greenwashing and turn away from the brand.

Moreover, brands might be cautious about making false promises by using specific sustainability terminology which would require accountability and instead become excellent copywriters when they invent catchy descriptors of their products such as "pure and fair", "cruelty-free", "conscious", "Off The Grid" or "Re-Nylon" (Beard, 2008). These are again misleading terms and say nothing about the true practices of the brand.

Sustainability and marketing

The idea of integrating sustainability into marketing arose around the 1970s, when it was also known as "green marketing" and dealt with an "ecologically concerned consumer". It is important to note that sustainability marketing deals with issues of ecology and society, whereas sustainable marketing is a term connected to an ongoing and successful form of marketing, not connected to ecological or societal concerns (Kumar et al., 2012).

According to Polonsky (2001), green marketing requires a business to evaluate itself deeply and revisit its entire marketing mix to understand where sustainable behaviour is embedded and where it needs to be developed. The business might need to modify specific points along its entire supply chain, including the marketing of products. It must be more than just following government regulations (which might be connected to fines if not adhered to) and set actionable objectives. It is not simply enough to promote products or design activities but might include elements such as targeting, green pricing, green design and product development, green positioning, the greening of logistics, the marketing of waste, the greening of promotion and green alliances (Polonsky, 2001 in Charter and Tischner, 2001).

Green marketing continued as a necessity over the decades, and the contemporary consumer sentiment means that most brands have to disclose their sustainability efforts through brand communication channels at a minimum. This is because Gen Z and Millennial consumers want to shop from brands that make the world a better place. This leads to the term "sustainability marketing", which is not yet clearly defined.

Based on available literature and a study by Kemper and Ballentine (2017), this book proposes to focus on four distinct types that can be ranked on a scale from unsustainable at one end to moderately, advanced and highly sustainable at the other end. They consist of greenwashing, sustainable product focus, sustainable lifestyle focus and institutional change focus (see Figure 11.7).

Greenwashing in sustainability marketing

As detailed earlier in the chapter, greenwashing is a most unsustainable way of marketing. In the context of sustainability marketing, it tries to use communication and marketing tactics to mislead consumers (and other stakeholders) about the sustainability efforts of a particular business and quality of products. According to Pearse (2012), big brands, including fashion brands, resort to "slogans and logos" to make a green impression on consumers. Of the many tactics they employ in marketing, their humble green approach includes a limited number of sustainable products accompanied by intense advertising or campaigns that boast about targets to reduce emissions without admitting that the company's growth and production increase will automatically increase all the negative effects on the environment. Part of the communication strategy of greenwashing includes CEOs, spokespeople and celebrities who deliver speeches, participate in promotional campaigns and collaborations. Brands might even resort to the most powerful stars available to back their claims: the government. Pearse sees these efforts as part of a large industry that employs teams of greenwashing experts who set up advertising and PR campaigns to gain credibility. If you look at the marketing mix, it is not well balanced as the focus is heavily set on promotion.

Auxiliary sustainability marketing

The next type is moderate but honest sustainability marketing called auxiliary sustainability marketing and focuses on the production of sustainable products.

Auxiliary sustainability marketing focuses on environmental, social and economic dimensions of production mainly and consumption to a smaller extent. This focus on sustainability is integrated throughout the entire marketing mix and the product mix. This means that sustainable products might be recyclable or materials reusable and possibly endeavour to offer a cradle-to-cradle design or offer repairs. There will be recyclable or biodegradable packaging, too. Auxiliary sustainability marketing works to ensure positive change happens within established structures such as free markets, government interventions and business models (Kemper and Ballentine, 2017). The case examples in this chapter show two brands - LOEWE and Freitag - that use auxiliray sustainability marketing and are developing into the next stage of reformative sustainability marketing.

Reformative sustainability marketing

A more advanced form of sustainability marketing called reformative sustainability marketing builds on the preceding auxiliary approach through the promotion of sustainable lifestyles and behavioural changes.

Reformative sustainability marketing is aware that the current consumption levels are unsustainable, based on limited global resources and inequity between developed and developing nations. Therefore, reformative sustainability marketing moves away from using marketing to push a product but instead promotes sustainable lifestyles to "demarket" certain harmful or undesirable products/services and alters how sustainability is marketed. It also acknowledges that marketing promotes consumption and that this cannot be seen as sustainable, which means it promotes sustainable products (like in auxiliary sustainability marketing) while advocating for sustainable lifestyles. Consumers are seen as changemakers who are empowered to lead sustainable lifestyles. There is also interest in cooperation with governments and NGOs to help with the promotion of sustainable lifestyles, to educate consumers or even introduce regulations (Kemper and Ballentine, 2017). Brands such as Finisterre and Deploy are good examples of fashion brands confidently engaging in reformative sustainability marketing and are on their way to reach transformative sustainability marketing, since they both have achieved B-Corporation certification. Certified B Corporations are legally required to meet a minimum standard of performance that will yield overall positive stakeholder impact and to consider the impact of their decisions on all other stakeholders — their suppliers, workers, customers, communities, and the environment as well as future generations. (Kassoy, 2022)

Transformative sustainability marketing

The highest form of sustainability marketing is called transformative sustainability marketing. It builds on both the auxiliary and reformative approaches and believes that there is a need for the transformation of current institutions, norms and critical reflection.

Transformative sustainability marketing acknowledges that the problems are multifaceted and that efforts for change need to be made by multiple stakeholders (including governments, companies and consumers). Simply producing sustainable goods or leading a sustainable lifestyle cannot suffice to ensure a healthy ecosystem because this system still revolves around social norms of consumerism and ideologies of capitalism, which are then enforced through marketing. It questions the contemporary business philosophy and advocates for social entrepreneurship with new philosophies and business models.

> Consequently, TSM acknowledges the weaknesses of the current economic system and challenges us to question our preconceived notions of the "good" of capitalism and neo-liberal economics, and its associated assumptions and ideology. [TSM] aims to change institutions that inhibit a transition to a sustainable society.
>
> (Kemper and Ballentine, 2017)

Brands that engage in this form of sustainability marketing are rare. However, one example is Patagonia, which is exemplary in its efforts, but in terms of global fashion brands, there is little competition. Most fashion brands that fulfill the requirements of transformative sustainability marketing are small in scale and local and this chapter features a case example and interview with SOLIT Japan which is acting in a transformative way, specifically in terms of inclusion and sustainability.

Theory frameworks proposing solutions for sustainability and sustainability marketing

Interesting theory models and approaches have come to light in recent years and decades. All preach that the life cycle of fashion needs to change and that various actors throughout the entire fashion system need to participate in

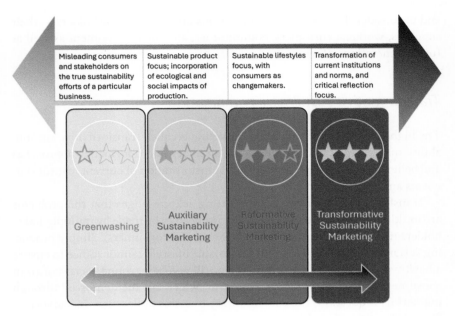

Figure 11.7 Four types of sustainability marketing. Adapted from Kemper and Ballentine (2017). The stars give a rating from zero to one, two and three stars, with the latter being the most advanced form of sustainability marketing.

order to make a change. There are concepts such as the 3 Rs, which encourage us to reduce, reuse and recycle; or the 10 Rs, which prompt for respect, responsibility, refuse, reduce, rethink, repurpose, reuse, repair, recycle and restore (Telford and Wrekin, 2021).

For fashion, Rotimi et al. (2021) propose a "conceptual framework for sustainability" (CFS) showing sustainable garment end-of-life-cycle practices in the achievement of strategic competitive advantage. This framework puts the responsibility on everyone throughout the supply chain to the end consumer, asking for reuse, recycle, recover and redistribute, and educating and engaging stakeholders.

The triple-A approach to ethical activism

If change can start with the consumer (as proposed by auxiliary sustainability marketing), a practical and effective take on the numerous sustainability or

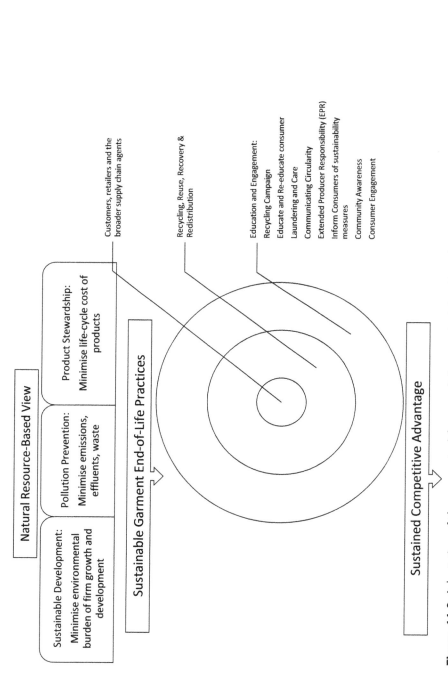

Natural Resource-Based View

Sustainable Development:
Minimise environmental
burden of firm growth and
development

Pollution Prevention:
Minimise emissions,
effluents, waste

Product Stewardship:
Minimise life-cycle cost of
products

Sustainable Garment End-of-Life Practices

Customers, retailers and the
broader supply chain agents

Recycling, Reuse, Recovery &
Redistribution

Education and Engagement:
Recycling Campaign
Educate and Re-educate consumer
Laundering and Care
Communicating Circularity
Extended Producer Responsibility (EPR)
Inform Consumers of sustainability
measures
Community Awareness
Consumer Engagement

Sustained Competitive Advantage

Figure 11.8 Adaptation of the conceptual framework for sustainability (CFS) for end-of-life-cycle practices in the achievement of strategic competitive advantage. Source: Rotimi et al. (2021) in Mitterfellner (2023)

garment life-cycle models would be the "triple-A approach to ethical activism", which is intended to be accessible to all customers and does not expect a pre-existing understanding of sustainability in fashion but does invite customers to partake in activism.

If consumers are strong, brands cannot manipulate them and need to adapt their practices, so activism is the way forward. Consumers can educate themselves by acquiring vital knowledge about what is right and wrong in the fashion system. They can act on this knowledge to consume in a better way. Finally, by setting personal ethical goals, unsustainable ways of consuming fashion can be avoided. This is a simple and interactive way to become an ethical activist.

The triple-A approach to ethical activism consists of the following actionable points:

Acquire knowledge

Acquire knowledge about what is wrong with the fashion system. For example:

1. Visit websites such as the Fashion Revolution or Labour Behind the Label and educate yourself.
2. Investigate the brands you like and find out how their garments are made. If there is not enough information, you should cross them off your shopping list.
3. Watch the documentary *The True Cost*.
4. Look through the Sustainable Fashion Glossary, set up by Condé Nast and the Centre for Sustainable Fashion, London College of Fashion, University of the Arts London, to uncover mysterious terms such as "systems thinking" and many others.
5. Hold your piece of clothing to your ear. Perhaps you can hear the story of the person who made it.

Act

Your activism can change consumption habits and help improve the state of the fashion industry. For example:

1. Break the consumption habit and swap garments with your friends or rent a garment.
2. Explore vintage stores, charity shops and online resale platforms.

3. Fall in love again with what you already have. Putting away clothes for half a year and then rediscovering them in a box can be almost as good as going shopping.

4. Mend, upcycle, restyle what you already own, or ask a designer to do it for you. You can also support a small ethical designer and ask for custom-made pieces.

5. Save up and invest in a classic designer piece, luxury or crafted item that you intend to keep forever.

Avoid

Set ethical goals for yourself that you abide by. This will break the chain of unethical consumption.

1. Do not immediately give to charity. Charity items do help but are known to cause giant dumps and landfills of clothing in Third World countries, such as Africa. According to D-Waste, the African continent has up to 20 of the world's 50 largest dumpsites. And Not Just a Label reports that for-profit recyclers export 45 per cent of our First World clothing donations to Third World countries.

2. Avoid shopping from brands and stores that cannot provide a transparent account of how and where their products are made. Check out the Fashion Transparency Index provided annually by the Fashion Revolution, which lists 250 of the largest global fashion brands and retailers.

3. Avoid fashion advertising, avoid sales and avoid impulse buying. According to euromarketing.com, consumers spend $5,400 annually on impulse purchases of food, clothing, household items and shoes. At night, do not shop. Moonlight and insomnia shopping are never good ideas.

4. Unfollow influencers who promote hauls and throwaway fashion and who make you feel somehow less worthy or prompt you to check out their brands. *The Huffington Post* reported that Instagram influencers fuel our destructive addiction to fashion.

5. Follow the advice from Adbusters and buy nothing. It is as simple as that. Adbusters was launched by Kalle Lasn in the mid-1990s as a Canada-based anti-capitalist publication which promotes a "Buy Nothing Day", stopping our capitalist shopping habits. It is also famous for its spoof fashion ads.

Even a few of these steps will help people be more ethical consumers, change their own values and change how millions of people produce fashion and how

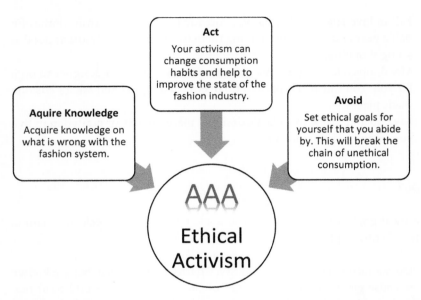

Figure 11.9 The triple-A approach to ethical activism. First published in Mitterfellner (2023).

millions of people consume fashion. This approach, however, does not alleviate brands and supply chain actors from their responsibility and can only complement the responsibility that everyone should bear. As per the concept of reformative and transformative sustainability marketing, the other stakeholders should also be involved in these efforts.

Sustainable Development Goals (SDGs)

According to Ellen Pabst von Ohain (Mitterfellner, 2023), what is needed is a transparent, universally-agreed-on, comprehensive set of criteria that will define what sustainable practices are for a brand or enterprise, tailored to specific industries. The United Nation's SDGs are fast becoming the go-to reference in providing suggested points of alignment for companies, according to what is applicable to that firm and its industry. The UN understands, too, that no company can address all 17 areas adequately. But it is a start and one that allows a workable template for firms. This would be aligned with transformative sustainability marketing as proposed by Kemper and Ballentine (2017).

How did the 17 SDGs come about? Originally, they were

> an extension of the Millennium Development Goals — set in 2000 and of which mercifully there were only eight (…). The idea was to hold up a mirror to the world and to help marshal the resources to improve the reflected image.
>
> (Pilling, 2023)

The Millennium Summit of 2000 was attended by world leaders who debated world problems and then agreed on eight goals originally developed by the Organization for Economic Cooperation and Development (OECD):

Values and Principles
Peace, Security and Disarmament
Development and Poverty Eradication
Protecting Our Common Environment
Human Rights, Democracy and Good Governance
Protecting the Vulnerable
Meeting the Special Needs of Africa
Strengthening the United Nations

However, the OECD is political in its nature as it is an intergovernmental organization with 38 member countries which was founded in 1961 to advance economic progress and world trade. The 38 members are predominantly Western power nations. This is because the OECD was established to ensure the continuation of the Marshall Plan (which was rejected by the Soviet Union and its satellite states). There is more critical information on this background in the "Ethical considerations" at the end of this chapter.

The current 17 SDGs are as follows (each goal is supported by specific targets, with 169 in total) (United Nations, 2024):

SDG 1: No Poverty
SDG 2: No Hunger
SDG 3: Good Health and Well-Being
SDG 4: Quality Education
SDG 5: Gender Equality
SDG 6: Clean Water and Sanitation

SDG 7: Affordable and Clean Energy
SDG 8: Decent Work and Economic Growth
SDG 9: Industry and Infrastructure
SDG 10: Reduced Inequality
SDG 11: Sustainable Cities and Communities
SDG 12: Responsible Consumption and Production
SDG 13: Climate Action
SDG 14: Life Below Water
SDG 15: Life on Land
SDG 16: Peace, Justice and Strong Institutions
SDG 17: Partnerships for the Goals

SDG 12, Responsible Consumption and Production, is often considered to be highly relevant to the fashion industry and fashion marketing.

As per the World Bank and the SDG Fund, SDG 12 advocates "for the sustainable production and consumption of goods and services" with the aim to fulfil this goal by 2030. This is coupled with national growth (and improving the standard of living) that must not deplete natural resources or cause the degradation of the environment through pollution or problematic waste management. Within SDG 12, there are 11 subcategories such as the use of natural resources, reduction of waste generation, promotion of universal understanding of sustainable lifestyles, and encouraging companies to adopt sustainable practices and report on them (Textile Exchange, 2024).

The SDGs call for sustainable consumption and require that resources are not wasted, but rather recycled and safely managed. If either production or consumption is not sustainable, economic output will be constrained, leading to more pollution, greenhouse gas emissions and the loss of biodiversity. In the SDG framework, the responsibility to ensure sustainable production and consumption patterns is shared by governments, the private sector and citizens.

The SDGs and World Bank call for action by governments and the private sector. Actions by governments should make the effort to limit fossil fuel subsidies, as fossil fuel subsidies create incentives to prioritize unsustainable production and discourage the use of renewable resources. This is a short-term measure that contributes to greenhouse gas emissions and climate change, counteracting SDG 7 and SDG 13. Most countries use fossil fuel subsidies to some extent, and some spend more than 5 per cent of their national income, with Iran and Lebanon at the top, devoting 19 and 13 per cent, respectively.

Actions by the private sector call for companies to use recycled materials, renewable energy, limit their biodiversity impacts and more. Some enterprises have taken these actions, partly driven by consumer demand and by goals set by governments and the SDGs. The World Bank praises high-income countries whose companies have been producing sustainability reports. But in low-income countries, there is no more than one company producing sustainability reports. "Even when companies publish sustainability reports, it may not lead to action. This makes it challenging to assess progress in this area from the private sector" (The World Bank Group, 2024).

Returning to the idea of four types of sustainability marketing, it is then possible to map out the different sustainable frameworks and also apply them to an individual brand or business, rating whether they are suitable for auxiliary, reformative or transformative sustainability marketing. For auxiliary sustainability marketing, which includes sustainable products by companies, there is mostly scope for the 3 Rs, 10 Rs, 3As of ethical activism, and the three pillars. In the advanced form of sustainability marketing, which is the reformative type, companies are endorsing a sustainable lifestyle. Thus, in addition to the 3 Rs, 10 Rs, the three pillars, corporate social responsibility efforts, the conceptual framework for sustainability, the triple bottom line framework and the SDGs come into play. The 3As of ethical activism would not apply here, as the framework is based on an initiative solely led by the consumer. Lastly, in the transformative sustainability marketing type, the highest option, all possible theoretical frameworks apply (including others that are not listed in this chapter) because here action is necessary from the brands, consumers and institutions to achieve a complete system change which counteracts capitalist practice.

Specifically for assessing a brand's sustainability marketing, the following figure and questions can help achieve the best results and avoid greenwashing:

- In which way are our products and services sustainable?
- How do we communicate this to customers and stakeholders?
- How do we encourage and support our customers to live a more sustainable lifestyle?
- Where are we actively trying to change the political, social and environmental systems and norms?
- Are there particular frameworks or certifications that can underpin our efforts? How can this be embedded in our business strategy and marketing activities?
- Are there any elements that could be perceived as greenwashing in our brand communication? How do we ensure not to mislead or overpromise?

Figure 11.10 The various sustainability theory frameworks matched with the four types of sustainability marketing as an assessment tool for brands. Adapted from Kemper and Ballentine (2017). The stars give a rating from zero to one, two and three stars, with the latter being the most sustainable.

Case example: SOLIT Japan

SOLIT Japan is a ground-breaking company that creates clothing which is fully inclusive and adapts to individuals with physical challenges such as illness or disability. It was founded in 2020 by Misaki Tanaka and has already won prestigious awards, including gold in the iF Design Award 2022 for the product category; the Beyond Millennials 2023 (Business Insider Japan) award; and the Circulation System of Clothes around Medical Field at the crQlr Awards, a global award for designing a circular economy in 2021.

SOLIT's vision is "achieving an all-inclusive society where nobody and nothing is left behind". According to SOLIT, this would call for a market formation (economic zone) where multiple stakeholders, such as companies, councils and organizations from a broad range of disciplines participate. The "Eastern philosophical approach to inclusive design" is the foundation of how SOLIT approaches its work. It is a pluralistic philosophy which values each individual, their complexity and mutual influence (SOLIT, 2024). This is evident in the entire structure of the company and the supply chain, which has a very human and sustainable approach.

For example, the company carefully selects talented and diverse employees from different nationalities, languages, sexualities, living environments, housing, ages, professions and occupations. Working as a team, every member is invited to be a decision-maker.

SOLIT works with factories in partnership and chooses those that guarantee to treat their workers well, giving new staff the opportunity to acquire sewing skills that can further their careers.

In terms of sustainability, the brand produces minimal quantities so that no excess is created, which would contribute to the overuse of raw materials and pollution and burden the environment. The fabrics used are durable and are expected to last for a long time, extending their lifespan. Other initiatives include the release of deadstock to customers, repairs and upcycling of worn garments and working with recycling partners.

Most importantly, instead of producing standardized designs, SOLIT allows the wearer to customize the items by choosing elements such as the type of buttons (for example regular, magnetic, snap or Velcro).

For instance, the "Dawn" collection can be worn by consumers with different needs. It consists of a jacket and trousers. For the jacket, comfort is an important design element. SOLIT explains:

> This "Dawn Jacket" is characterized by its ease of wear and ease of movement, even for those who do not like such jackets. The arm opening is designed to be wide enough to allow even those with limited arm and shoulder movement to easily slip the sleeves through. Wide gussets on the sides allow smooth movement around the shoulders, making the jacket less tiring to wear. The back is in a raglan style to facilitate daily arm forward movement, such as when working at a desk, washing hands, or moving by wheelchair. In addition, to prevent the chest area from sagging or wrinkling when sitting, the buttons are positioned higher than usual, and the vent, a cutout in the back of the jacket, was purposely not made to maintain a smart silhouette.
>
> (SOLIT, 2024)

For desk workers' and wheelchair users' needs, special attention was given to the design of the cuffs, which can wear out easily through friction. This has been solved by making the folded cuff fabric a strong nylon. This material has a higher thread strength than the outer fabric and can be washed at home. The problem of "sleeves that don't fall down but can't be rolled up" has been solved by incorporating ribs at the back of the jacket cuffs so that the jacket sleeves can be tucked up like a blouson.

The Dawn trousers are designed for wheelchair users and people who work at a desk a lot, with emphasis on the beauty of the shape when sitting down. The trousers are therefore slightly longer in the back, and the waist is elasticated, allowing for easy adjustment by simply pulling the strings, even for those with paralyzed hands or weak strength. The waist front can be selected from a front-opening fake or two types of zippers, solving the respective problems of "zipper bites and makes it painful" and the inconvenience of using the restroom without a zipper.

Inclusion is built into every detail, such as the side pockets which can have Velcro fastenings that will stop them from opening when sitting

Figure 11.11 The "Dawn" collection by SOLIT Japan includes trousers and a jacket which give comfort, ease of wear and customization to diverse needs. The shirts in this image are from the "Broad" and "Jersey" collections and are the first shirt collections which SOLIT developed. Shirt on the left: Broad; shirt in the middle: Broad; shirt on the right: Jersey.) With kind permission from Misaki Tanaka.

Figure 11.12 A close-up of SOLIT's adaptable trousers with inner strings that allow for individual waist adjustment. With kind permission from SOLIT.

down. The design will allow for a catheter opening and medical use of the pockets, too. And for the back pockets, the choice is to have real ones or faux ones.

Figure 11.13 A close-up of an adaptable shirt by SOLIT Japan. There is a choice of buttons for the customer, including magnetic buttons for ease of use. With kind permission from SOLIT.

Interview with Misaki Tanaka

Figure 11.14 Misaki Tanaka, the founder of SOLIT. With kind permission from Misaki Tanaka.

Misaki Tanaka is a serial social entrepreneur and social designer based in Tokyo, Japan. She ran an NGO on disaster prevention and climate change for eight years. After that, she became the head of a PR firm specializing in solving social issues and is the founder of SOLIT, Inc., a harmonized design solution company. She won the iF Design Award 2022 Gold and the A' Design Award Bronze.

Q: What was the motivation to start SOLIT?

MT: While working for an NGO on climate change and natural disasters, I felt uncomfortable when I visited the mountains of waste created by the fashion industry. Later, one of my classmates in postgraduate school was a wheelchair user, and I discussed with him that there were not many clothes that he wanted to wear but could. I felt that, even though so much is thrown away in the world, why was the person in front of me saying there wasn't any? I decided to solve that gap with the power of business.

Q: Who are the main people behind SOLIT, and how does their background help to develop the company?

MT: The members of SOLIT are a group of professionals working in different fields. From fashion professionals and medical and welfare professionals to creators and PR and marketing specialists; professionals from a wide variety of fields have come together as one team, overcoming differences and attributes such as disabilities, sexualities and nationalities in sympathy with the concept of an "all-inclusive society".

Because each member has different expertise across sectors and domains and different values towards things, it takes time to come up with one idea everyone can agree on, but we believe this is an important step for us to respect and embrace individualities and each person's uniqueness.

Q: SOLIT has a very unique position on sustainability and inclusivity. Could you explain more about this?

MT: When we talk about sustainability, we often talk about part of a whole flow, such as "materials" or "carbon dioxide". When we think about how to make the earth, people, animals and plants sustainable without leaving anything behind, we look at it in terms of flows and systems, and our strength and characteristic is that we are based on the basic premise that we must not forget that there are diverse beings and people with diverse values even within these flows and systems.

Q: What types of products does SOLIT offer?

MT: Currently released items are produced after having discussions with the producer to determine which items can be made to order/minimum lot production. We produce shirts, jackets and pants for casual or formal wear with simple designs and colours that can be worn in a genderless way.

Q: How is the feedback from the people who purchase the product?

MT: Eighty per cent of SOLIT's buyers are customers without particular physical disabilities who sympathize with SOLIT's sustainability and inclusion, but about 20 per cent are people with real experiences of not being able to wear the clothes they want in the past. In particular, wheelchair users and people with paralysis in their limbs may not be able to wear shirts with buttons or have no formal clothing options such as jackets. Many people with such physical challenges often give us positive feedback about their social participation, such as the fact that they can now attend formal events such as weddings.

Q: What kinds of products would SOLIT like to offer in the future?

MT: We want to give people more choice in the things we need to live, such as food, clothing and housing. We started with fashion, which is the most familiar thing to people, but we are now developing stationery and furniture in collaboration with companies that have strengths in this field, and in the future, we want to design a wide range of daily necessities, including architecture, parks, bedding and cars.

Q: Could you tell me more about the "Traceability of the empathy axis"?

MT: Nowadays, the world is discussing the importance of "traceability", in which companies disclose information about where and how their products are produced and how much impact they have on the environment. In the near future, more detailed information on the nationality, gender, age and past history of producers will also be disclosed, and it may become commonplace for consumers to make purchasing decisions based on such transparency.

While we believe that this quantitative and clearly worded information should exist for "ease of understanding", we also believe that some information may be lost when evaluated and categorized according to certain criteria.

We, therefore, considered what the ideal state of traceability would be in the "all-inclusive" future that we are aiming for.

As a sample, we decided to collect and publish information that is more personal, more tangible and less easy to judge, unlike conventional information that is made public. This means that the decision-making criteria are not based on some set criteria or values, but on the viewer's own criteria, which is the purchase experience starting from "empathy".

- What if the person in charge of raw material processing and your favourite musician were the same?
- What if the person in charge of production management finds commonality in the way he spends his holidays?
- What if you want to support the dream of the person in charge of sales?

Usually, we hesitate to buy a product because of unconscious prejudice, such as "because the country of production is here", but when we come into contact with the various human qualities behind the product, we are freed from this bias. Wouldn't it be nice to have such information disclosure?

This way of thinking led us to start our traceability project based on the empathy of consumers.

Q: How do you understand the idea of "anti-lookism"?

MT: SOLIT believes in diversity. However, in expressing this, we do not want to present diversity only on the surface. What we want is for each person to be truly diverse – not just in appearance, but also in invisible values and ideas, and the differences between them.

It goes without saying that expressing diversity is essential for diverse people to have the opportunity to challenge themselves and to move the hearts of those who see their output.

That said, it is too much against our ideology to use those differences as a marketing tool. What we want is for each of us to be together for the future that we truly aspire to.

We want to communicate diversity, not just the visible diversity of a group of diverse beings, but the diversity of all of them.

For this reason, we ask all photographers, videographers, models and stylists involved in the photos and videos that appear on the SOLIT website, social networking sites and other information sources to share our vision of the future and to be sympathetic and supportive of it.

Q: What is the project "AWAKE"?

MT: SOLIT's products are produced based on a system that ensures that only the necessary amount is delivered to the necessary people, without the mass production and mass disposal that the conventional fashion industry has promoted, so as not to burden the environment and diverse people as much as possible.

However, some products remain in our warehouses due to prototypes made to create better products, out-of-spec products such as those with scratches and stains that inevitably occur in the production process, and user order errors. However, if these products can meet people who will utilize them with love, they can still shine and have value.

AWAKE is a project that aims to sell, donate and create new encounters for such items with people who will cherish and wear these products, instead of letting them remain in warehouses or being thrown away.

We name this project AWAKE, aiming to awaken items that have been asleep and to increase the number of opportunities for people to find items they have been interested in.

We also hope that we can witness such wonderful encounters that will wake up someone who has always thought that new items are the most beautiful and let them understand the different values in clothing.

Q: Where are your products available right now for purchase?

MT: You can purchase our products on our EC site: https://SOLIT -japan.com/en/collections/products

Q: Could you tell me more about the D&I [diversity and inclusion] lectures and training that SOLIT offers?

MT: We closely work with other businesses across sectors and domains and provide one-stop solutions for everything they need to achieve their inclusion goals.

Based on our expertise in production design and knowledge of diversity and inclusion, we provide extensive consulting services, supporting other businesses to promote diversity and inclusion within their organization and through their businesses.

Ethical considerations

The ethical considerations of this chapter focus on the SDGs, as most of the content already deals with questions of ethical and sustainable practice in fashion. In theory, any business that adheres to ethics would automatically adhere to sustainable practices and the honest marketing of them. However, as highlighted in every chapter of this book, there are many businesses that do not embed ethical principles in their actions. So when it comes to sustainability, there is a high risk of greenwashing which is misleading the consumer regarding the sustainable practices of a brand.

The SDGs are signposts which some brands use as a benchmark for their sustainability efforts or future goals. Again, in principle, the SDGs can be seen as a sensible approach to embedding sustainable practices. However, the SDGs are seen as problematic by some experts. For one, they are overly ambitious and unrealistic in their implementation, having a negative effect on the poorest members. "It is argued that the SDGs, their 169 targets and 232 indicators, and the state and corporate driven processes behind their development serve to exacerbate the large-scale bias; promote an approach to formalisation that risks marginalising the poorest and entrenching inequality" (Hirons, 2020).

Second, their origin is political. As mentioned earlier in this chapter, the SDGs are based on The Millennium Summit of 2000, which in turn was an idea by the OECD. The OECD had 38 mostly Western member countries and was founded in 1961 to stimulate economic progress and world trade. The reason the OECD was established was to help administer the Marshall Plan (which was rejected by both the Soviet Union under Stalin and its satellite states) – a plan conceived in 1948 during the aftermath of WWII to help Europe recover.

William Clayton, who was the first Under Secretary of State for Economic Affairs, recalled the birth of the Marshall Plan, OEEC and OECD in his article from 1963:

> The committee, informally organized into the Committee for European Economic Cooperation under the chairmanship of Sir Oliver Franks was then set up formally, in the Spring of 1948, under the title of Organization for European Economic Cooperation (OEEC). This organization fully justified the faith of Secretary Marshall and his advisers, because it managed to secure the removal of many of the restrictions on imports between European countries. In time, the United States and Canada became associate members of this organization; still later, it was changed to Organization for Economic Cooperation and Development (OECD), which is its present name. The United States and Canada are now full members of OECD.

This automatically leads to the third problem: The Marshall Plan was criticized as American economic imperialism. With the evolution into the SDGs, they also impose a Western bias and Western values as the only solution for a multipolar world. Furthermore, the SDGs impose neo-colonialism and neo-globalism on the very nations that were originally exploited by colonialism.

According to McEachrane (2019), "There is an elephant in the room of sustainable development. Namely, the very relationship between the developed and developing world of domination and subordination and its historical roots in colonialism". McEachrane laments that the unsustainability which exists today is a direct result of historical control over the use of natural resources and cheap labour, which only benefited one type of consumer: European states and European colonial-settler states. Looking at this history, McEachrane (2019) finds "a bottom line of maximising profit and economic growth (which) included colonisation of foreign lands and peoples, a transformation of landscapes and societies across the world, enslavement, genocides, wars and systemic racial discrimination".

This history lasted many centuries, resulting in a well-established, developed world, but it continues to be dominated by the same European descendants of the same European colonial states (McEachrane, 2019).

Looking further into the legacy of colonialism and globalization, pollution comes into question.

Studies have revealed that direct foreign investment from post-colonials into BRIC nations or other underdeveloped countries has an environmental trade-off. Economic growth that is triggered by foreign direct investment leads to an increase in biomass energy consumption and a consequent increase in pollution as well as increased carbon emissions (Barış-Tüzemen and Tüzemen, 2022; Mitterfellner, 2023). Although this can be mitigated over time as those nations learn to develop more sustainably, the environment takes a negative toll that is difficult to reverse. Furthermore, in order to apply sustainable measures, the developing nations must again rely on foreign sustainability techniques, which can include the SDGs.

With this in mind, there is also a significant financial incentive when using the SDGs. According to a report by the World Resource Institute, much profit is to be made from poor and emerging countries taking on Western developmental blueprints. The report shows "that achieving the SDGs in just four sectors—food and agriculture, cities, energy and materials, and health and well-being—would create $12 trillion of new market opportunities by 2030". It would create new jobs, of which 90 per cent would be in developing countries: 85 million jobs created in Africa and 220 million jobs created in China, India, and the rest of developing and emerging Asia (Jaeger et al., 2017).

The funding for all this comes from the former colonial countries, and they are the ones reaping the benefits. "A growing number of Western countries are making their aid packages contingent on going 'green' when African nations simply can't afford it", says Ayuk, African Energy Chamber chair (Ryan, 2022).

Then there is a valid debate around the definition of climate change. There are scientists who have proposed that CO_2, which officially is labelled as a trace gas and is present in the atmosphere at a mere 0.04%, is not a threat to the planet. In fact, of that 0.04 per cent, 97 per cent is produced by nature and only 3 per cent by human activities. Moreover, without a certain amount of CO_2 in the atmosphere, life could not exist. These facts coupled with natural phases of planetary heating and cooling throughout its entire history would mean that global warming is triggered with or without human activity. Although these facts are not welcomed by the mainstream narrative, they are supported by studies and do give a chance to look at the problem from different angles, rather than apply a blanket approach with punitive measures for people and countries (Pilmer, 2009).

What does this mean for businesses that want to use the SDGs as part of their marketing and sustainability efforts? They must carefully examine what each SDG means and whether the actions would indeed exploit developing countries and benefit only Western postcolonial trade.

Finally, however the financial pressures might look, businesses have the option of introducing and adhering to generally fair and responsible practices - even if they are not specifically aligned with the SDGs or similar frameworks. Porter and Kramer (2011) suggested applying a business model based on creating shared value (CSV) that changes the concept of capitalism, which is purely profit-driven, and instead incorporates ethical values into its very core. The idea is that healthy businesses are directly linked to the surrounding communities with which a mutually respectful and fair partnership should be established. The authors question the profit-driven values of companies: "How else could companies overlook the well-being of their customers, the depletion of natural resources vital to their businesses, the viability of key suppliers, or the economic distress of the communities in which they produce and sell?" (Porter and Kramer, 2011, p. 64). This is another solution amongst many and has been developed further through Social Value initiatives which could be the best way moving forward.

Further reading

Barış-Tüzemen, Ö. and Tüzemen, S. (2022) The Impact of Foreign Direct Investment and Biomass Energy Consumption on Pollution in BRICS Countries: A Panel Data Analysis. *Global Journal of Emerging Market Economies* 14(1), 76–92. Article first published online: January 4, 2022; Issue published: January 1, 2022. https://doi.org/10.1177/09749 101211067092

Beard, N. D. (2008). The branding of ethical fashion and the consumer: A luxury niche or mass-market reality? Fashion Theory, 12(4), 447–467. http://doi.org/10.2752/175174108X346931

Charter, M. and Tischner, U. (2001) *Sustainable Solutions: Developing Products and Services for the Future.* Sheffield: Greenleaf Publishing.

Clayton, W. L. (1963) GATT, The Marshall Plan, and OECD. *Political Science Quarterly* 78(4), 493–503. Published by: Oxford University Press. Available at: https://www.jstor.org/stable/2146352

Duncan, S. (2021) *The Ethical Business Book: A Practical, Non-preachy Guide to Business Sustainability (Concise Advice).* 2nd edn. London: LID Publishing.

Elkington, J. (2018a) 25 Years Ago I Coined the Phrase "Triple Bottom Line." Here's Why It's Time to Rethink It. *Harvard Business Review.* Available at: https://hbr.org/2018/06/25-years-ago-i-coined-the-phrasetriple-bottom-line-heres-why-im-giving-up-on-it

Elkington, J. (2018b) *The Elkington Report: Zen and the Triple Bottom Line.* Green Biz. Available at: www.greenbiz.com/article/zen-and-triple-bottom-line

Freitag Group (2023) Freitag Impact Report 2022. Available at: 230927_freitag_impact_report_2022_en.pdf

Gerralda, J. (2015) *Loewe Case Study: Sustainability and Durable Luxury.* Madrid: IE Business Publishing. Available at: https://iepublishing.ie.edu/en/loewe-case-study-sustainability-and-durable-luxury

Kassoy, A. et Al. (2022) Patagonia asks all business leaders to look at themselves in the mirror. B Corporation (online). Available at: https://www.bcorporation.net/en-us/news/blog/b-lab-founders-message-patagonia/

Kemper, J. A. and Ballentine, P. W. (2017) What Do We Mean by Sustainability Marketing? *Journal of Marketing Management* 35(3–4), 277–309. https://doi.org/10.1080/0267257X.2019.1573845

LOEWE Foundation. (2023). Craftprize. Available at: http://craftprize.loewe.com/en/home

Mclaughlin, A. (2020) Freitag wants you to swap your old bags for Black Friday. Creative Review (online). Availble at: https://www.creativereview.co.uk/freitag-anti-black-friday/

Mitterfellner, O. (2023) *Luxury Fashion Brand Management: Unifying Fashion with Sustainability.* Abingdon: Routledge.

Orange, E. and Cohen, A.M. (2010). From eco-friendly to eco-intelligent. The Futurist, 44(5), p.28.

Pearse, G. (2012) Greenwash: Big Brands and Carbon Scams. Melbourne: Black Inc.

Pilmer I. (2009) Heaven and earth – Global warming the missing science. Lanham: Taylor Trade Publishing

Polonsky, J. (2001) Green marketing in Charter, M., and Tischner, U. (ed.) *Sustainable Solutions: Developing Products and Services for the Future.* Sheffield: Greenleaf Publishing.

Rauturier, S. (2022) *Greenwashing Ēxamples: 8 Notorious Fast Fashion Claims and Campaigns.* Good on You. Available at: https://goodonyou.eco/greenwashing-examples/

Ravago, M.-L. V., Balisacan, A. M., and Chakravorty, U. (2015). The principles and practice of sustainable economic development. In Sustainable Economic Development. Edited by Balisacan et al. Academic Press.

Robinson, D. (2021) What Is Greenwashing? Earth.org. Available at: https://earth.org/what -is-greenwashing/

Rotimi, E. O. O., Topple, C. and Hopkins, J. (2021) Towards a Conceptual Framework of Sustainable Practices of Post-consumer Textile Waste at Garment End of Lifecycle: A Systematic Literature Review Approach. *Sustainability 13, 2965.* https://doi.org/10.3390 /su13052965

SOLIT (2024) Available at: https://SOLIT-japan.com/en

Telford and Wrekin (2021) The 10 R's of Sustainable Living. Telford & Wrekin Council ICT Development Team. Available at: http://sustainabletelfordandwrekin.com/get -involved/did-you-know/10-rs-of-sustainable-living

Textile Exchange (2024) The UN's Sustainable Development Goals are universal, holistic, and measurable. Available at: https://textileexchange.org/sdgs/

The World Bank Group (2024) Atlas of Sustainable Development Goals 2023 – Available at: Responsible consumption & production | SDG 12: Responsible consumption & production (worldbank.org)

United Nations (n.d.) Sustainable Development Goals. Available at: https://sdgs.un.org/ goals

University of Alberta, Office of Sustainability (n.d.) What is Sustainability. Available at: www.mcgill.ca/sustainability/files/sustainability/what-is-sustainability.pdf

Trend forecasting and innovation
Trends and opportunities

12

Chapter topics

The Fashion Carousel

The future of fashion marketing and communication, indeed the entire fashion system, is closely connected to the occurrence and re-occurrence of trends and the cyclical economic nature which impacts society. Thus, the "Fashion Carousel" is a figurative representation of the regular and cyclical nature of the fashion system which seems to be ever-changing and innovating while simultaneously rotating and recycling ideas from the past (figure 12.1). It is designed as a tool which can be applied at any moment to observe the current state of the fashion industry. By stepping back and gaining a broader picture of how it interconnects, just like you would observe a colourful carousel at a fair, you can spot areas that need change. This first step is an an observation, and the second step includes ethical considerations so that a better fashion system

DOI: 10.4324/9781003449157-12

The Fashion Carousel – with ethical considerations

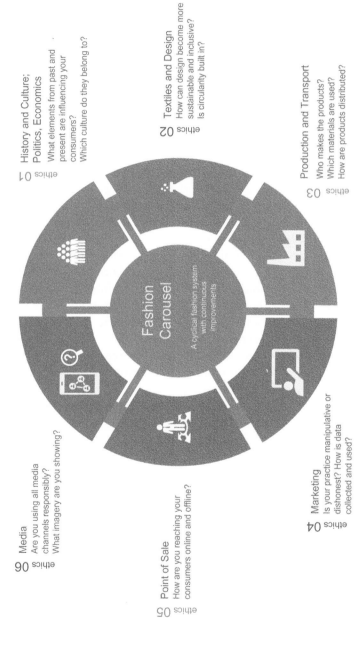

History and Culture;
Politics, Economics
What elements from past and
present are influencing your
consumers?
Which culture do they belong to?
ethics 01

Textiles and Design
How can design become more
sustainable and inclusive?
Is circularity built in?
ethics 02

Production and Transport
Who makes the products?
Which materials are used?
How are products distributed?
ethics 03

Marketing
Is your practice manipulative or
dishonest? How is data
collected and used?
ethics 04

Point of Sale
How are you reaching your
consumers online and offline?
ethics 05

Media
Are you using all media
channels responsibly?
What imagery are you showing?
ethics 06

Fashion
Carousel
A cyclical fashion system
with continuous
improvements

Figure 12.1 The Fashion Carousel with ethical considerations, is a figurative representation of the regular and cyclical nature of the fashion system which prompts a re-evaluation of each element and improvement of the system. Author's original illustration.

and cycle can be achieved. Working in marketing and business, including the fashion industry, will inadvertently present us with questions for ethical consideration. Looking at future trends in particular, it is up to this and the next generation to decide how deeply we dive into the brain functions of humans, whether artificial intelligence would pose a security threat, how much marketers should manipulate emotions, exploit our insecurities, and harm nature and populations for the sake of making a profit. For this purpose, the Fashion Carousel with ethical considerations is a guideline to help fashion students and professionals reflect on and improve the fashion system.

But first, let's look at the Fashion Carousel and its components. It includes textiles, design, production, retail, marketing, media and technology. Further elements are culture, history, politics and economics. These are components that form the basis of the fashion system, taking fashion garments from the initial textiles, through the entire supply chain resulting in retail and the supporting marketing activities. It also contains the important components of culture and history and politics and economics, which exert a huge influence on what is produced for fashion and arguably are not linear but recurrent. Arguably, each component has room for improvement and each component can be supported by theories and frameworks which are explained in this chapter.

For instance,the Economic Wave Theory is presented as the starting point for each new cycle of the carousel, fostering innovations (or re-inventions) which result in fashion and trends and the diffusion and adaptation by the public, before a new cycle begins. Marketing activities support the diffusion of these innovative trends. Because trends are closely connected to economic and social developments, which is reflected in the word "Zeitgeist" - they can be picked up on through trend forecasting.

Observing the cyclical nature of fashion design, represented by the spinning motion of the Fashion Carousel, we see that in every era certain trends were prominent and return again and again. Fashion pieces such as shoulder pads, for example, saw different uses (and materials) in the last 2000-plus years.

> They were part of a Roman Centurion's dress, later appearing in medieval armour suits for men. European military coats at the end of the seventeenth century featured external shoulder pads called epaulettes. In the late 1800s American football players received shoulder padding as protection from injury. In the 1930s they were introduced into womenswear and later in the 1980s became the silhouette of the power suit for women. Yet again in 2009, Olivier Rousteing presented a collection for Balmain which emphasized the shoulders. Most likely, we will see the shoulder pads in fashion over and over again.

Mini skirts are another interesting type of clothing, which, throughout history, transferred from men to women, making themselves prominent in the twentieth century, so much so that a "Hemline Index" was created, establishing a connection between the fluctuating length of a hemline and political, economic and social events.

Heels were worn by women and men alike in the last centuries, representing class, status, wealth, social position and style. Now mostly attributed to womenswear, the shape and size of a heel change with seasons and shoemakers.

The tight-fitting sheath dress of ancient Egypt, adorned with jewels, precious stones and metals, became highly fashionable in the 1920s when the tomb of Tutankhamun was discovered and inspired a collection by Karl Lagerfeld for Chanel in the twenty-first century.

The preceding fashionable examples could seem trivial if they were not connected to significant manifestations of our society such as the military, politics, economy, class, or ancient civilizations. Indeed, fashion recognizes, interprets and expresses various events in society, politics, economy, technology and even law.

Economic wave theory

Taking economy as one important impulse for fashion, there is evidence of a correlation between economic trends, innovation and the resulting fashion trends, which are an expression of societal changes. Here too, the idea proposed is that a free economy flows in waves and has a cyclical nature of ups and downs and can be seen as a starting point for the Fashion Carousel (figure 12.1) Various theories have been developed on the cyclical nature of economic trends and the length of a cycle, ranging from a few years to several decades. The following economists suggested waves and cycles of different lengths: Nikolai Kondratiev (54 years), Simon Kuznets (18 years), Clément Juglar (7-11 years) and Joseph Kitchin (about 4 years). Finally, the Austrian economist Joseph Schumpeter, who later in his life became a professor at Harvard University, took all these theories and combined them into one, bringing the theory by Kondratiev to the attention of the Western world.

The original "Kondratiev waves" is a theory invented by the Russian scientist Nikolai Kondratiev in the early twentieth century Soviet Russia. Sometimes they are referred to as K-waves, economic longwaves, or supercycles; and the inventor's name is sometimes spelled Kondratieff.

A Kondratiev wave is an evolutionary long-term economic cycle in a free capitalist economy, believed to result from technological innovation and produce a long period of prosperity during the expansion phase, but at a certain point it halts during a stagnation phase and ultimately results in economic

Figure 12.2 Russian economist Nikolai Kondratiev lived from 1892 to 1932 and invented the "Kondratiev waves". Author's original illustration.

downturn during a recession. This cycle or wave would last between four to six decades on average and always ensure that an economy would thrive again. These waves have later been divided into four distinct seasons that correlate with the economic movement at a certain period of time: spring for economic awakening, summer for the peak season, autumn for the downturn and winter for the full recession (Barbuto, 2023).

Although modern economists have opposing opinions on whether this theory is accurate and acceptable, the ones who acknowledge its validity recognize several such waves which are all connected to innovation and social change. Five distinct Kondratiev waves have been recognized since its invention, with discussions pointing towards an imminent sixth one (Kenton, 2018).

If you return to Chapters 1 and 2, you can look at developments of the industrial revolution and the changes which the fashion industry experienced, comparing them to Kondratiev's waves. The industrial revolution and consequent production of cloth and then clothing run in parallel with the first Kondratiev wave. The innovation of railways and electricity helped to expand advertising and public relations, while petrochemicals and the automotive industries sped up and facilitated a global production and consumption of fashion en masse

Table 12.1 Kondratiev waves from past to future

Kondratiev Wave	Duration of wave	Innovation	Transformation of	Industry benefit
First Kondratiev wave	1780 to 1830	Steam engine	Energy	Textile industry
Second Kondratiev wave	1830 to 1880	Steel and rail industries	Energy	Mass transportation
Third Kondratiev Wave	1880 to 1930	Electricity and chemicals	Energy	Infrastructure, communication, production
Fourth Kondratiev wave	1930 to 1970	Petrochemicals, mass production and automobiles	Energy	Mass consumption
Fifth Kondratiev wave	1970 to present	Information technology and telecommunications	Information	ICT industry
Sixth Kondratiev wave	Present to future	Medicine, health and Biotech; post-information technology	Bioinformation digital information	Biotech industry Digital economy Digital Intelligence

during the second to fourth Kondratiev waves. Modern communication practices are connected to the fifth Kondratiev wave with the rise of digital media and devices. Finally, present-day innovations in medicine and health as well as biotech include studies of neuroscience, AI and genes which are connected to some of the latest trends in the fashion industry, as illustrated later in this chapter. With every wave, it was either energy or information which was converted and harnessed.

Understanding how economic waves work can give a competitive advantage in understanding the connection between innovation, which in turn can set trends and affect consumers.

The focal point of the Kondratiev waves is the drivers of economic upturn and prosperity (i.e. spring and summer) which are initiated through disruptive innovations and new technology.

These innovations go through phases that coincide with time: research and development, introduction of the innovation, growth, maturity and finally decline. The corresponding theory is the "diffusion of innovations" concept developed by Everett Rogers. He was one of the first people to note universal factors which explain societal changes and innovation.

However, when these new technologies go through the motion of being adopted by the masses, they become cheap, outdated and obsolete, and economic benefit stagnates (this is equal to the autumn and winter phase by Kondratiev).

Diffusion of innovations theory

In the early 1960s, the diffusion of innovations theory (DOI) was developed by Everett M. Rogers, who stipulated that new ideas and technology spread through society from the very early stages of research and development, through to introduction, growth, maturity and decline. Rogers defined four main elements in the diffusion of innovations: an innovation is communicated through certain channels, over time, among the members of a social system (Rogers, 2003). Thus, any innovation is not accepted uniformly by all members of a society; it is a gradual development, potentially reaching 100 per cent of a population.

The innovation

Rogers describes the first and very crucial part of his theory – the innovation itself – in the following way:

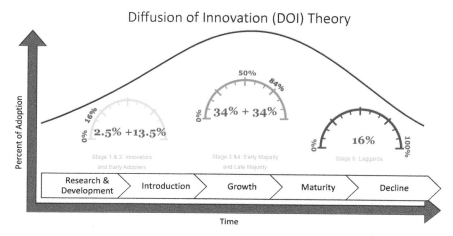

Figure 12.3 Diffusion of innovations.

> An innovation is an idea, practice, or object perceived as new by an indi-
> vidual or other relevant unit of adoption. The idea need not be objec-
> tively new as measured by the lapse of time since its use or discovery but
> merely perceived as new and innovative. The newness of an innovation
> does not just involve new knowledge, but also persuasion, or a decision
> to adopt. Someone may have known about an innovation for some time
> but may not yet have adopted or rejected it.
>
> (Rogers, 1987, p. 114)

In his later observation after the 1970s, Rogers notes that sometimes an innovation can be a re-invention, meaning that an innovation undergoes change or
modification by a user in the process of adoption and implementation. This,
he believes, makes for a more rapid diffusion and adoption of the innovation
because it becomes customizable. (Here we can see a strong connection to the
fashion industry and the re-invention of styles.)

Rate of adoption and communication

According to Rogers, the rate of adoption by individuals in any society has a
relative speed which can be "measured as the number of individuals who adopt
a new idea in a specified period, such as a year". This can be visualized as a
numerical indicator of the steepness of the adoption curve for an innovation
(Rogers, 2003).

Five variables influence the success of the adoption in any given society, including the perceived attributes of the innovation, the nature of the social system and its norms, and the communications channels that help inform the public of the innovation. For Rogers, it will spread better if mass communication is deployed rather than word of mouth (Rogers, 2003).

The diffusion and adopter categories

The diffusion itself starts from the innovation and grows in percentage over time, reaching more and more members of a society. The social distribution according to Rogers is divided into the innovators who represent the first 2.5 per cent of the group to adopt an innovation, followed by 13.5 per cent as early adopters, 34 per cent as early majority, 34 per cent as late majority and lastly 16 per cent as laggards (CFI Team, 2024). To him, these are ideal types and not necessarily true representations of a society which has deviations and exceptions (Rogers, 2003).

The five adopter categories have specific characteristics:

Innovators: Characterized by venturesomeness, due to a desire for the daring and the risky. Being an innovator has several prerequisites, such as the ability to understand new technology, have resources to produce the prototypes or absorb financial losses during the development process. The innovator must be able to cope with a high degree of uncertainty about an innovation at the time he or she adopts it.

Early adopters: Characterized by "the highest degree of opinion leadership in most systems". Potential adopters look to early adopters for advice and information about an innovation. The early adopter is considered by many to be "the individual to check with" before adopting a new idea. The social characteristics of earlier adopters mark them as more educated, of higher social status and the like. They are wealthier and have larger-sized units. Socioeconomic status and innovativeness appear to go hand in hand (Rogers, 2003).

Early majority: Characterized by those who adopt new innovations before the average person. They form a link between the very early adopters and the late majority which helps the diffusion process among mainstream society.

Late majority: Characterized by those who are sceptical of change and will only adopt an innovation after it's been generally accepted and adopted by the majority of the population. Like the early majority, the late majority makes up one third of the members of a system. Adoption may be both an economic necessity for the late majority and the result of increasing peer

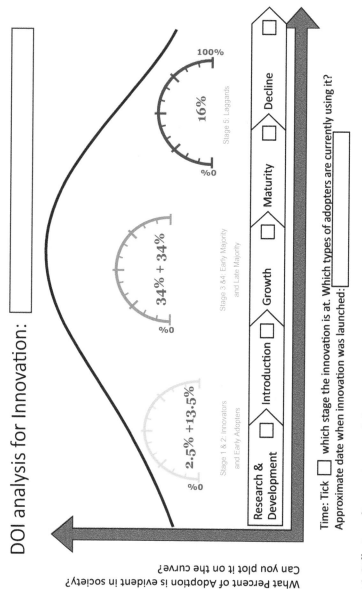

Figure 12.4 Diffusion of innovations worksheet 1.

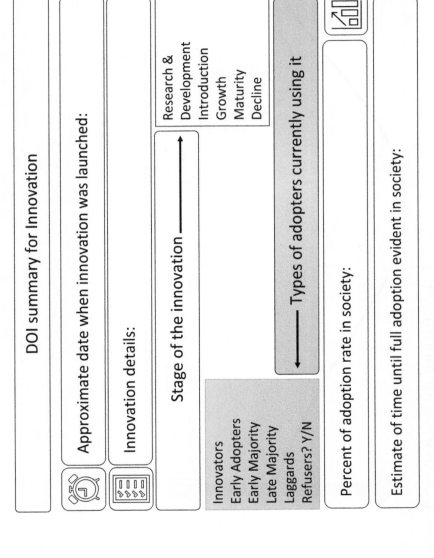

Figure 12.5 Diffusion of innovations worksheet 2.

pressures. Innovations are approached with a sceptical and cautious air, and the late majority do not adopt until most others in their system have already done so.

Laggards: Characterized by those who are very traditional and conservative – they are the last to accept change. They hold no opinion leadership that is noteworthy and can be socially isolated. They might be in a precarious economic position that forces them to be extremely cautious in adopting innovations.

Rogers (2003) later notes that there are even those who completely refuse innovations. Called "people who said no to innovation", he is referring to social groups such as the Old Order Amish who are forbidden from adopting any innovations of the modern world. Yet, despite this, he praises them for being very innovative in adopting innovations that are consistent with their Amish cultural values.

In the worksheets provided, you can brainstorm on an innovation (existing or proposed) and map it along the DOI framework and then summarize your findings.

Rogers on the diffusion of fashion trends

Interestingly, Rogers (2003, pp. 216–217) makes a connection to fashion, providing a good explanation of microtrends in fashion (or fads) which are explored in more detail next:

> Status Aspects of Innovations: One motivation for many individuals to adopt an innovation is the desire to gain social status. (...) For certain innovations, such as new clothing fashions, the social prestige that the innovation conveys to its adopter is almost the sole benefit the adopter receives. In fact, when many other members of a system have also adopted the same fashion, an innovation such as shorter skirts or a bare midriff may lose its prestige value to earlier adopters. This gradual loss of status conferral on the part of a particular clothing innovation provides pressure for yet newer fashions. Many clothing fashions are fads, innovations that represent a relatively unimportant aspect of culture, which diffuse very rapidly, mainly for status reasons, and then are rapidly discontinued.

Evolution of fashion trends and trend forecasting

Modern trend forecasting for the fashion industry has undergone an evolution over several centuries, with particular developments in the latter half of the twentieth century, and is now a global industry which offers professional future forecasts by specialist agencies. Together with the understanding of external shifts such as economic cycles and political changes, and the use of AI and algorithms, trend forecasting agencies effectively help businesses detect consumer behaviour patterns and trends, helping designers and marketers alike to position themselves competitively for the future. Trends are perceived to be current and future-focused; however, they are not new as such. In this context, an evolution of fashion trends can be observed throughout history and, in the following example, European history.

Fashion was reserved for the European aristocrats and upper classes, who communicated about it in tightly knit circles and competed with each other between Italy, France, Spain, the Netherlands, Russia and England, setting trends at their respective courts. Thus, the nobility was the only social class that could afford extravagant fashion and dominated tastes for centuries, with Italian courts setting the fashion trends until the middle of the fifteenth century (Mentges, 2011).

A significant shift occurred during the sixteenth century, when Europe slowly emerged from the Dark Ages and transitioned into the Renaissance. Travellers began to bring back textiles and garments from distant voyages, introducing new sartorial ideas from trade with America, Asia and the Ottoman Empire, each of which of course had its own unique fashion and materials. Moreover, the merchants established a class of their own and developed into competitors for the nobility. Mentges (2011) believes that an important medium for disseminating fashion among European countries was the "richly illustrated costume books which enjoyed a strong European-wide reception between 1532 and 1600" and which were available in multiple languages such as Italian, Dutch and French.

This correlates with Ballmer and Tobias (2016) who date back the first notable trend forecasting to the manufacturers' sample books or trade catalogues from the 1700s, which may resemble modern trend-forecasting catalogues. With merchants and middle classes rising and establishing themselves in European cities by the eighteenth century, fashion trends were prominent in Paris, London, St Petersburg and Vienna – and became a social language expressing their values, new financial power, political views (rejecting sumptuary laws or standards set by the nobility) and affiliation (Mentges, 2011).

Of course, fashion production and forecasting became even more prominent during the industrial revolution in Europe, which saw the clothing and textiles trade expand, and created the need to better predict and set upcoming colour and style trends. It is also noteworthy that communication played a role in accelerating information on fashion. As mentioned in Chapters 1 and 2, the advances of the industrial revolution brought the distribution of printed news-papers and magazines, the telegraph and telephone with it at first, later com-plemented by radio, cinema and television. With industrialization, Western fashion moved from class fashion to consumer fashion, which is especially true in our postmodern society (Crane, 2000; Kawamura, 2011).

Whilst London had established itself as a trend-setter for menswear, dur-ing the eighteenth century, France had established itself as the main leader of women's fashion – both in terms of producing sought-after styles and in terms of the craftsmanship and know-how to do so. France was celebrated and envied in its dominant position so much so that it had to protect itself from ruthless competition through coordinated regulation and professional associations. The Chambre Syndicale de la Haute Couture was one such pro-tective association and was founded in 1868. "In that environment, the drive by foreign department stores to adapt couture to domestic mass production set up the conditions in which reporting, sketching, and eventually forecasting would thrive" (Ballmer and Tobias, 2016).

The celebrated styles of Paris travelled out of Europe across the Atlantic and became very popular in North America. At the beginning of the twentieth century, America and its large department stores were looking at France and its production of colours, textiles and styles as a trend indicator and sent their own "spies" to help copy some of the world's most renowned designs. Gaining access to fashion shows meant that you were in an insider's heaven where you could learn about the visions and creations of the couturiers and designers. Selling the copied fashion made in the USA (versus imported from France) meant higher profits for retailers. Notably, the mediators between France and the US were fashion journalists, relaying accurate information back to their sponsors who would then manufacture very similar garments in the USA.

> By the 1920s, with fashion production cycles firmly established in Paris and with department stores operating as the retail powerhouses in world cities, reporting services proliferated. For example, Evans quotes American Vogue managing editor Edna Woolman Chase's recollection that the "instant the collections have taken place, and days before the buyers" purchases can reach the United States by ship or even plane, an admirably drawn, accurately documented portfolio of all the best French models is on the desk of almost every Seventh Avenue manufacturer. It is an international spy system to turn the military green with envy.
>
> (Ballmer and Tobias, 2016)

In response to Paris's most prominent role in creating desirable trends, America's very own Textile Color Card Association of the USA (TCCA) was set up and began to consult brands and stores on which colours to produce and sell in order to meet popular customer demands.

By 1930, the TCCA played a major role in defining the colours and their names for all manner of fashion as well as government-related items such as uniforms, ribbons, medals and flags. Another 20 years later, the TCCA membership of subscribing businesses grew internationally. This expansion led to the creation of industry-specific trends and colour books sponsored by those industries and direct trend consulting was offered to individual companies (Hollandand and Jones, 2017).

However, in Europe the stronghold of its own fashion forecasting continued: from the late 1950s onwards, agencies such as France's Promostyl, Nelly Rodi and Li Edelkoort's Trend Union emerged, offering colour, trend and visual forecasts in inspirational and often quirky books for a serious price.

Further agencies followed, such as the UK's WGSN (Worth Global Style Network) in the late 1990s and Trendstop and Stylus after 2000. Today, these agencies still operate and have global offices around the world. The shift here was clearly from runway collections to all echelons of the fashion industry, and trend services were offered to mass-produced brands just as much as ready-to-wear clients. The objective now is to keep up with the fast pace of the industry with a speedy time to market.

WGSN is a very powerful and strong influencer in trend reports and trend prediction. It was founded by brothers Julian and Marc Worth in London in 1998, growing explosively and changing owners to parent company Ascential in 2005. The service (like most of the modern trend-forecasting agencies) looks at a broad variety of influences on the fashion industry, such as textiles, colour, fashion, catwalks, lifestyle, interiors, cosmetics, marketing, consumer behaviour, retail and innovation. Critics of trend forecasting agencies have pointed out that behemoths such as WGSN are so influential in their forecasts that they are influencing textile manufacturers years before any fashion trends can emerge. This, in theory, means that any fashion brand is selecting materials today that were dictated by WGSN years ago, taking away their own power of decision-making and making the predictions a self-fulfilling prophecy (Seto, 2017).

Additionally, European textile fairs and trade exhibitions such as Premiere Vision, Pitti Filati and Techtextil grew to become authorities on textile trends and now help the entire fashion industry prepare for the upcoming seasons by providing insights into the raw material trends which are turned into clothes.

Futurology or trends to be aware of

Forecasting is integral to human nature, the desire to be prepared for the future and outsmarting forces such as weather, unforeseen events, competitors or even fate and ensuring an auspicious outcome. There is forecasting for business and finance, economy (as detailed in the Economic Wave Theory earlier on), meteorology, geology and ecology, politics and law, etc. – and fashion.

"Futurology" is one term that describes the attempt to predict the future based on current trends and is criticized for being of a subjective and biased nature due to interpretations rather than facts. The *Oxford Dictionary of Philosophy* even describes futurology as "mainly a pseudo-science, given the complexities of social, political, economic, technological, and natural factors" (Blackburn, 2008).

Futurology in fashion – which can simply be seen as a catalyst for social events – looks at short-term and long-term issues of society, science, technology, politics and consumer behaviour alike. Qualitative data and quantifiable data such as statistics and AI assist in analyzing the potential of these sometimes emerging and quiet developments or loud and lasting occurrences, which are labelled as micro-, macro- and megatrends. But what is the difference between them?

The available literature does not always agree, but the general consensus is that microtrends are short-lived fads that quickly become obsolete. They can, however, continue to grow into macrotrends that have a broader social reach and remain alive for longer. The longest trends are megatrends and represent major shifts in society.

Developments such as neuroscience and machine learning, emotions and curation, Gen Z and Gen Alpha, emerging markets and globalization, inclusivity, and sustainability are arguably macrotrends that fashion brands have been engaging with. As these trends develop, it is equally important not to lag behind in adopting an ethical approach to the use and application of these advances. Table 12.2 explores the rapid developments from the ethical angle.

Trend-driven Innovation

Innovations can start trends, but equally, trends can be used to foster innovative thinking in businesses. Mason et al. (2015) propose a systematic approach to understanding societal shifts fuelling consumer trends and harnessing them to offer new products or services. The authors developed a "Consumer Trend Canvas" (CTC), which is a visual aid to innovation thinking and design. With

Table 12.2 Global trends fashion needs to be aware of

AI and metaverse	Both AI and the metaverse are notable technological advances of recent times.
	The rapid development of AI and its accessibility to the general public pose questions of risk versus benefit across many sectors.
	Large language models (LLMs) are classified as generative AI technology, which is able to generate content, much like a dialogue with a real human, based on large data sets and training. While this can improve work output, speed and accuracy, LLMs have been found to be autoregressive wherein "they use past data to predict future data in generating responses; this probabilistic process means outputs can be inconsistent, often changing depending on the wording of queries". Alarmingly, false information and even AI "hallucination" have been noted (Blease and Torous, 2023).
	There is also a notable difference in development between the East and West: China is offering Baidu's Ernie bot due to restrictions on OpenAI's ChatGPT.
	In terms of security, AI can be used in conjunction with our health and digital identification and allow for biometric security, which includes acoustic authentication technology (pioneered by NEC), keystroke verification, fingerprints, iris and face recognition, behaviour recognition, emotion detection and more.
	Within a very short time of its launch, a phenomenon called "AI fatigue" has set in. AI is overwhelming and concerning at the same time, leading some people to embrace human creations in traditional physical forms more than before.
	According to Mintel (2023), 81 per cent of Indonesian consumers believe that AI will make them treasure creations by humans more, including art and books.
	The metaverse embeds a digital interface into consumers' lives, who are predicted to spend one hour or more per day in the metaverse by 2026, with Gen Alpha experiencing the most social enthusiasm. The metaverse also offers events – a market valued at $114 billion in 2021, and expected to grow by 21.4 per cent annually until 2030 (Mintel).

(Continued)

Table 12.2 Global trends fashion needs to be aware of (*Continued*)

In fashion, NFTs have been bridging the physical and digital worlds with varying rates of success: Gucci had a collaboration with Superplastic resulting in SUPERGUCCI NFTs, co-created by Gucci's Creative Director Alessandro Michele and synthetic artists Janky & Guggimon; Karl Lagerfeld offered his miniature self in the form of NFT collectibles, consisting of 777 digital figurines sold for €77 each, with a wardrobe which users could digitally change through subsequent digital drops. (7 was Karl Lagerfeld's favourite number.)(Meanwhile, in 2024, Hermès is in an ongoing lawsuit facing artist Mason Rothschild over the Metabirkin NFTs.

Blockchain technology is being increasingly used to facilitate supply chain transparency, and avatars form a personal expression in a digital landscape. The world's largest luxury conglomerate, LVMH, leads an accelerator programme

"La Maison des Startups", which invites start-ups to help solve challenges in the world of luxury, such as 3D/virtual product experience and the metaverse, dynamic translation of natural language into database query language and more. An application of this is the new LV Diamonds collection, which will see the mine-to-finger journey of the stones certified by the Aura Blockchain Consortium for traceability purposes (Templeton, 2024). Beauty retailer Sephora is also fortifying its digital presence with a new immersive, customizable 3D gaming-like Web3 platform, designed exclusively with beauty enthusiasts in mind. (Flavia, S., 2023)

It is predicted that AI will be implemented in the metaverse, where it will offer virtual spaces that simulate real-life or fantasy scenarios. This is no longer augmented reality versus virtual reality, but augmented virtual reality or AVR. We will increasingly hear more about mixed reality (MR or XR).

Finally, in terms of marketing, the most advanced companies make use of algorithms, AI (e.g. Etro's recent AI campaign), digital advertising, global social media channels (with variations between West and East), personalization and consumer targeting through personalized data, and measuring campaign success with data analytics.

(*Continued*)

Table 12.2 Global trends fashion needs to be aware of (*Continued*)

Neuroscience for curated experiences	Neuroscience is a modern science of the nervous system and brain, part of which aims to uncover how it works by using insightful technology such as MRI brain scanners. Areas that this science might serve include traditional and digital marketing by trying to tap into consumers' emotions, mood, memory and impulses.
	Neuroscience has revealed that humans are driven by emotions and many decisions are emotion-based rather than the rational result of our brain's activity. It is thus lucrative for marketers to tap into consumers' emotions to connect them to the brand and influence purchase decisions through the use of "neuromarketing", which, according to Bentahar(2023) will be "the future of marketing strategy".
	One way of enhancing the positive emotional appeal and consumer engagement is by offering a curated shopping experience.
	The definition of curation is "the selection and care of objects to be shown in a museum or to form part of a collection of art, an exhibition", as stated by the *Cambridge Dictionary* (2019) and it has been a common practice in museums. However, over the last decades, it has been applied to marketing and retail as well as online environments.
	Offline, consumers enter department stores and flagship stores like a museum, experiencing a carefully selected display of objects, often interactive. Concept stores such as 10 Corso Como, the now-closed Colette or Dover Street Market achieved a fusion of cultural space, commerce and exhibition space, setting trends in what is "cool". Despite digital advances, consumers still enjoy physical retail and will gravitate towards experiential locations.
	Online websites are aiming to deliver the same experience through "curated commerce" and digital experience platforms (DXP), which are able to offer consumers meaningful and personalized experiences across all platforms and devices (Gartner, 2023). Of course, with the consumer behaviour data that digital platforms can collect, a more tailored experience can be offered to each individual visitor.
	According to De Kruiff (2023), the future in digital fashion will be "hyperverticalization" – a tapestry of intertwining values that digital consumers insist upon, such as inclusivity, diversity and integrity with cutting-edge technology, which can include AI, VR, AR and more.

(*Continued*)

Table 12.2 Global trends fashion needs to be aware of (*Continued*)

	In China, curation via digital platforms is in an advanced stage, with livestream shopping booming and performed by humans and virtual streamers alike. This multitude of online resources paired with real-time interaction offered, video streaming, online games and social interactions have had an impact on how the younger generations partake in culture and cultural interactions (Ding and Chai, 2022).
Post-Covid economy and shift of global powers	The pandemic has left many consumers with dire realities and strained budgets, having intensified existing social inequalities, with notable negative health outcomes for groups who were already disadvantaged in society (British Academy, 2021).
	Those communities all over the world are experiencing daily cost-of-living angst, fuelled by inflation and uncertainty and will gravitate towards brands that offer transparency in their pricing, honest messaging and the option to pay in instalments (e.g. Klarna, Shahry, AsiaPay).
	This new and rising market for financial services includes digital options such as neo-banks (digital-only banks), cryptocurrencies and financial wellness platforms.
	According to Ding and Chai (2022), our consumption habits have changed due to digital capitalism becoming more diversified and convenient and offering personalized experiences.
	"In China, the consumption sector related to digital capitalism has registered a growth rate far exceeding that of the overall gross domestic product (GDP), becoming the cornucopia for digital capital worldwide. Shopping on online platforms has taken the front seat in retailing because of its strengths in smart popping-up, correlation matching, one-click
	ordering, one-day delivery, whole-process tracking and taking in consumers' feedback for improvement".
	This is part of the counterbalance to struggling countries; emerging economies such as the BRICS are on their way to becoming developed countries.
	They have financial infrastructure, GDP growth, established industries or increasing industrialization, social stability, and an overall high growth rate.
	They are a lucrative investment for established brands because those countries have a rising middle class with numerous customers who have relatively recently obtained more disposable income and are eager to buy into designer brands.

(*Continued*)

Table 12.2 Global trends fashion needs to be aware of (*Continued*)

Sustainability	Sustainability famously means "meeting our own needs without compromising the ability of future generations to meet their own needs".
	It includes environmental, economic, social and overall ethical aspects and should ideally create a world where ecological integrity is maintained, communities can thrive and human rights are respected (McGill, 2019).
	The sustainability trend continues to permeate consumers' minds and their purchase behaviour. They are keen to have sustainable products and buy guilt-free. Equally, manufacturers and brands have to demonstrate that their practices are indeed sustainable.
	However, any ethical and sustainable practices that brands communicate are questionable with consumers understanding that facts could potentially be twisted, thus greenwashing and making false claims.
	Sustainability also permeates the entire consumer lifestyle, including choices of where to live, what travel destinations to choose and what to eat. In terms of fashion choices, vintage and resale options are becoming increasingly popular, together with alternative materials that do not harm animals or nature and allow for circularity. The EY Future Consumer Index (2022) shows that 72 per cent of consumers believe companies should be championing better social and environmental outcomes.
Wellness in a diverse and inclusive world	Post-pandemic, consumers have discovered the importance of self-care while simultaneously still battling with post-Covid anxiety.
	According to Mintel (2023), brands can have a direct effect on consumers' personal health and well-being by offering them a social world where they can create and share experiences, strengthening social ties.
	At the same time, people have become more aware of individualistic needs and are seeking meaningful solitude, even when they work from home or in hybrid settings.
	The metaverse finds significance here, too, with 65 per cent of global consumers using it to improve their health (virtual fitness) or find virtualized calm (meditation) (Brynn and Baron, 2023).

(*Continued*)

Table 12.2 Global trends fashion needs to be aware of (*Continued*)

Escapism is on the rise, paired with nostalgia for the past, with the latter being attributed to Gen Z. A longing for nostalgic stability is an antidote to global challenges and when travelling, consumers start their journey by looking at health, wellness and relaxation offers at the airports (Airport Dimensions, 2023). They venture on to holistic wellness retreats, where their need for experiential holidays does not leave an imprint on nature. Travel destinations must provide "respite from hyperstimulated modern lifestyles" (Shardlow, 2024).

A large contributing factor to consumer wellness is the need to feel diversity and inclusion both in everyday life and through the brands that consumers choose. With brands embracing a wide scope of sizes and body shapes, ethnicities and genders, the trend is steadily encompassing many industries, including fashion, which has a history of being highly excluding.

its simple layout, it offers a handy framework to understand a consumer trend and then apply it to create a true innovation.

In connection with the Economic Wave Theory, one can see that in times of economic downturn (autumn phase and winter phase) innovations have lifted economies out of stagnation and back into prosperity. Picking up on the sentiment amongst people that can be attributed to a specific time, or the "Zeitgeist", we can analyse more accurately what it is that consumers might need.

The step-by-step guide to using the trend canvas is as follows:

Table 12.3 The step-by-step guide to using the Consumer Trend Canvas (CTC). (Mason et al., 2015)

01 Choose A Trend	Based on your trend research, accessible trend reports from agencies and marketing research, choose a trend (preferably an established or macro trend that will last several future seasons).
02 Analyze Your Trend	**Inspiration** Start with the real-world innovations that illustrate a trend in action. Why? Because seeing the brand visions, business models, products/services/experiences and marketing/campaigns being created by organizations (including corporations, startups, nonprofits or governmental organizations) validates that a trend exists and shows its evolution over time. Plus, it provides an easy way to tangibly understand a trend, gain inspiration and show what it can mean for your customers.

(*Continued*)

Table 12.3 The step-by-step guide to using the Consumer Trend Canvas (CTC). (Mason et al., 2015) (*Continued*)

02 Analyze Your Trend	**Basic needs:** We're all human. Trends – and behavior more broadly – are ultimately rooted in our basic, fundamental, rarelyifever-changing human needs, wants and desires. Identifying these basic needs and desires isn't rocket science, or even deep social science. They are the forces that have been shaping personal and social relations for centuries, if not millennia. Points to consider might be these: Social status / Self-improvement / Entertainment / Connection / Security / Identity / Relevance / Health & wellbeing / Fairness / Trust / Loyalty / Peace of mind / Convenience / Support **Drivers of change** While people's basic needs rarely change, consumers are constantly faced with technological, societal and economical change. Without this change, trends simply wouldn't exist. To help simplify the broad drivers of change that exist in the world, we divide them into two types: Shifts are the long-term, macro changes that are playing out across years, or even decades, that will shape both the direction and flavor of a specific trend. Triggers are the more immediate changes that drive the emergence of a consumer trend. These can include specific technologies, political events, economic shocks, environmental incidents, and more. Action Think about 2-3 changes in the last 5-10 years that has made this trend emerge and add them to the Shift section. Identify 2-3 changes from the last 6 months – 5 years to narrow down your exploration of the Triggers. **Emerging expectations** Trends emerge when basic human needs, external change and new innovations combine to create new expectations among consumers. The secret to understanding a trend, and the opportunities it presents, lies in finding the points of tension between what people currently have, and what they want or expect. Action Look back at the Basic Needs, Drivers of Change and Innovation examples identified on your canvas. To pinpoint 3-5 emerging expectations to add to the canvas, start with the following prompts: 'This trend creates new desires for…'; 'Because of this trend people can't live without…'; 'After interacting with these innovations you would expect…'.

Table 12.3 The step-by-step guide to using the Consumer Trend Canvas (CTC). (Mason et al., 2015) (*Continued*)

03 Apply The Insight	When you're thinking about applying a consumer trend, it helps to consider how and where it could impact your business, through the lens of these four areas:
	Brand Vision
	How will the deeper shifts underlying this trend shape your company's long-term vision?
	Business Model
	Can you apply this trend to launch a whole new business venture or brand?
	Product / Service / Experience
	What new products and services could you create in light of this trend? How will you adapt your current products and services?
	Marketing / Campaign
	How can you incorporate this trend into your campaigns, show consumers you speak their language, and that you simply 'get it'? Think beyond demographics – it's not about peoples' gender, age, or what they say but about what they do: their needs, desires and expectations. You may already have a customer segment in mind for whom you need to develop a new innovation for. However, we encourage you to think beyond your existing customers, to new groups you could target.
	Need further inspiration? Look at what extreme users are currently doing. New consumer behaviors usually start with certain (niche) segments, before evolving and spreading throughout the mass market.
04 Capture Your Ideas	This is where the magic happens! By referring back to the insights you generated during the analyze phase, and making connections between the two halves of the canvas, you will now uncover truly novel concepts and ideate new consumer-facing innovations.
	Action
	Innovate! Write down every idea that emerges from your conversation. At this stage, no idea is a bad idea. Even the ones you dismiss could be valuable in the weeks and months to come.
	Finally...
	Pick the best innovation idea, and complete the Big Idea Worksheet to summarize where it has come from, along with the emerging expectations your idea is fulfilling (and exceeding). This gives you a focused, one-page summary that is ready to share with your colleagues and business leaders.

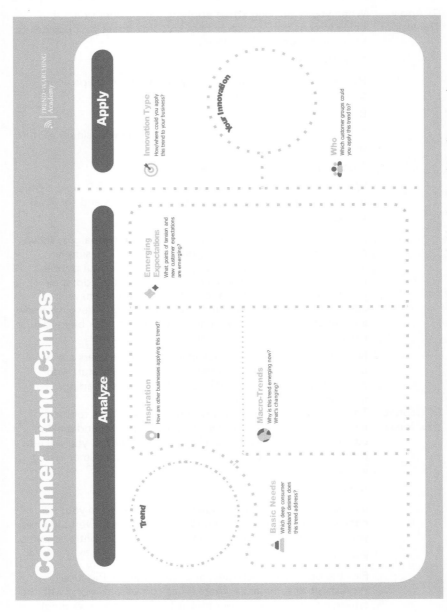

Figure 12.6 A blank Consumer Trend Canvas with instructions. Kindly provided by the TrendWatching Academy.

L'esprit du temps *or the Zeitgeist*

L'esprit du temps is the French expression meaning the "spirit of the times", describing a unique sentiment amongst people that can be attributed to a specific time period or even a longer era, which then is *l'esprit de l'epoche*. Within this time frame, trend forecasters can perfectly detect the state the consumers are in and how fashion brands can cater to their needs.

In some trend forecasting literature, the German version of this term, *Zeitgeist* (pronounced ['tsaɪtgaɪst]) is used in conjunction with the spirit of the times (Holland and Jones, 2017). The *Duden* (2023) defines it as "a mental attitude or general sentiment which is characteristic for a specific historical time" and was first mentioned by Herder in 1769. It also represents sentiment (thoughts and feelings) during a particular time, but the time can take any span and is not defined.

Briefly looking at the German language from which this word has been taken, you can express it in several forms: *Zeitgeist* is the noun, *zeitgeistig* or *zeitgeistlich* are the adjectives, which mean that something meets the current sentiment. The Komparativ, or comparative, which is the form of the adjective used to express a difference, would be *zeitgeistlicher*, the Superlativ is *am zeitgeistlichsten*. Lastly, with the suffix *-keit* and the article *die*, the adjective is turned into a noun: *die Zeitgeistlichkeit*. This suffix is known to create very abstract concepts, and thus whereas Zeitgeist is something that exists in society on its own, Zeitgeistlichkeit is an activity. This noun signifies the ability to be in the present moment, for something or someone to experience and live out the Zeitgeist as a reality. Zeitgeistlichkeit means that the trend forecasters can perfectly detect the state the consumers are in and how fashion brands can cater to their needs.

Interview with Kirstine Fratz

Kirstine Fratz is a cultural scientist and Germany's most renowned Zeitgeist researcher. She explores the influence of Zeitgeist on our cultural development and how to harness it for creating a better future. Kirstine advises companies and institutions such as Unilever, Gucci, Facebook, Audi and even the Church. She is an international speaker on Zeitgeist topics, a lecturer at universities, a board member at German Real Estate, a TED speaker and an author.

Homepage: https://zeitgeistforschung.com/en/home-en/

Figure 12.7 Kirstine Fratz. With kind permission.

Q: You are a "Zeitgeist researcher". Can you give us more details on what this means, please?

KF: We understand a lot about trends, but hardly anything about the Zeitgeist. The force that drives cultural change in the background. While trends are mostly clearly discernible, Zeitgeist reveals access to the cultural subconscious. A subtle crack in the societal matrix can be enough to recognize new cultural potential and to create a pull that adds unimaginable things to our culture.

In this sphere of autonomous cultural change, beyond institutions and interests, Zeitgeist research is active. A field of research that started over a 100 years ago and, through its interdisciplinary approach, is currently contributing to a deeper understanding of creativity and change.

As a Zeitgeist researcher, my role involves delving into the collective psyche of society, uncovering its underlying longings, aspirations and trends that shape various aspects of life including culture, economy and politics.

By understanding the Zeitgeist, organizations can better adapt to changing cultural dynamics, anticipate future trends and create innovative solutions that resonate with people's deepest desires and needs for new life experiences.

Q: Looking at the linguistic significance, what is your personal under-standing of the term "Zeitgeist" and how can someone make sense of it not knowing the German language of origin?

KF: The term "Zeitgeist" encompasses the spirit, mood or cultural context of a particular period in time. It reflects the collective beliefs, attitudes and values that shape society at a given moment.

Even without knowing its German language origin, one can under-stand "Zeitgeist" by recognizing its broader linguistic significance. It essentially refers to the prevailing mindset or prevailing cultural atmosphere of a specific time. By observing societal trends, cultural expressions, psychosocial microevolution and historical events, one can grasp the essence of the Zeitgeist without needing to know the specific German term.

Q: What are consumers focused on in these current times?

KF: One of my Zeitgeist maxims is: "Zeitgeist is the permission to recover from prevailing conditions, in all shapes and colours". A prime field to observe this statement is the type of vacations we take to rejuvenate ourselves from daily life and the drugs we preferentially consume to compensate for the system in which we live. Presently, it's fascinating to note that vacations often revolve around healing. There's an increasing number of concepts in the realm of mental health, some of them drug-based, and vacations focused on mental well-being, for example modern curated retreats where only one par-ent takes a vacation while the other continues with family duties. The experience of a harmonized self has replaced some traditional travel mentalities.

Talking about drugs as a great indicator of how a society is doing, looking into the beverage industry is always interesting. Products are now infused with various active substances like mushrooms and herbs to support a more intense but although coherent quality of life. Additionally, the phenomenon of sober curiosity, the longing to experience life all aware and curious, is quite noticeable. This marks a shift towards a need for a different life experience as usual, away from the well-established techniques of numbing and compensating. That will impact various aspects of life and therefore consumers' expecta-tions on business and products. In observing these phenomena, I ask, "What is the new empty field of longing? What is the next shift in evolutionary life experiences people wish to have, and how can one support that within their own industry?" Similarly, one can effectively keep an eye on what the next empty field of longing might be.

Q: Do you see any shifts due to the pandemic?

KF: The pandemic has shaken deep-seated beliefs about how life should function. Besides the realization that remote work is a viable option and the acknowledgement of the disproportionate mental load on mothers during lockdowns, it has prompted numerous new and profound questions about health, consumption, work and the use of technology. Old belief systems have experienced a crisis, leading to an openness to new ways of thinking and acting. Personally, I've noticed a significant shift in interest towards Zeitgeist research. There's a growing need for a new meta-concept to better understand transitions rather than simply passing judgement on them.

Q: What immediate future do you see in terms of consumer trends?

KF: The immediate future in terms of consumer trends could likely revolve around a heightened emphasis on personal autonomy and interconnectedness. Consumers are seeking products and services that promise to support their individual growth and development while fostering meaningful connections with others. This reflects a deeper understanding of human dynamics and a recognition of the importance of preserving personal agency within an increasingly dynamic world. As we navigate this societal experiment, alongside advancements in artificial intelligence, it's intriguing to consider how this generation will shape the world by prioritizing values such as connection and personal development. Furthermore, these two values mark the two basic needs of every living system. Today, we have the opportunity to collectively reflect on what powerful hierarchical systems in politics, society and, yes, even marketing based on pressuring standards have done and continue to do to life through their fundamental structure.

Q: What long-term shifts and trends do you foresee?

KF: In the long term, I foresee a continued shift towards a mindset of minimizing harm and maximizing support across various aspects of life. This shift is evident in our increasing awareness of the need for environmental conservation, climate action and consideration for our fellow human beings. Unlike in the past, when partners or employees were often forced into adaptation processes regardless of collateral damage, today there is a decline of tolerating such approaches. This attitude permeates all areas of life, as seen, for example, in evolving concepts of early childhood education, which often reflect the current Zeitgeist.

Moreover, there is a growing demand within businesses for leaders who prioritize nurturing and empowerment over destructive behaviours. While aggressive and authoritarian leadership styles may have been celebrated in the past, they are now viewed with suspicion, indicating a significant shift in societal values. Understanding how this development unfolds and identifying the intermediate steps will be crucial in navigating a promising future landscape for our society and institutions.

This indeed presents an opportunity within the Zeitgeist dynamic to cultivate a spirit that seeks to break free from outdated paradigms. However, there is a risk inherent in this tension: movements and groups may cling to traditional power structures, seeking to maintain their dominance and sense of superiority. These forces can effectively influence the collective mindset, offering security and identity within familiar patterns, even as new and more optimistic life philosophies struggle to gain widespread acceptance. Which represents an eternal dynamic our ancestors had to battle with before.

Q: What is your appraisal of the significance of digital developments, such as AI, the metaverse, and digitalization?

KF: In terms of Zeitgeist competence and longing-identification, AI and digitalization enable Zeitgeist Spirit Makers to delve deeper into understanding societal longings and aspirations. By asking AI the question "What wants to become?" rather than "How should it be?" these technologies empower individuals and organizations to uncover hidden potentials within societal structures. This understanding could then be leveraged to create new cultural homes and enhance the overall quality of life.

In all future scenarios involving AI and the metaverse, it remains crucial to observe how technology truly interacts with the human experience. From there, entirely new insights and needs will emerge, to which we will continually need to react and adapt, as long as, hopefully, humans will be the centre of this development.

Q: How should brands prepare themselves for the near future?

KF: Brands should prepare themselves for the near future by deeply understanding and aligning with the Zeitgeist dynamic, which thrives on the human need for connection and their evolutionary collective longings. This entails recognizing the subconscious longings expressed through customer relationships, branding strategies, marketing efforts and cultural products like kindergarten concepts and Netflix series.

To effectively prepare, brands must adopt a targeted perspective on the world. They should analyze what is causing friction, what no longer works, what calls for connection or disentanglement, and which beliefs have shifted. These insights are essential for navigating the Zeitgeist dynamics that permeate all aspects of society and uncovering new areas of longing that demand innovative solutions.

Moreover, brands should actively engage with Spirit Makers who adeptly navigate the Zeitgeist dynamics, identifying societal fissures and fostering new levels of quality of life and entrepreneurial spirit. Developing Zeitgeist competence is crucial for the dynamic evolution of leadership, business models and the cultivation of Spirit Makers within organizations. This future skill will enable brands to stay attuned to the changing needs of consumers.

Q: Are there any cyclical occurrences you have noted? Any consumer sentiment, trends or events that we are experiencing in a new cycle?

KF: One notable cycle involves the shifting focus towards creating new structures for work, family, love relations and personal development while striving to minimize harm. This cycle reflects a growing awareness and emphasis on empathy and understanding of evolving societal needs and longing.

Spirit Makers, who distinguish themselves through their empathy for evolutionary longings, play a crucial role in this cycle. They prioritize understanding what wants to emerge rather than prescribing how things should be. By attuning themselves to the feelings and emotions prevalent in society, they adapt their leadership styles, business strategies and personal development approaches to foster coherence and alignment with the Zeitgeist.

As we move forward, it's important to remain vigilant about how culture and consumers seek to create coherence in the near future. Recognizing and navigating these cyclical occurrences will be essential for businesses and leaders to stay relevant, adaptive and empathetic in meeting the evolving needs of society.

Interview with Roger Tredre on trends

Roger Tredre, journalist, author and lecturer, is course leader in MA Fashion Communication at Central Saint Martins, London. From 1999 to 2006, he was editor-in-chief of trend forecasting giant WGSN. He has also edited the trends magazine *Viewpoint* and contributed to magazines and newspapers worldwide, and has most recently worked as a consultant editor at *Vogue Business*. He is co-author of *The Great Fashion Designers*, now in its second edition (2019).

Neuroscience and machine learning

The latest developments in neuroscience give opportunities to target customers more effectively, while artificial machine learning means we might adapt to a life alongside intelligent machines, humanoid robots or other life-imitating machines. In fashion, retail giants have been using machine-learning algorithms to forecast demand and set prices for years already. According to Amit Sharma (2016), retailers would be better off if they started thinking more like tech companies, using AI and machine learning not just to predict how to stock stores and staff shifts, but also to dynamically recommend products and set prices that appeal to individual consumers.

Figure 12.8 Roger Tredre.

Q: How do you see the future of fashion in relation to these technological advances?

RT: The fashion industry has always wanted to understand consumers better, but the volatility and unpredictability of fashion represent a challenge for AI and machine learning. That said, these technologies used carefully can massively improve the likelihood of creating the right kind of clothes for the right kind of customers at the right time. That is why fashion companies, particularly in the mainstream, are investing heavily in AI. My view is that they will never completely replace gut instinct and the chance element behind many trends, both micro and macro.

Emotions and curation

Emotionally charging brand comms means turning them into a powerful mechanism that can engage the viewer to such an extent that he or she feels compelled to share the ad within social media channels, thus turning the comms into a viral sensation. But what does it mean if people voluntarily help a brand to spread its advertising?

Emotions also play a big part in the need for curated spaces. Concept stores or curated online selections, along with copy text, make shopping for fashion experiential and engaging. There is a need for spaces that let people unwind from a fast-paced lifestyle, and these are ironically shops.

Q: There seems to be a contradictory trend of strong emotional involvement by consumers in the brands whilst at the same time they need to detox from them, ironically, often in the same space. What is your view on this?

RT: Talking about physical space first: if the brand can support the consumer in the process of unwinding or playing, then there is no need for a hard sell. When I pass by a Starbucks mid-morning, I know there is a strong likelihood that I will find a comfortable sofa to sit on and check my emails. The purchase of a cappuccino is not the key appeal for me. I go into Starbucks for a pleasant experience tinged with a low-key emotion. A retailer who provides more reasons to visit a store beyond the purchase of product inevitably widens the customer base. Through social media, brands can also widen their appeal by tapping into and supporting the values of their customers. There is a calculated risk, of course, that consumers can become tired by *every* brand seeking to emotionally engage. Some members of Generation Z are already cynical about all this!

Sustainability

The current "green" trend has been developing for some years now and has reached many consumers who want to shop guilt-free, regardless of whether it is luxury, fast fashion or throwaway fashion. Brands can no longer ignore the dark side of fashion especially after the media continues to publish accusations of human rights violations or dangerous chemicals in the poorest countries of the world where tons of garments are made every day.

Whether it is fast fashion's H&M or a luxury brand like Gucci, all are keen to certify that their supply chain meets the SA8000 Standard of the independent inspection group Bureau Veritas. The efforts by brands are evident.

> Q: How do fashion brands cater to the ethical needs of consumers, and how can they do this through communications? Do you see any dangers in "greenwashing" the consumers (i.e. pretending to be sustainable only to be then found out)?

> RT: Consumers, in my view, are very aware of the likelihood of so-called greenwashing because there's been so much of it about. Fashion companies have to engage at a very senior executive level to work out how best to guarantee ethical sourcing and sustainable production. The momentum from consumers and consumer pressure groups has been building much faster in recent years, although not fast enough – to the frustration of many in the sustainable fashion movement. The important point is that it is still building. The heightened awareness globally about plastic bags, for example, which spread very rapidly in 2018 showed the power of the media in spreading the message. Besides using social media and in-store displays, fashion brands can put across their message by making more use of that most basic of things – the hangtag on a garment – to pass on a sustainable message and to provide traceable information.

Inclusivity

Inclusivity has become a major talking point in the fashion industry in recent years. Emerging designers showing at London Fashion Week, such as Ashley Williams and Sinead O'Dwyer, have been among the key proponents of a more inclusive industry, but the broader market has responded too, with niche companies offering fashion targeted at people of colour as well as a broader variety of sizes and target age groups.

Q: What can be learned from this is that the trend to communicate inclusivity to consumers and offer suitable products has been slowly growing over several decades, only to explode in the last years. Is it now at a level where consumers expect brands to have a stance on inclusivity and diversity? Can fashion truly be inclusive? After all, it is an industry that has a strong focus on the slim and beautiful, often fair-skinned, and has a long-standing history of social exclusion.

RT: Fashion has often played on social exclusion to incite consumer desire for product, but the Millennials and Gen Z are sophisticated and aware of the ways in which they are being played. Brands encouraging social inclusiveness – translating into a sense of "brands for the people" – have become more important.

There is absolutely no doubt in my mind that an emphasis on and provision for inclusivity and diversity are going to be long-term wins for fashion brands as well as society in general. Not all fashion brands can serve all consumers, but it is the spirit and intent that matter too. In this respect, the advertising campaigns under the United Colors banner for Italian knitwear brand Benetton by Oliviero Toscani in the 1980s were well ahead of their time. I met and interviewed Toscani during his golden years. He was an arch-provocateur, always with a twinkle in his eye. By the end of his time at Benetton, he appeared to have run out of steam.

In the future, brands may even play a political role in a charged global political landscape: brand advertising has the power to be much more than simply a means of selling products. Expect to see the braver ones stand up for liberal values in an illiberal climate.

Emerging markets and global outlook for the next generations

The next important generation that fashion marketers will have to address is Gen Alpha, who will presumably grow up with an understanding of sustainability and inclusivity, AI and new communication channels, as well as gadgets, and a form of emotional and educated consumerism, making it vital for brands to tap into that demographic group with the right communication and marketing approach. Furthermore, these young consumers will be based in emerging economies, which offer great opportunities but also challenges to brands.

Q: How do you perceive the future in this global and young world? And what must fashion brands consider in order to thrive in the future?

RT: The challenge will be how to bring together emotion, human "realness" and the advantages of technology to connect with Gen Alpha. The young consumers in urban China and Southeast Asia are extremely sophisticated in their use of technology, but there are also concerns over surveillance and the lack of privacy, which may create a more wary kind of consumer. The value and enjoyment of social interaction in the physical space of the shopping mall or flagship store will lead to a comeback of brick-and-mortar stores driven by a new generation of retailers who blend the selling of products with entertainment and experiential fun.

Ethical considerations

For the future, it is important to use a framework such as the Fashion Carousel to improve the fashion industry while it undergoes further cycles. This means that any participant in the industry must positively influence at least one section within the carousel and facilitate change, be it the supply chain, the marketing practices, the understanding of cultural developments, etc.

In terms of the cyclical nature of fashion trends, the understanding of economic wave theory can help to produce innovations at the right time – but these need to adhere to ethical considerations and best practices.

For example, current innovations in AI pose many ethical questions: There is a huge amount of personal data that is collected by AI-powered interfaces to train the machine learning mechanisms, but there is little to no accountability regarding the safety measures of the collected data. Furthermore, advances in technology allow for user identification by saving unique biological markers such as our auditory profile, fingerprints and irises, and in marketing circles, it can be our online behaviour and preferences. Whilst this can offer security to consumers and personalization as a positive outcome, there is danger in the misuse of our most personal human attributes and the deletion of our human rights.

The problem of machine versus human was already a topic nearly 60 years ago. In 1967, an episode titled "Court Martial" of the original *Star Trek* series that was written by Gene Roddenberry presented a case where the starship's computer was considered to be superior to mankind, and a false accusation was made against Captain Kirk based on the computer's data. A famous quote from the episode is by the character Cogley (played by Elisha Cook Jr.), Kirk's lawyer:

> And I repeat! I speak of rights! A machine has none. A man must! My client has the right to face his accuser. And if you do not grant him that right, you have brought us down to the level of the machine. Indeed, you have elevated that machine above us. I ask that my motion be granted. And more than that, gentlemen, in the name of a humanity fading in the shadow of the machine, I demand it. I demand it!
>
> (IMDb, 2024)

Thus, our innovations should never make the mistake of making humans serve a machine. In more recent times, author Malcolm Gladwell gave advice along the same lines:

> The trick to interacting with machines is to remember that they are machines. And we are a fundamentally different thing. They think differently than us and they are not a version of us. They are a wholly different tool that is there to serve us, not the other way around.
>
> (Johnson, 2018)

Further reading

Ballmer, A. and Tobias, J. (2016) Trend Forecasting: Collecting the History of the Future. *Art Libraries Journal 42*(1), 19–25. https://doi.org/10.1017/alj.2016.40

Airport Dimensions (2023) News & Insights. Available at: https://airportdimensions.com/news-and-insights?tab=2

Bartlett, D. (2013) *Fashion Media: Past and Present.* London: Bloomsbury Academic.

Bentahar, A. (2023) Neuromarketing: The Future Of Marketing Strategy. Forbes (online). Available at: https://www.forbes.com/councils/forbesagencycouncil/2023/07/13/neuromarketing-the-future-of-marketing-strategy/

Blackburn, S. (ed.) (2008) *The Oxford Dictionary of Philosophy.* 2nd edn. Oxford University Press. https://doi.org/10.1093/acref/9780199541430.001.000

Cambridge Dictionary (2019) Curation. Available at: https://dictionary.cambridge.org/dictionary/english/curation#google_vignette

CFI Team (2024) Diffusion of Innovation. Available at: https://corporatefinanceinstitute.com/resources/economics/diffusion-of-innovation/

Coleman, R. et al. (2007) *Design for Inclusivity: A Practical Guide to Accessible, Innovative and User-Centred Design (Design for Social Responsibility).* Abingdon, UK: Routledge.

Crane, D. (2000) *Fashion and its Social Agendas: Class, Gender and Identity in Clothing.* Chicago: University of Chicago Press.

Flavia S. (2023) Sephora's Beauty Annual Event Embraces NFTs and Metaverse. Cryptoflies. Available at: https://blog.cryptoflies.com/sephoras-beauty-annual-event-embraces-nfts-and-metaverse/

Gartner (2023) The Gartner Magic Quadrant for Digital Experience Platforms. Available at: https://www.gartner.com/en/webinar/445907/1051512

Holland, G. and Jones R. (2017) *Fashion Trend Forecasting*. London: Laurence King Publishing.

Kawamura, Y. (2011) *Doing Research in Fashion and Dress: An Introduction to Qualitative Methods*. New York: Berg.

Kondratiev, N. D. (2014) *The Long Waves in Economic Life. Reprint of 1935 English Translation*. Eastford, CT: Martino Fine Books.

Mason, H. (2015) *Trend-Driven Innovation: Beat Accelerating Customer Expectations*. Hoboken: John Wiley & Sons.

Mentges, G. (2011) European Fashion (1450–1950). In European History Online (EGO), published by the institute of European History (IEG), Mainz 2011-06-03. Available at: http://ieg-ego.eu/mentgesg-2011-en

Murphy, P. E., Laczniak, G. R. and Harris, F. (2016) *Ethics in Marketing*. Abingdon, UK: Routledge.

O'Neill, M. (2017) *The Future is Now: 23 Trends That Will Prove Key to Business and Life*. London: Matt Publishing.

Porter, M. E. and Kramer, M. R. (2011, January–February) The Big Idea: Creating Shared Value, Rethinking Capitalism. *Harvard Business Review 89*(1/2), 62–77.

Raymond, M. (2010) *The Trend Forecasters Handbook*. London: Laurence King Publishing.

Rogers, Everett M. (2003) *Diffusion of Innovations*. 5th edn. Free Press. Available at: ProQuest Ebook Central, http://ebookcentral.proquest.com/lib/westminster/detail.action?docID=4935198

Bibliography and further reading

4A's (2019) *Home Page – 4A's*. Available at: www.aaaa.org/ [Accessed 22 May 2016].

Aaf.org (2019) *WHO WE ARE | AAF*. Available at: www.aaf.org/iMIS/AAFMemberR/ WHO_WE_ARE/AAFMemberR/Who_We_Are/Who%20We%20Are.aspx?hkey= 40e639f5-03ef-4f0d-aee5-806cc047ae68 [Accessed 2 Jul. 2016].

Abrahamian, A. (2016) Rise in Advertising as North Korea Embraces Nascent Consumerism. *The Guardian*. Available at: www.theguardian.com/world/2016/jun/17/rise-in-advertising- as-north-korea-embraces-nascent-consumerism [Accessed 20 Jun. 2016].

Advertising Research Foundation (2019) *The ARF*. Available at: https://thearf.org/ [Accessed 20 Dec. 2016].

Airbus.com (2004) *Flight Operation Briefing Notes*. Available at: www.airbus.com/fileadmin/ media_gallery/files/safety_library_items/AirbusSafetyLib_-FLT_OPS-HUM_PER-SEQ04.pdf [Accessed 6 Jul. 2015].

Akbareian, E. (2015) American Apparel's New CEO on Making the Brand Less Suggestive. *The Independent*. Available at: www.independent.co.uk/life-style/fashion/news/ american- apparels-new-ceo-set-to-tone-down-the-brands-sexualised-imagery-100384 59.html [Accessed 20 Jun. 2016].

Altman, J. (2022) *Hidden Man: My Many Musical Lives*. Sheffield: Equinox.

AMA (2024) *Branding*. American Marketing Association (online). Available at: https://www. ama.org/topics/branding/

Amies, N. (2023) 'Glass Generation' struggling with information overload, psychologists warn. The Brussels Times (online). Available at: https://www.brusselstimes.com/ 433926/glass-generation-struggling-with-information-overload-psychologists-warn

Amos, C., Holmes, G. and Strutton, D. (2008) Exploring the Relationship between Celebrity Endorser Effects and Advertising Effectiveness: A Quantitative Synthesis of Effect Size. *International Journal of Advertising* 27(2), 209–234. https://doi.org/10.1080/02650487.2008. 11073052

Amosa, A. and Haglund, M. (2002) From Social Taboo to "Torch of Freedom": The Marketing of Cigarettes to Women. *Tobacco Control 9*, 3–8. Available at: https://tobaccocontrol.bmj.com/content/tobaccocontrol/9/1/3.full.pdf [Accessed 12 Jun. 2016].

The ANDYs (2019) *About – ANDY Awards*. Available at: www.andyawards.com/about/ [Accessed 2 Jul. 2016].

Arakawa, T. (2018) Ear Acoustic Authentication Technology: Using Sound to Identify the Distinctive Shape of the Ear Canal. *NEC Technical Journal 13*(2), Special Issue on Social Value Creation Using Biometrics. Available at: https://www.nec.com/en/global/techrep/journal/g18/n02/180219.html

ASA (2024) Annual Report 2023: Building our world-leading AI capability. Available at:https://www.asa.org.uk/news/annual-report-2023.html

Athique, A. (2013) *Digital Media and Society: An Introduction*. Cambridge: Polity.

Atwal, G. and Bryson, D. (2014) *Luxury Brands in Emerging Markets*. Basingstoke: Palgrave Macmillan.

Awasthi, A. K. and Choraria, S. (2015) Effectiveness of Celebrity Endorsement Advertisements: The Role of Customer Imitation Behaviour. *Journal of Creative Communications 10*(2), 215–234. https://doi.org/10.1177/0973258615597412

Ballmer, A. and Tobias, J. (2016) Trend Forecasting: Collecting the History of the Future. *Art Libraries Journal 42*(1), 19–25. https://doi.org/10.1017/alj.2016.40

Bamat, J. (2015) Grenoble turns over a new leaf. France 24. Avaialble at: https://webdoc.france24.com/grenoble-green-revolution/

Barbuto, J. (2023) *Kondratieff's Economic LongWave*. The Economic LongWave. Available at: https://www.youtube.com/watch?v=HYS44SxglcA&ab_channel=TheEconomicLongWave

Barr, J. (2018) Do|Co|Mo|Mo|Japan|02 : Dojunkai Apartments : Tokyo : Dojunkai Corporation. John Barr Architects. Available at: https://www.johnbarrarchitect.com/post/2018/10/09/docomomojapan02-dojunkai-apartments-tokyo-dojunkai-corporation

Bartlett, D., Cole, S. and Rocamora, A. (2013) *Fashion Media*. London: Bloomsbury.

Beard, N. D. (2008). The branding of ethical fashion and the consumer: A luxury niche or mass-market reality? Fashion Theory, 12(4), 447–467. http://doi.org/10.2752/175174108X34693

Becdach, C. et al. (2023) *Ready for Prime Time? The State of Live Commerce*. McKinsey & Company. Available at: https://www.mckinsey.com/capabilities/growth-marketing-and-sales/our-insights/ready-for-prime-time-the-state-of-live-commerce

Belfanti, C. (2008) Was Fashion a European Invention? *Journal of Global History 3*(3), 419–443.

Bendoni, W. K. (2017) *Social Media for Fashion Marketing: Storytelling in a Digital World*. London: Bloomsbury.

Bentahar, A. (2023) *Neuromarketing: The Future of Marketing Strategy*. Forbes. Available at: https://www.forbes.com/sites/forbesagencycouncil/2023/07/13/neuromarketing-the-future-of-marketing-strategy/

Berlendi, C. (2011) *The Role of Social Media Within the Fashion and Luxury Industries*. Saarbrücken: Lap Lambert Academic.

Bischoff, W. (2006) *"Grenzenlose Räume"–Überlegungen zum Verhältnis von Architektur und städtischem Geruchsraum*, From Outer Space: Architekturtheorie außerhalb der Disziplin

(Teil 2) 10. Jg., Heft 2, September 2006. Wolkenkuckucksheim – Cloud-Cuckoo-Land – Vozdushnyi Zamok Available at: www.cloud-cuckoo.net/openarchive/wolke/deu/Themen/052/Bischoff/bischoff.htm [Accessed 20 Sept. 2015].

Blasberg, D. (2014) Harper's Bazaar, Marc and Sofia: The Dreamy Team. Available at: www.harpersbazaar.com/fashion/designers/a3169/marc-jacobs-sofia-coppola-0914/

Blease, C. and Torous, J. (2023) ChatGPT and Mental Healthcare: Balancing Benefits with Risks of Harms. *BMJ Mental Health 26*(1), e300884. https://doi.org/10.1136/bmjment-2023-300884

Boumphrey, S. (2015) Strategies for Consumer Market Success in China. Euromonitor Market Research Blog. Available at: http://blog.euromonitor.com/2015/08/strategies-for-consumer-market-success-in-china.html [Accessed 15 Mar. 2017].

Breward, C. (1994) Femininity and Consumption: The Problem of the Late Nineteenth-Century Fashion Journal. *Journal of Design History 7*(2), 71–89. Available at: www.jstor.org/stable/1316078 [Accessed 2 Jul. 2016].

Britannica, The Editors of Encyclopaedia (2017) "Golden Age of American Radio". Encyclopedia Britannica, 6 Jun. 2017. Available at: https://www.britannica.com/topic/Golden-Age-of-American-radio. Accessed 18 December 2023

British Academy (2021) The COVID Decade: Understanding the Long-term Societal Impacts of COVID-19. London: The British Academy. https://doi.org/10.5871/bac19stf/9780856726583.001

Bruhn, M. and Köhler, R. (2011) *Wie Marken wirken*. München: Franz Vahlen.

Brynn, V. and Baron, K. (2023) *Moving the Metaverse On: Future-Proofing Brand Strategies*. Stylus. Available at: Moving the Metaverse On: Future-Proofing Brand Strategies (stylus.com)

Brynn, V. and Baron, K. (2023) *Moving the Metaverse On: Future-Proofing Brand Strategies*. Stylus. Available at: Moving the Metaverse On: Future-Proofing Brand Strategies (stylus.com)

Buergi, T. and Spafford, M.-E. (2010) Freitag: Designing a Brand from Nothing but Waste. FHNW University of Applied Sciences and Arts Northwestern Switzerland. The Case Centre [online] Reference no. 810-031-1. Available at: www.thecasecentre.org

CACI (2020) ACORN user Guide. Available At: https://www.caci.co.uk/wp-content/uploads/2021/06/Acorn-User-Guide-2020.pdf

Caird, J. (2016) "A Character That Will Live Forever": How We Made the Levi's Flat Eric Ads. *The Guardian*. Available at: www.theguardian.com/media-network/2016/mar/31/levis-flat-eric-advert-puppet [Accessed 6 Jun. 2016].

Carter, C. and Steiner, L. (2004) *Critical Readings: Media and Gender*. Maidenhead: Open University Press (McGraw-Hill Education).

Cartner-Morley, J. (2012) Victoria's Secret v Agent Provocateur: Lingerie Stores Turn Up the Heat. *The Guardian*. Available at: www.theguardian.com/fashion/2012/oct/23/lingerie-agent-provocateur-victorias-secret

Castro, R. and Lewis, T. (2011) *Corporate Aviation Management*. Chicago: Southern Illinois University Press.

Chaffey, D. (2009) *E-Business and E-Commerce Management*. 4th ed. Harlow: Prentice Hall.

Chaffey, D. and Smith, P. R. (2017) *Digital Marketing Excellence: Planning, Optimizing and Integrating Online Marketing.* 5th ed. Abingdon: Routledge.

Chang, R. J. (2022). The countries with the most billionaires 2022. Forbes.com. Available at: www.forbes.com/sites/richardjchang/2022/04/05/the-countries-with-the-most-billi onaires-2022/?sh=36073c78b57e

Charlesworth, A. (2014) *Digital Marketing: A Practical Approach.* Abingdon: Routledge.

Charlesworth, A. (2022) *Digital Marketing: A Practical Approach.* 4th ed. Abingdon: Routledge.

Charter, M. and Tischner, U. (2001) *Sustainable Solutions: Developing Products and Services for the Future.* Sheffield: Greenleaf Publishing..

Citra (2024) Kuwait National ICT Figures. Citra Communication & Information Technology Regulation Authority. Available at: https://citra.gov.kw/sites/en/Pages/ict_indicators.aspx

Claritas (2015) MyBestSegments. Available at: https://segmentationsolutions.nielsen. com/mybestsegments/Default.jsp?ID=30&menuOption=segmentdetails& pageName=Segment%2BExplorer&id1=CLA.PNE [Accessed 7 Jan. 2017].

Collister, P. (2015) The Directory Big Won Rankings 2015. *The Directory.* Available at: www. directnewideas.com/bigwon/ [Accessed 9 Sept. 2016].

Cope, J. and Maloney, D. (2016) *Fashion Promotion in Practice.* New York: Fairchild.

Cortese, A. J. (1999) *Provocateur: Images of Women and Minorities in Advertising.* Boston: Rowman & Littlefield.

Cozens, C. (2003) Barnardo's Shock Ads Spark 330 Complaints. *The Guardian.* Available at: www.theguardian.com/media/2003/nov/24/advertising2 [Accessed 7 Jan. 2017].

Crane, D. (2000) *Fashion and Its Social Agendas: Class, Gender and Identity in Clothing.* Chicago: University of Chicago Press.

Credle, S. (2023) My Most Immortal Ad: Susan Credle on Levi Strauss & Co's 'Swimmer'. Little Black Book [online]. Available at: https://www.lbbonline.com/news/my-most-immortal-ad-susan-credle-on-levi-strauss-cos-swimmer/

Crestodina, A. (2018) Blogging Statistics and Trends: The 2018 Survey of 1000+ Bloggers. Available at: www.orbitmedia.com/blog/blogger-trends/

Cull, N. J., Culbert, D. and Welsh, D. (2003) *Propaganda and Mass Persuasion: A Historical Encyclopedia, 1500 to the Present.* Santa Barbara: ABC-Clio Inc.

Cullers, R. (2012) Ikea "Regrets" Airbrushing Women Out of Its Saudi Catalog. *Adweek.* Available at: www.adweek.com/adfreak/ikea-regrets-airbrushing-women-out-its-saudi-catalog-144140 [Accessed 10 Jun. 2015].

Curtis, A. (2011) *Five Years after Banning Outdoor Ads, Brazil's Largest City Is More Vibrant Than Ever.* Center for a New American Dream. Available at: www.newdream.org/resources/sao-paolo-ad-ban [Accessed 3 Jun. 2016].

Da Silva, M. (2020) Making sense of visual pollution: The "Clean City" law in São Paulo,Brazil in Davis, T. and Mah, A. (ed.) *Toxic truths: Environmental justice and citizen science in a post-truth age.* Manchester: Manchester University Press. pp.158-174. Available at: https://doi.org/10.7765/9781526137005.00019

De Kruiff, W. (2023) *Fashioning the Future: How Tech Brings New Experiences to Consumers and Luxury Brands.* The Drum. Available at: Fashioning the future: How tech brings new experiences to consumers and luxury brands | The Drum

Dejean, M. (2014) *Pourquoi supprimer les pubs des rues? Le maire de Grenoble répond* 25/11/14 15h44 Les Inrockuptibles. Available at: www.lesinrocks.com/2014/11/25/actualite/suppression-pub-rues-grenoble-on-retrouve-lidentite-reelle-ville-11537533/ [Accessed 3 Nov. 2016].

Dencheva, V. (2023) *Leading Platforms for Influencer Marketing Worldwide as of January 2020.* Satatista. Available at: https://www-statista-com.uow.idm.oclc.org/statistics/1241723/platforms-influencer-marketing/

Dencheva, V. (2024) *Influencer Marketing Market Size Worldwide from 2016 to 2024.* Statista. https://www-statista-com.uow.idm.oclc.org/statistics/1092819/global-influencer-market-size/

Desmet, D. et al. (2015) Speed and Scale: Unlocking Digital Value in Customer Journeys. Available at: www.mckinsey.com/insights/operations/speed_and_scale_unlocking_digital_value_in_customer_journeys?cid=digital-eml-alt-mip-mck-oth-1511

Diamond, J. (2015) *Retail Advertising and Promotion.* New York: Fairchild .

DigitalCrew (2024) KOL And Influencer: What Is The Difference? Available at: https://www.digitalcrew.agency/kol-and-influencer-what-is-the-difference/

Ding, X. and Chai, Q. (2022) The Rise of Digital Capitalism and the Social Changes It Caused: How to Develop the Digital Economy in Socialist China. *China Political Economy* 6(1), 35–43. Emerald Publishing Limited. 2516-1652. https://doi.org/10.1108/CPE-10-2022-0017. Available at: CPE-10-2022-0017_proof 35..43 (emerald.com)

Drury, G. H. (1985) *The Historical Guide to North American Railroads.* Milwaukee: Kalmbach Publishing Co.

Duden (2023) "Zeitgeist". Available at: https://www.duden.de/rechtschreibung/Zeitgeist

Duncan, S. (2021) *The Ethical Business Book: A Practical, Non-Preachy Guide to Business Sustainability (Concise Advice).* 2nd ed. London: LID Publishing.

DynamicAction (2015) Now You're Talking: Four Customer Segmentation Secrets Revealed by Agent Provocateur. Available at: www.dynamicaction.com/now-youre-talking-four-customer-segmentation-secrets-revealed-by-agent-provocateur/

Dyvik, E.H. (2024) Forecast of the world population in 2022 and 2100, by continent. Statista. Available at: https://www.statista.com/statistics/272789/world-population-by-continent

Elkington, J. (2018a) 25 Years Ago I Coined the Phrase "Triple Bottom Line." Here's Why It's Time to Rethink It. *Harvard Business Review.* Available at: https://hbr.org/2018/06/25-years-ago-i-coined-the-phrasetriple-bottom-line-heres-why-im-giving-up-on-it

Elkington, J. (2018b) The Elkington report: Zen and the triple bottom line. *Green Biz.* Available at: www.greenbiz.com/article/zen-and-triple-bottom-line

Ellis, N. et al. (2011) *Marketing:A Critical Textbook.* London: Sage Publications.

Epstein, E. J. (1982) Have You Ever Tried to Sell a Diamond? *The Atlantic.* Available at: www.theatlantic.com/magazine/archive/1982/02/have-you-ever-tried-to-sell-a-diamond/304575/

EY (2022) *EY Future Consumer Index: The Era of the Conscious Consumer.* Press Release. Available at: EY Future Consumer Index: The Era of the Conscious Consumer | EY Ireland

Fennis, B. M. and Stroebe, W. (2010) *The Psychology of Advertising.* Psychology Press.

Flora, L. (2015) *Kering Sustainability is a Business Imperative for Global Luxury Industry.* Jingdaily.com. Available at: https://jingdaily.com/kering-sustainability-is-a-business-imperative-for-global-luxury-industry/

Freitag (2024a) Best Closed: Our Material Cycles. Available at: https://www.freitag.ch/en/material-cycle

Freitag (2024b) Our Journey to Circularity. Freitag. Available at: https://www.freitag.ch/en/circularity-roadmap?_gl=1*axoz8g*_gcl_au*ODEyOTA5NzAwLjE3MTE5NjgzMzQ

Friedman, U. (2015) How an Ad Campaign Invented the Diamond Engagement Ring. *The Atlantic*, 13 Feb. Available at: www.theatlantic.com/international/archive/2015/02/how-an-ad-campaign-invented-the-diamond-engagement-ring/385376/ [Accessed 28 Aug. 2016].

Garber, M. (2015) "You've Come a Long Way, Baby": The Lag Between Advertising and Feminism. *The Atlantic*. Available at: www.theatlantic.com/entertainment/archive/2015/06/advertising-1970s-womens-movement/395897/

Glover, G. (2023) Russia Got Richer Even as the War in Ukraine Raged on Last Year, While the West Shed Trillions of Dollars of Wealth. Business Insider [Online]. Available at: https://www.businessinsider.com/war-in-ukraine-russia-richer-millionai res-billionaires-uhnw-wealth-ubs-2023-8

Goffman, E. (1976) *Gender Advertisements*. New York: Harper Torchbooks.

Graham, B. and Anouti, C. (2018) *Promoting Fashion*. London: Laurence King.

Grazia (2018) *Grazia*: An Eclectic Mix of Fashion, Beauty, Current Affairs and News that Celebrates Women. Available at: www.bauermedia.co.uk/uploads/Grazia.pdf [Accessed 1 Jan. 2019].

Hanbury, M. et al. (2023) *The Rise, Fall, and Latest Stumbles of Victoria's Secret*. Business Insider. Available at: Victoria's Secret: Rise, Fall, Comeback of Lingerie Giant (businessinsider.com)

Hays, K. (2019) Ads In the September Issues: A Multiyear Breakdown. WWD (online). Available at: https://wwd.com/feature/ads-in-the-september-issues-a-multiyear-break down-1203276718/

Higgins, D. (2015) Plan Ahead When Importing Goods to Your Doorstep. Available at: www.japanupdate.com/2015/01/plan-ahead-when-importing-goods-to-your-doorstep/

Hines, T. and Bruce, M. (2007) *Fashion Marketing*. 2nd ed. Abingdon: Routledge.

Hirons, M. (2020) How the Sustainable Development Goals Risk Undermining Efforts to Address Environmental and Social Issues in the Small-scale Mining Sector. *Environmental Science & Policy* 114, 321–328. ISSN 1462-9011, https://doi.org/10.1016/j.envsci.2020.08.022. Available at: https://www.sciencedirect.com/science/article/pii/S1462901120305335

Hoang, L. (2016) Can Cost-Cutting Save Fashion Magazines? *Business of Fashion*. Available at: www.businessoffashion.com/articles/intelligence/cost-cutting-fashion-magazines-hearst-time-inc-conde-nast?utm_source=Subscribers&utm_campaign=ce6e732d6e-&utm_medium=email&utm_term=0_d2191372b3-ce6e732d6e-418254849

Hofstede Insights India (2024) Country Comparison Tool: India. Available at: https://www. hofstede-insights.com/country-comparison-tool?countries=india

Holland, G. and Jones, R. (2017) *Fashion Trend Forecasting*. London: Laurence King Publishing.

Hooley, N. et al. (2020) *Marketing Strategy and Competitive Positioning*. 7th ed. Harlow: Pearson.

Howley, C. L. (2009) Dressing a Virgin Queen: Court Women, Dress, and Fashioning the Image of England's Queen Elizabeth I. *Early Modern Women 4*, 201–208.

Huaxia (2020) Discover China: Kingdom of Dreams and Reality in Eastern China. Xinhua Net. Available at: http://www.xinhuanet.com/english/2020-06/24/c_139164513.htm

Hughes, H. (2021) Loewe launches bag made from surplus leather. Fashion United. Available at: https://fashionunited.uk/news/fashion/loewe-launches-bag-made-from-surplus-leather/202103165445

IMDb (2024) "Star Trek" Court Martial (TV Episode 1967): Elisha Cook Jr.: Cogley. IMDb. Available at: https://www.imdb.com/title/tt0708425/characters/nm0176879

Interfax in Statista (2024) Year-over-year gross domestic product (GDP) growth rate in Russia from January 2019 to January 2024. Statista. Available at: https://www-statista-com.uow.idm.oclc.org/statistics/1009056/gdp-growth-rate-russia/

Jaber (2022) In Sá, M.J. and Serpa, S. (2023) Metaverse as a Learning Environment: Some Considerations. *Sustainability 2023*(15), 2186. https://doi.org/10.3390/su15032186

Jackson, T. and Shaw, D. (2009) *Mastering Fashion Marketing*. Basingstoke: Palgrave Macmillan.

Jaeger, J. et al. (2017) *By the Numbers: How Business Benefits from the Sustainable Development Goals*. World Resources Institute. Available at: https://www.wri.org/insights/numbers-how-business-benefits-sustainable-development-goals

Jhally, S. and Kilbourne, J. (1979) *Killing Us Softly: Advertising's Image of Women*. San Francisco: Kanopy Streaming, 2014.

Johnson, C. (2018) Malcolm Gladwell's Take On Artificial Intelligence at The World Government Summit. *Forbes Magazine* (Online). Available at: https://www.forbes.com/sites/yec/2018/04/03/malcolm-gladwells-take-on-artificial-intelligence-at-the-world-government-summit/

Karolini, D. (2015) the6milliondollarstory. Available at: www.the6milliondollarstory.com/dont-crack-under-pressure-feat-cara-delevigne-for-tag-heuer/

Kassoy, A. et Al. (2022) Patagonia asks all business leaders to look at themselves in the mirror. B Corporation (online). Available at: https://www.bcorporation.net/en-us/news/blog/b-lab-founders-message-patagonia

Kawamura, Y. (2005) *Fashion-Ology: An Introduction to Fashion Studies*. New York: Berg.

Kawamura, Y. (2011) *Doing Research in Fashion and Dress: An Introduction to Qualitative Methods*. New York: Berg.

Keaney, M. (2007) *Fashion and Advertising (World's Top Photographers Workshops)*. London: RotoVision.

Kemper, J. A. and Ballentine, P. W. (2017) What Do We Mean by Sustainability Marketing? *Journal of Marketing Management 35*(3–4), 277–309. https://doi.org/10.1080/0267257X.2019.1573845

Kendall, N. (2015) *What is a 21st Century Brand? New Thinking from the Next Generation of Agency Leaders*. London: Kogan Page.

Kent, S. (2021) The Sustainability Gap How Fashion Measures Up. In *The Business of Fashion*. Edited by Amed, I., Young, R., and Crump, H. Available at: https://www.businessoffashion.com/reports/sustainability/measuring-fashions-sustainability-gap-download-the-report-now/

Kenton, W. (2018, Feb.) Kondratieff Wave. Investopedia. Available at: www.investopedia.com/terms/k/kondratieff-wave.asp

KesselsKramer (2013) *Advertising for People Who Don't Like Advertising*. London: Laurence King Publishing.

Khong, J. (2023) *2024 Global Consumer Trends: South APAC Webinar*. Mintel. Available at: 2024 Global Consumer Trends: South APAC Webinar – Mintel

Kilbourne, J. (1999) *Can't Buy ME Love: How Advertising Changes the Way We Think and Feel*. New York: Touchstone.

Kloss, I. (2012) *Werbung: Handbuch für Studium und Praxis*. 5th edn. München: Vahlen.

Korean Cultural Centre UK (n.d.) Hallyu (Korean Wave). Available at: https://kccuk.org.uk/en/about-korea/culture-and-arts/hallyu-korean-wave/

Kotler P. et al. (2009) *Marketing Management*. 13th edn. Harlow: Pearson Education Ltd.

Kotler, P. (2012) Chicago Humanities Festival. Available at: http://chicagohumanities.org/events/2012/america/marketing-with-philip-kotler [from a conference recording] [Accessed 5 Jun. 2016].

Kumar, V. et al. (2012) Evolution of Sustainability as Marketing Strategy: Beginning of New Era. *Procedia - Social and Behavioral Sciences 37*, 482–489. ISSN 1877-0428, https://doi.org/10.1016/j.sbspro.2012.03.313. Available at: https://www.sciencedirect.com/science/article/pii/S1877042812007926

Laird, P. (2001) *Advertising Progress: American Business and the Rise of Consumer Marketing*. Baltimore: Johns Hopkins University Press.

Lane, W. R., Whitehill K. K. and Russel, T. J. (2008) *Kleppner's Advertising Procedure*. 17th edn. New Jersey: Pearson Prentice Hall.

Lea-Greenwood, G. (2012) *Gaynor: Fashion Marketing Communications*. John Wiley & Sons.

Lemelson–MIT. (n.d.) Massachusetts Institute of Technology. Available at: http://lemelson.mit.edu/resources/henry-ford [Accessed 18 Jun. 2016].

Lett, J.-C. (2017) Riba Guixà Welcomes Second LVMH Métiers d'Art Artist in Residence. Available at: www.lvmh.com/news-documents/news/riba-guixa-welcomes-second-lvmh-metiers-dart-artist-in-residence/

Levinson, J. C. (2016) Guerilla Marketing. Available at: www.gmarketing.com/index.php

Lewino, F. and Dos Santos G. (2015) Les trois versions de "La Sortie des usines Lumière". *Le Point*. Available at: www.lepoint.fr/culture/les-trois-versions-de-la-sortie-des-usines-lumiere-27-03-2015-1916316_3.php [Accessed 23 Nov. 2016].

Li, V. (2021) Ethics Check: Mintel Global Consumer Trend 2022. Mintel (online) Available at: https://clients.mintel.com/content/trend/ethics-check?fromSearch=%3Ffreetext%3Dethics%26resultPosition%3D2

Life Magazine (1947) 14 Apr. 1947. Available at: https://books.google.de/books?id=ik0EAAAAMBAJ&pg=PA60&lpg=PA60&dq=adler%27s+elevator+

shoes&source=bl&ots=EtiqRxsR9A&sig=w8pDcM2faZM-imh6ZtuvZR9iNfg&hl=en&sa=X&ved=0ahUKEwi9-f-jzdbNAhVK7 xQKHdsxDHMQ6AEIcDAP#v=onepage&q=adler%27s%20elevator%20shoes &f=false [Accessed 3 Jul. 2016].

LOEWE (2023a) Careers at LOEWE. Available at: www.loewe.com/eur/en/information/ careers-at-loewe.html

LOEWE (2023b) LOEWE x Sustainability. Available at: www.loewe.com/eur/en/ information/sustainability-at-loewe.html

LOEWE (n.d.) Loewe x Sustainability. Available at: www.loewe.com/eur/en/information/ sustainability-at-loewe.html

LOEWE Foundation (2023). Craftprize. Available at: http://craftprize.loewe.com/en/ home

LOEWE Foundation (n.d.). Blog. Available at: www.blogfundacionloewe.es/en/

London, B. (2015) As Celebrities Lead the Trend for Genderless Fashion, Selfridges Axes its Separate Women and Menswear Departments in Favour of Three Floors of Unisex Clothes. *Daily Mail*. Available at: www.dailymail.co.uk/femail/article-3002605/As-celebrities-lead-trend-genderless-fashion-Selfridges-axes-separate-women-menswear-departments-favour-three-floors-unisex-fashion.html [Accessed 28 Dec. 2016].

LVMH (2014) News: Don't Crack Under Pressure: The TAG Heuer challenge. LVMH [online]. Available at: https://www.lvmh.com/news-documents/news/dont-crack-under-pressure-the-tag-heuer-challenge/

LWG. (2023). Leather Working Group: About Us. Available at: www.leatherworkinggroup. com/about

Macmillan Dictionary (2019) Propaganda. Available at: www.macmillandictionary.com/ dictionary/british/propaganda [Accessed 3 Jan. 2019].

Macmillan Dictionary (2019) Propagate. Available at www.macmillandictionary.com/ dictionary/british/propagate [Accessed 3 Jan. 2019].

Majidi, M. (2023) *TV Advertising Worldwide - Statistics & Facts*. Statista. Available at: TV advertising worldwide - statistics & facts | Statista (oclc.org)

Manral, K. (2011) The Difference between Above-the-Line and Below-the-Line Advertising. Available at: www.theadvertisingclub.net/index.php/features/editorial/3256-differen ce-between-above-the-line-and-below-the-line-advertising

Marketing-Schools (2012) Marketing with Celebrities: How to use Celebrities in Advertising. Available at: www.marketing-schools.org/consumer-psychology/marketing-with-cele brities.html [Accessed 7 Nov. 2015].

Mau, D. (2014) The 2014 September Issues by the Numbers. *Fashionista*. 23 Jul. Available at: http://fashionista.com/2014/07/september-issue-ad-pages

McDonough, W. and Braungart, M. (2001). The Next Industrial Revolution. In *Sustainable Solutions: Developing Products and Services for the Future*. Edited by Martin Charter, et al. Sheffield: Greenleaf Publishing.

McEachrane, M. (2019) *Does Sustainable Development Have an Elephant in the Room? The Inherently Unequal Relationship between the Developed and Developing World Is Hindering Sustainable Development*. Al Jazeera. Available at: https://www.aljazeera.com/opinions/ 2019/10/10/does-sustainable-development-have-an-elephant-in-the-room

McGill (2019) *What is Sustainability?* Available at: www.mcgill.ca/sustainability/files/sustainability/what-is-sustainability.pdf

Mclaughlin, A. (2020) Freitag wants you to swap your old bags for Black Friday. Creative Review (online). Availble at: https://www.creativereview.co.uk/freitag-anti-black-friday

Melkadze, A. (2022) Average Delivery Time of Online Orders in Russia H1 2021, by City. Statista. Available at: https://www-statista-com.uow.idm.oclc.org/statistics/1206552/average-delivery-time-of-online-orders-in-russia-by-city/

Melkadze, A. (2023) Leading online stores in Russia 2022, by sales value. Statista: Available at: https://www-statista-com.uow.idm.oclc.org/statistics/1006643/leading-online-stores-russia/

Mentges, G. (2011) European Fashion (1450-1950), in: European History Online (EGO), published by the institute of European History (IEG), Mainz 2011-06-03. Available at: http://ieg-ego.eu/mentgesg-2011-en

Merriam-Webster (2019) Ethic. Available at: www.merriam-webster.com/dictionary/ethic [Accessed 8 Feb. 2019].

Mintel (2015) 56% of Americans Stop Buying From Brands They Believe Are Unethical. Available at: www.mintel.com/press-centre/social-and-lifestyle/56-of-americans-stop-buying-from-brands-they-believe-are-unethical [Accessed 2 Aug. 2018].

Mitterfellner, O. (2023) Luxury Fashion Brand Management: Unifying Fashion with Sustainability. Abingdon: Routledge

Moore, G. (2012) *Basics Fashion Management: Fashion Promotion 02: Building a Brand through Marketing and Communication.* Lausanne: AVA Publishing.

Moriarty, S. et al. (2019) *Advertising & IMC: Principles & Practice.* 11th ed. Harlow: Pearson.

Müller, S. and Gelbrich, K. (2015) *Interkulturelles Marketing.* Munich, Germany: Vahlen.

Muratkovski, G. (2013) Urban Branding: The Politics of Architecture. Design Principles and Practices: An International Journal — Annual Review Volume 6, 2013. https://doi.org/10.18848/1833-1874/CGP/v06i01

Muratore, P. (2014) Ad People, Don't Get Stiffed by Dead Celebrities. *Ad Age.* Available at: http://adage.com/article/cmo-strategy/marketers-beware-dead-celebs-ads/292427

Muratovski, G. (2011) The Role of Architecture and Integrated Design in City Branding. *Place Branding and Public Diplomacy 8*(3), 195–207.

Navarro, J. G. (2023) *Most Trusted ad Channels Worldwide 2021.* Statista. Available at: Global consumer trust in advertising by format | Statista (oclc.org)

Navarro, J.G. (2024) Advertising worldwide – statistics & facts. Statista. Available at: https://www.statista.com/topics/990/global-advertising-market/#topicOverview

NFT Stars (2023) RWA and NFTs: The Future of Investments and Ownership Rights. Medium. Available at: https://medium.com/nft-stars/rwa-and-nfts-the-future-of-investments-and-ownership-rights-f9e1163778a8

NHK World (2023) *China's Live Commerce Village. Rerun June 2, 2023.* NHK World. Available at: https://www3.nhk.or.jp/nhkworld/en/tv/asiainsight/20230602/2022345/

Noel, C. P. (2010) Shock Advertising: Theories, Risks, and Outcomes Analyzed Using the Case of Barnardo's. *Inquiries Journal/Student Pulse.* Available at: www.inquiriesjournal.com/a?id=305

NRS (2015) National Readership Survey: Social Grade. Available at: www.nrs.co.uk/nrs-print/lifestyle-and-classification-data/social-grade/ [Accessed 20 Aug. 2015].

Nudd, T. (2016) Diesel Awkwardly Stuffs Every Online Obsession Into a New Global Ad Campaign. *AdWeek*,19 Jan. Available at: www.adweek.com/adfreak/diesel-awkwardly-stuffs-every-online-obsession-new-global-ad-campaign-169067

O'Brien, P. (2022) Remembering the Minitel: How France Was Online before the Rest of the World. France 24. [video online] Available at: https://www.france24.com/en/tv-shows/tech-24/20221209-remembering-the-minitel-how-france-was-online-before-the-rest-of-the-world

O'Neill, A. (2023) Gross Domestic Product (GDP) Growth Rate in the BRICS Countries 2000–2028. Satatista. Available at: https://www-statista-com.uow.idm.oclc.org/statistics/741729/gross-domestic-product-gdp-growth-rate-in-the-bric-countries/

Onishi (2005) cited in Hanaki et al (2006) Hanryu Sweeps East Asia: How Winter Sonata is Gripping Japan. *International Communication Gazette* 69(3). https://doi.org/10.1177/17480485070765

Orange, E. and Cohen, A.M., 2010. From eco-friendly to eco-intelligent. The Futurist, 44(5), p.28

Oxford College of Marketing (2013) The Extended Marketing Mix: Physical Evidence. Available at: https://blog.oxfordcollegeofmarketing.com/2013/08/09/marketing-mix-physical-evidence-cim-content/ [Accessed 20 Nov. 2018].

Oyster (2011) Scott Schuman Makes Lots of Money and Hates Girls. *Oystermag*, 1 Oct. Available at: www.oystermag.com/scott-schuman-makes-lots-of-money-and-hates-girls#1RsX2TqmsjKk5qZL.99

Pearse, G. (2012) Greenwash: Big Brands and Carbon Scams. Melbourne: Black Inc.

Perlman, S. and Sherman, G. J. (2010) *Fashion Public Relations*. New York: Fairchild.

Pilling, D. (2023) Why the SDGs Are a Bad Idea. *Financial Times* [online] Available at: https://www.ft.com/content/ceedd447-a6d1-4773-9a8a-e3b25a50645c

Polonsky, J. (2001) Green marketing in Charter, M., and Tischner, U. (ed.) *Sustainable Solutions: Developing Products and Services for the Future.* Sheffield: Greenleaf Publishing

Polonsky, J. (2001) Green marketing in Charter, M., and Tischner, U. (ed.) *Sustainable Solutions: Developing Products and Services for the Future.* Sheffield: Greenleaf Publishing

Posner, H. (2011). *Marketing Fashion.* New York: Laurence King Publishing.

Pouillard, V. (2013) The Rise of Fashion Forecasting and Fashion Public Relations, 1920–1940: The History of Tobe and Bernays. In *Globalizing Beauty: Consumerism and Body Aesthetics in the Twentieth Century.* Edited by Hartmut, B. and T. Kühne. Palgrave Macmillan, pp. 151–169.

Pravda (2007) Bomb Explodes at McDonald's Restaurant in St.Petersburg. *Pravda*, 19 Feb. Available at: www.pravdareport.com/news/hotspots/87528-mcdonalds

PRSA (2016) About Public Relations. Available at: www.prsa.org/aboutprsa/publicrelationsdefined/#.V3jWvKLdIq8 [Accessed 30 Aug. 2016].

Qin, Z. S. (2021) *How China's livestream industry is Revolutionizing Ecommerce.* The China Project. Available at: https://thechinaproject.com/2021/02/03/how-chinas-livestream-industry-is-revolutionizing-ecommerce/

Raimund, L. (2008) *Consumers: In a State of Sensory Overload.* Munich, Germany: Grin Verlag.

Rao, A. (2010) Second TVC for Cadbury Dairy Milk's "Shubh Aarambh" Released. *Campaign India*, 6 Sep. Available at: www.campaignindia.in/article/second-tvc-for-cadbury-dairy-milks-shubh-aarambh-released/412695

Ravago, M.-L. V., Balisacan, A. M., and Chakravorty, U. (2015). The principles and practice of sustainable economic development. In Sustainable Economic Development. Edited by Balisacan et al. Academic Press

Reic, I. (2017) *Events Marketing Management: A Consumer Perspective*. Abingdon: Routledge.

Remy, N., Catena, M. and Durand-Servoingt, B. (2015) *Digital Inside: Get Wired for the Ultimate Luxury Experience*. McKinsey&Company, Jul. Available at: www.mckinsey.com/~/media/mckinsey/industries/consumer%20packaged%20goods/our%20insig hts/is%20luxury%20ecommerce%20nearing%20its%20tipping%20point/digital_insi de_full_pdf.ashx [Accessed 11 Sept. 2016].

Richardson, T. (2020) The Kate Effect: The Duchess of Cambridge is asking 5 Big Questions about early years. University of Northampton (online) Available at: https://www.northampton.ac.uk/news/the-kate-effect-what-will-the-duchess-of-cambridges-survey-tell-us-about-early-years/

Rigby, D. K. (2015) Customer Segmentation. Bain & Capital, 10 Jun. Available at: www.bain.com/Images/BAIN_GUIDE_Management_Tools_2015_executives_guide.pdf

Rogers, E. M. (1981) Diffusion of Innovations: An Overview. In *Use and Impact of Computers in Clinical Medicine. Computers and Medicine*. Edited by Anderson, J.G. and Jay, S.J. New York, NY: Springer. https://doi.org/10.1007/978-1-4613-8674-2_9

Rogers, Everett M. (2003) *Diffusion of Innovations*. 5th ed. Free Press. Available at: ProQuest Ebook Central, http://ebookcentral.proquest.com/lib/westminster/detail.action?doc ID=4935198

Rotimi, E. O. O., Topple, C. and Hopkins, J. (2021). Towards a Conceptual Framework of Sustainable Practices of Post-consumer Textile Waste at Garment End of Lifecycle: A Systematic Literature Review Approach. *Sustainability 13*, 2965. https://doi.org/10.3390/su13052965

Ryan, C. (2022) ESG in Africa is 'Colonialism 2.0' LinkedIn. Available at: https://www.linkedin.com/pulse/esg-africa-colonialism-20-ciaran-ryan/

Ryan, D. and Jones, C. (2016) *Understanding Digital Marketing: Marketing Strategies for Engaging the Digital Generation*. 4th ed. London: Kogan Page.

Ryan, P. (2016) A Brand Case Study: The Superdry Appeal. *The Branding Journal*. Available at: www.thebrandingjournal.com/2016/03/the-superdry-appeal/

Ryder, B. (2024) Korean and Thai Stars Dominate Milan Men's Fashion Week. *Jing Daily*. Available at: https://jingdaily.com/posts/korean-and-thai-stars-dominate-milan-men-s-fashion-week

Scheier, C. and Held, D. (2006) *Wie Werbung wirkt: Erkenntnisse des Neuromarketing*. Munich, Germany: Haufe Lexware Gmbh.

Scheier, C. and Held, D. (2012) *Was Marken erfolgreich macht: Neuropsychologie in der Markenführung*. Munich, Germany: Haufe Lexware Gmbh.

Seiter, C. (2016) The Psychology of Social Media: Why We Like, Comment, and Share Online. Available at: https://blog.bufferapp.com/psychology-of-social-media

Seto, F. (2017) How Does Trend Forecasting Really Work? *High Snobiety*, 5 Apr. Available at: www.highsnobiety.com/2017/04/05/trend-forecasting-how-to/

Shardlow, E. (2024) *Wellness Travel Trends: 2024/25*. Stylus. Available at: Wellness Travel Trends: 2024/25 (stylus.com)

Sharma, A. (2016) How Predictive AI Will Change Shopping. *Harvard Business Review*, 18 Nov. Available at: https://hbr.org/2016/11/how-predictive-ai-will-change-shopping [Accessed 25 Nov. 2016].

Sharp, A. (2019) *Escape the Corset: #탈코*. *Leeds Human Right Journal* [Online]. University of Leeds. Available at: https://hrj.leeds.ac.uk/2019/11/29/escape-the-corset-%ED%83%88 %EC%BD%94/

SINUS Markt- und Sozialforschung GmbH (2015) Information on Sinus Milieus. Available at: www.sinus-institut.de/fileadmin/user_data/sinus-institut/Downloadcenter/201508 05/ 2015-01-15_Information_on_Sinus-Milieus_English_version.pdf

Smith, P. R. and Zook, Z . (2016) *Marketing Communications: Offline and Online Integration, Engagement and Analytics*. 6th edn. London: Kogan Page.

Smith, P. R. and Zook, Z. E. (2016) *Marketing Communications: Offline and Online Integration, Engagement and Analytics*. 6th ed. London: Kogan Page.

Solomon, M. R. (2020) *Consumer Behavior: Buying, Having, and Being*. 13th ed. London: Pearson.

Springer, P. (2008) *Ads to Icons: How Advertising Succeeds in a Multimedia Age*. London: Kogan Page.

Statista (2016) Anzeigenumsätze (brutto) der Elle in den Jahren 2010 bis 2018 (in Millionen Euro). Available at: http://de.statista.com/statistik/daten/studie/486439/umfrage/anz eigenumsaetze-der-frauenzeitschrift-elle/ [Accessed 11 Sept. 2016].

Statista (2023a) Least Trusted Digital Advertising Channels Worldwide as of September 2021. Available at: Least trusted digital ad media 2021 | Statista (oclc.org)

Statista (2023b) *Digital Advertising Spending Worldwide from 2021 to 2026*. Statista. Available at: Digital ad spend worldwide 2026 | Statista (oclc.org)

Stutchbury, P. (2016) Architecture Foundation Australia and the Glenn Murcutt Master Class. Available at: www.ozetecture.org/2012/peter-stutchbury [Accessed 3 Dec. 2016].

Taflinger, R. F. (2011) Advantage: Consumer Psychology and Advertising. Kendall Hunt. Available at: https://online.vitalsource.com/#/books/9781465252685

Tag Heuer (2019) Cara Delevigne. Available at: www.tagheuer.com/en/cara-delevingne

Taylor, J. (2015) The Many Muses of Karl Lagerfeld, From Kendall Jenner to Tilda Swinton. *Observer*, 18 Aug. Available at: http://observer.com/2015/08/the-many-muses-of-karl-lagerfeld-from-kendall-jenner-to-tilda-swinton/ [Accessed 10 Feb. 2016].

Telford and Wrekin (2021) The 10 R's of Sustainable Living. Available at: http://sustainable telfordandwrekin.com/get-involved/did-you-know/10-rs-of-sustainable-living

Templeton, L. (2024) Exclusive: Louis Vuitton Debuts LV Diamonds Line With Mine-to-finger Traceability. WWD [online]. Available at: https://wwd.com/accessories-news/ jewelry/louis-vuitton-lv-diamonds-monogram-star-cut-mine-to-finger-traceability-aura-blockchain-gia-recognized-1236159847/

Thomala, L. L. (2023) *Influencer/KOL Marketing in China - Statistics & Facts*. Statista. Available at: Influencer/KOL marketing in China - statistics & facts | Statista

Tungate, M. (2007) *Adland: A Global History of Advertising*. London: Kogan Page.

Tye, L. (2002) *The Father of Spin: Edward L. Bernays and the Birth of Public Relations*. New York: Henry Holt (Owl Books).

UN Broadband Commission (2016) China, India Now World's Largest Internet Markets. Unescopress, 15 Sep. Available at: www.unesco.org/new/en/media-services/single-vi ew/news/china_india_now_worlds_largest_internet_markets [Accessed 9 Oct. 2016].

United Nations (n.d.) Sustainable Development Goals. Available at: https://sdgs.un.org/ goals

University of Alberta, Office of Sustainability (n.d.) What is Sustainability. Available at: www.mcgill.ca/sustainability/files/sustainability/what-is-sustainability.pdf

University of Twente (2017) *Two Step Flow Theory*. Available at: www.utwente.nl/en/bms/ communication-theories/sorted-by-cluster/Mass-Media/Two_Step_Flow_Theory-1

University of Wisconsin Sustainable Management (2023) The Triple Bottom Line. Available at: https://sustain.wisconsin.edu/sustainability/triple-bottom-line/, https://online.hbs. edu/blog/post/what-is-the-triple-bottom-line

Van Gelder, K. (2024) E-commerce Worldwide - Statistics & Facts. Statista. Available at: https://www-statista-com.uow.idm.oclc.org/topics/871/online-shopping/#topic Overview

Vecchi, A. and Buckley, C. (eds.) (2016) *Handbook of Research on Global Fashion Management and Merchandising*. Hershey, PN: IGI Global.

Veja (2024) Project: Leather. Available at: https://project.veja-store.com/en/single/leather

Villani, S. (2001) Impact of Media on Children and Adolescents: A 10-Year Review of the Research. *Journal of the American Academy of Child & Adolescent Psychiatry* 40(4), 392–401.

Von Kameke, L. (2023) *Leading Influencer Types Prompting Product Purchase Decisions in the Asia-Pacific Region as of May 2023, by Country or Territory*. Statista. Available at: APAC: top influencer types prompting product purchases by country 2023 | Statista (oclc.org)

Wang, H. (2016) #Brand Transliteration: How to Translate and Protect Your Brand for the Chinese Market. *CCPIT Patent and Trademark Law Office*. Available at: www.ccpit-patent.com.cn/node/3795

Watson, A. (2024) *U.S. Magazine Industry - Statistics & Facts*. Statista. Available at: https:// www-statista-com.uow.idm.oclc.org/topics/1265/magazines/#topicOverview

Whitelock, A. (2013) *Elizabeth's Bedfellows*. London: Bloomsbury Publishing.

Williamson, J. (1978) *Decoding Advertisements: Ideology and Meaning in Advertising*. London: Marion Boyars.

Wind, Y. and Douglas, S. P. (2001) *International Market Segmentation*. Wharton School, University of Pennsylvania and CESA. Available at: https://faculty.wharton.upenn.edu/ wp-content/uploads/2012/04/7213_International_Market_Segmentation.pdf

Winship, J. (1987) *Inside Womens' Magazines*. London: Pandora.

The World Bank Group (2024) Atlas of Sustainable Development Goals 2023 – Available at: Responsible consumption & production | SDG 12: Responsible consumption & production (worldbank.org)

Wren, B. (July 2022) Sustainable Supply Chain Management in the Fast Fashion Industry: A Comparative Study of Current Efforts and Best Practices to Address the Climate Crisis. *Cleaner Logistics and Supply Chain* 4, 100032. https://doi.org/10.1016/j.clscn.2022.100032

Xin, B. et al. (2023) Strategic Product Showcasing Mode of E-commerce Live Streaming. *Journal of Retailing and Consumer Services 73*, 103360. ISSN 0969-6989, https://doi.org/10.1016/j.jretconser.2023.103360. Available at: https://www.sciencedirect.com/science/article/pii/S0969698923001078

Yiddish Radio Project (2002) Exhibits. Sound Portraits Productions. Available at: www.yiddishradioproject.org/exhibits/history [Accessed 12 Jun. 2016].

Yiddish Radio Project (2002) Sound Portraits Productions. Available at: www.yiddishradioproject.org [Accessed 12 Jun. 2016].

Yurchisin, J. and Johnson, K. K. P. (2010) *Fashion and the Consumer*. Oxford: Berg.

Zarella, K. K. (2016) Diesels Renzo Rosso isn't Crazy just Genius. *Fashion Unfiltered*. Available at: http://fashionunfiltered.com/news/2016/diesel-s-renzo-rosso-isn-t-crazy-just-genius

Zeit Online (2012) Im Dienste der Werbung: Annoncen-Expeditionen feiern ihr hundertjähriges Bestehen. *DieZeit*, 17/1955. Available at: www.zeit.de/1955/17/im-dienste-der-werbung [Accessed 12 Jun. 2016].

Zweig, C. (1987) S.F.-Moscow Teleport–Electronic Détente. *Los Angeles Times* [Online]. Available at: https://www.latimes.com/archives/la-xpm-1987-12-09-vw-18480-story.html

Index